THE TWO ENDS OF THE LOG

"A university is a student at one end of a log and Mark Hopkins at the other." JAMES A. GARFIELD

~ THE TWO ENDS OF THE LOG ~

Learning and Teaching in Today's College

edited by Russell M. Cooper

UNIVERSITY OF MINNESOTA PRESS, Minneapolis

Library of Congress Catalog Card Number: 58-13186

PUBLISHED IN GREAT BRITAIN, INDIA, AND PAKISTAN BY THE OXFORD UNIVERSITY PRESS,
LONDON, BOMBAY, AND KARACHI AND IN CANADA BY THOMAS ALLEN, LTD., TORONTO

~§ J. L. MORRILL

Foreword

INSTITUTIONS of learning traditionally take pride in their antiquity — in contrast with individuals, who so often dread the mounting
number of their birthdays. The difference, I suppose, is in the faith
of educational institutions, among all others, that their indispensable
service to society is never done; that they must go forward eternally;
that the future offers always new challenges and a larger opportunity.
Some such awareness and conviction were the setting for the Centennial Conference on College Teaching which gave rise to this book.

One hundred years ago, after a compromise between two conten-
tious and actually competitive constitutional conventions, Minnesota
became a state and was admitted to the Union. The climate of controversy, so necessary to college professors characteristically inclined
to "think otherwise," thus received a historical validity in the life of
our state which endures to this day. It likewise provided an offsetting
warmth to the meteorological rigors of this region, so rigorous indeed
that our state is sometimes described as one in which the delicate die
young.

Nine years earlier than our becoming a state, the first territorial
assembly had passed an act providing for a system of free public
schools. In 1851, seven years before our statehood, the charter establishing the University of Minnesota was granted. Hamline University
was founded in 1854, and St. John's in 1857. By 1870, Gustavus Adolphus and Carleton had been established; and the normal schools at
Winona, Mankato, and St. Cloud.

From these beginnings, higher education in Minnesota has increased
— geometrically, one might say — with the number of colleges and
students, the number and variety of offerings and services expanding
far beyond the dreams of the founders.

And now the prospect, conservatively estimated, of doubled enrollments by 1970, and the possibility of new institutions, probably at the junior-college level, or new branches of existing ones. The longer future, of course, is as difficult to foresee as the present would have been to comprehend one hundred years ago.

The problem of improving instruction is the challenge confronting this conference — and the success of the teacher is the heart of the matter. There is nothing new about this; it has been so, always. Dean Cooper has reminded me, indeed, of a similar conference, sponsored by our university on this campus thirty years ago, on "Problems of College Education" — a conference likewise attended by teachers and administrators in large numbers, dealing with many aspects of teaching and its improvement, class size, student counseling, and the like. These were problems also in an earlier and quieter time.

And now the demands of an expanding and ever more specialized society, of an expanding knowledge, and of expanding student numbers pose new dimensions for the educational dilemma of quality and quantity. I have said the dilemma of quality *and* quantity, not quality *versus* quantity — for that *is* the challenge, I deeply believe, to which we must respond without surrender to the concept of an insoluble dichotomy.

As the president of a typically large university, I feel no competence to offer to you teachers any helpful advice in the exercise of your indispensable and too little appreciated function. Indeed, in making out my income tax this year, when I wrote *educator* in the space provided for occupation, I had the uneasy sense of having falsified my return!

So overwhelmingly preoccupied are we college presidents — a good many of us, at least, these anxious days — with the responsibilities for finding the means, physical and fiscal, to make more possible the success of our scholars and teachers, that we find ourselves increasingly and unhappily remote from the educative process itself. Our satisfactions, if any, must be largely vicarious.

And yet, most of us have been teachers at some time — and for four years, a long time ago, I had an assignment one aspect of which was the improvement of instruction at the freshman-sophomore level. Working with me at that time and with the faculties concerned were two distinguished visiting speakers at this conference, Dr. W. H. Cowley and Dr. Ralph Tyler. We were colleagues then at the Ohio State University — and I have been grateful all these years for the contribution they made to my education and more especially to the improvement of instruction at that university which was marked and measurable, as I am sure my Ohio State faculty friend, Dr. Edgar Dale, another of our guest speakers, would also testify.

At no time within my experience has there been such confusing controversy, some of it sensible but much of it senseless, over the aims and methods of education as at present. The rationalization of ignorance and prejudice has reached a new high, it seems to me. On the one hand we must contend with an anti-intellectualism which depreciates the vital place and prestige of the teacher. On the other, there are teachers who defeat their own function by an intellectual snobbery which expresses itself in a contempt for what the student doesn't happen to know as against what he might be taught to learn.

In a good many states there has been a growing divisiveness, damaging to both, between privately and publicly supported colleges and universities which happily we have not experienced in Minnesota. The good sense of our leaders in higher education and the cooperative approach to our problems through the Committee for the Continuing Study of Higher Education of our Minnesota Association have been responsible in large measure for our helpful and friendly relations.

We are hearing these days a curious disclaimer — not found in the training for other professions — of any relationship between the aims and the methods of teaching: the old and outworn assumption that the teacher is born and not made or trained; that a knowledge of subject matter carries the built-in capacity to teach it — assumptions which obviously belie the purposes and hoped-for benefits of a conference such as this one.

There is an exaggerated notion at the moment, especially at the secondary-school level, that curricular reform is the be-all and end-all of our difficulties, with a seeming forgetfulness of the fact that the curriculum is but an educational instrument of small significance except as it derives integrity and strength and effect from the capacity of the teacher to instruct and inspire.

I would suppose that every good and conscientious teacher is still himself a student, aware that there are always things yet to learn, eager to improve his teaching competence. It is this spirit which inspired the conference and which permeates this volume.

Preface

MODERN Jeremiahs have been predicting for some time that the day of quality instruction in our colleges is ended. They foresee a tidal wave of students flooding the institutions of higher education, jamming large lecture halls, and making precious personal interaction between student and professor virtually impossible.

Others, however, refuse to yield to such pessimism. They see in the swelling college populations a still greater opportunity for serving American youth and preparing them to participate in our rapidly shifting culture. They remember that the individual student is a separate human being, whether in a small or large group, and that education fails to take place at all until he is moved to examine phenomena independently and resolve problems in his own terms. If the coming decades offer a more challenging opportunity than ever before to help millions of students find themselves and prepare for intellectual leadership, the colleges simply must rise to this challenge.

It was in this determined spirit that the Association of Minnesota Colleges called a conference in April 1958 to re-examine the teaching job, assess the obstacles to learning, and appraise the most promising methods of college teaching in the days ahead. It was to be a representative conference composed of classroom teachers from the colleges of Minnesota and including all types of institutions and the many fields of subject matter.

It happened that 1958 was the centennial year for the state of Minnesota. Accordingly, at the suggestion of the Association, the state Centennial Commission endorsed the project as one of the official events of the centennial celebration. The Commission made a grant to help prepare and carry through the conference program. In addition, the Louis W. and Maud Hill Family Foundation granted funds to help cover expenses of delegates and thus ensure representative participation.

J. L. Morrill, president of the Association of Minnesota Colleges, appointed a committee to plan the program, procure the speakers, and make all necessary arrangements. The members were as follows:

J. Huntley Dupre, dean of Macalester College, co-chairman

Russell M. Cooper, assistant dean of the College of Science, Literature, and the Arts of the University of Minnesota, co-chairman

Sister Antonius, C.S.J., professor of chemistry at the College of St. Catherine

Howard Morris, associate professor of dairy husbandry at the University of Minnesota

Floretta Murray, professor of art at Winona State College

John Neumaier, dean of Hibbing Junior College

Dean M. Schweickhard, Commissioner of Education for the State of Minnesota

Invaluable leadership was also contributed by several subcommittee chairmen including Burton Paulu of the Television Committee; Hans E. Hopf and Howard F. Nelson of the Committee on Arrangements; William L. Nunn of the Banquet Committee; and William T. Harris of the Publicity Committee.

A total of 315 persons, representing virtually every institution of higher education in the state and chosen by those institutions on the basis of a quota system proportionate to student enrollment, attended the conference. Almost all were active classroom teachers and they came from many academic disciplines. The conference included 14 students, chosen because they were Minnesota delegates to the National Student Association and hence acknowledged leaders of student thought. It would have been hard to get a more representative group of persons concerned with college teaching.

This volume follows closely the organization and strategy of the conference. The interrelation of the several parts of the book, therefore, will have greater meaning if the reader understands the progression of thought at the conference.

On the first day, Thursday, April 17, attention was centered upon the students as the object of the entire educational process. The student therefore is the theme of the first section of this volume. Nevitt

Preface

Sanford has described the contemporary undergraduate, his interests and problems, and the campus and community influences affecting him. Drawing upon his scholarship as a psychologist and his recent researches at Vassar College, he has sketched the complexities of the problem and suggested ways for dealing with varying students more realistically. With this picture in mind, Wilbert McKeachie has outlined some of the factors involved in learning — factors to be conjured with if the contemporary student is to be challenged and won to the intellectual enterprise.

The Thursday afternoon discussions are represented in the next seven chapters of this volume. In each case an analyst prepared a background statement setting forth issues and current research related to the problem, and this thinking was assessed by discussants in the light of their own classroom experience. To ensure full participation, each discussion group was divided into two sections with separate chairmen and recorders. At the close of the afternoon, the two recorders for each topic prepared a resumé of the discussion and gave this to the analyst who could then revise his original statement in light of these new ideas. The seven chapters, therefore, represent the research and thinking of the several analysts but in addition they have been enriched by many ideas growing out of the conference itself.

At the conference banquet on Thursday evening, W. H. Cowley delivered the address which has become the tenth chapter of this volume. He has given a vivid account of the gradual change in American colleges during the past century, providing a background for the college teaching of today. This concern for dynamic teaching, conducted by persons adequately trained and dedicated to the job, forms a natural transition from the first section's emphasis upon the student to the second section's focus upon the professor. The Conference Committee was happy to permit the *Educational Record* to also publish this chapter in its issue for October 1958.

The chapters in the second section grew out of the Friday sessions of the conference. Dean Horace T. Morse of the University opened the day with his comments as a Roving Reporter concerning Thursday's group discussions, summarizing his own observations and the findings of the several recorders. (He performed the same function for the Friday discussions at the opening session on Saturday morning.) The major address on Friday morning was that by Reuben Gustavson showing the crucial importance of college teaching in the light of our technological civilization. The delegates were then divided into nine discussion groups according to respective subject-matter backgrounds and they addressed themselves to two questions: How can we cultivate our continued growth as teachers? and How can we improve our artistry of teaching? Each group had a chairman to lead the discussion and a recorder to report the findings. These nine recorders' reports were then probed and interpreted by Virginia Senders to become the twelfth chapter of this volume. The concern for teacher growth was climaxed on Friday afternoon by President Harold Taylor of Sarah Lawrence who presented his own provocative judgment on the matter.

The remainder of Friday afternoon was devoted to the evaluation of teaching. Ralph Tyler set forth the major dimensions of the problem after which the delegates divided into subject-matter groups as in the morning to pursue two additional topics: How can we evaluate teaching for over-all appraisal and faculty promotion? and How can we develop an analytical evaluation of teaching for the instructor's self-improvement? These afternoon discussions, duly summarized by the recorders, have been organized into the fifteenth chapter by Dean Morse.

The Friday evening and Saturday morning sessions again shifted emphasis — from the student and the professor to a consideration of ways whereby the two may more effectively organize their energies for more efficient learning. The Friday evening session included addresses by I. Keith Tyler and C. R. Carpenter on the nature and effectiveness of educational television, followed by a closed-circuit demonstration conducted by the University of Minnesota School of Dentistry. During this demonstration Burton Paulu of the Department of Radio and Television Broadcasting at the University of Minnesota served as chairman, aided by Dr. James R. Jensen of the School of Dentistry and Professor Hope Lunin Klapper of New York University. The National Association of Educational Broadcasters granted funds to help cover the expenses of this demonstration.

The Saturday sessions continued the emphasis on teaching methods with an address by Edgar Dale on the newer techniques of teaching. Following this, the delegates divided according to interest to discuss details of particular teaching devices. In each group, an analyst again presented a paper setting forth experience and research in the field and then revised his paper in light of the new insights gained through group discussion. These revised papers are the next several chapters of this book.

The final chapter is a paper by Dean Theodore C. Blegen delivered at the concluding luncheon of the conference and presenting through the eyes of a historian the dramatic role of higher education in building a new society.

Throughout the volume, bibliographical citations are noted in parentheses, rather than footnotes, and refer to a list of selected readings included at the end of the chapter.

A follow-up of the conference revealed that the discussions have already had an impact in many classrooms of the state and it is believed that the publication of the present volume will give impetus to further discussion and experimentation. The Conference Committee is grateful to the many speakers and delegates who contributed their thinking to the preparation of this volume and hopes the book will serve as an effective stimulus and resource for the further improvement of college teaching in America.

Table of Contents

THE TEACHING END

ENDS AND MEANS

THE LEARNING END

◄§ NEVITT SANFORD

The Professor Looks at the Student

To AVOID any possible alarm, I should announce at once that I am going to discuss students rather than professors. My title might easily suggest a lecture on the perceptual habits of professors, but this tempting subject had best be left for another time. A student said recently that he thought today's professors were looking at the students with a jaundiced eye. Other kinds of eyes have been noted among professors — naïve, baleful, even bleary. And it has seemed to some that professors were using various kinds of visual aids; these have ranged all the way from rose-colored spectacles to just a glass, through which things were viewed darkly. But let us assume that our professorial dignity and objectivity are going to be maintained, that we do not need visual aids, and that as is our custom, we are going to look at students with an eye that is clear and penetrating, but of course benign!

It is certainly true that most general statements about students today tend to be unflattering. This is no doubt partly because the terms we use, if they come from psychology or social science, are likely to have this aspect, and it is partly because in talking about students we are usually addressing ourselves to some problem, and this naturally draws attention to something that students ought to get over. Now and again someone rises to the students' defense, remarking that there are also a lot of good things that might be said about them, or that, in any case, students today are no worse than they used to be. This may make us feel just and objective, but it does not suggest anything that might be done.

Interestingly enough, students do not seem to mind being the objects of analytic and unflattering remarks. We of the Mellon Foundation program at Vassar College (the research group at present includes Donald Brown, Mervin Friedman, and Harold Webster, psychologists;

3

John Bushnell, anthropologist; and Richard Jung, sociologist) have published a great many statements about Vassar students, many of which statements sounded like scolding. Yet I believe it is fair to say that the students are not ill-disposed toward us. Of course, any student can consider that a remark about the conformity or other-directedness or social orientation of today's students does not apply to him or to her. But actually I think something more than this is involved. If students believe that remarks made about them are true, or nearly true, and are made in the spirit of scientific inquiry, they actually feel relieved, because it shows that their own efforts to evaluate themselves are not too wide of the mark, and because it supports their hope that when things are understood, it will be possible to improve them. More than this, students can see that criticisms of them are at the same time criticisms of the system they live in.

Returning to the perceptual orientation of the professor — and this time quite seriously — it seems that students may indeed be viewed from a number of different perspectives. One may view them singly or in groups. The professor or educator or research worker may adopt a short-time perspective embracing, let us say, the happenings of one year, or he may adopt a long-time perspective according to which the college experience is but a phase in a larger pattern of life. He may view students as people of a certain age and in a certain phase of development. He may view them simply as specimens of American society or of the several American social classes, and he may view them as performers in a particular social role. Students, like other people, are complex and many-faceted, and one has much choice as to what aspects he shall put in the focus of attention. An observer may concentrate on one or another aspect of their behavior, or he may direct attention to underlying personality structures; he may take any trait or characteristic of behavior or personality structure and then attend to its distribution in populations, or he may concern himself with the relations of such traits, one to another, within the individual person. Most of these perspectives are taken, from time to time, in my remarks here. I shall both offer some sweeping generalizations about the students of today, and attempt some analysis of the complicated processes to be found in individual students.

The perspective to be preferred is one that highlights the educational task itself. It is the professor or the educator who is looking at the student, and his main interest, it may be supposed, is centered on where the student stands with respect to the educational processes — on what kind of educational problem the student presents, and on what kind of potential he embodies.

A Model of the Educational Process

What is needed at the beginning is a model of the educational process itself. I should like to outline the model that we have found useful in our research. According to this scheme, prepared by Richard Jung, a college or university or training program is a productive institution. Materials, of somewhat diverse quality, enter the institution, there to be developed or shaped or molded in accordance with specified objectives — that is to say, qualities desired in the finished product. The educational or institutional processes presumably are carried forward in accordance with hypotheses concerning what kinds of actions will modify entering materials, in the directions determined by the objectives that have been defined. A student who enters such a productive institution and stays for two or four years, may or may not change. If he changes, this may or may not be in accordance with stated objectives. If he changes in accordance with stated objectives, this may or may not be due to educational procedures deliberately undertaken. If the entering student does not change in desirable ways, this may be due to resistance in the material itself, or to influences from outside the institution, or to the failure of the institution to bring to bear upon the entering material influences that could reasonably be expected to induce the desired changes. If one views the matter in this way, it becomes clear that the major task for educational research is to discover what processes will bring about desirable changes in given qualities of entering materials. The starting place, in other words, is the definition of the educational objectives.

The Problem of Educational Objectives

I am somewhat reluctant to bring up this subject, since it is difficult and controversial, but I do not see how we can tell what are the truly relevant things to say about students unless we have some notion of what somebody wants students to become. I should like to insist that the scientist can speak freely about objectives and study the conditions and processes that favor their attainment, without limiting the diversity that is prized so highly in our society, and without indicating the relative values of these various objectives.

In approaching this problem in our research, it has seemed best to use the term education in its narrow and traditional sense, to stand for the inculcation in the individual of the cultural heritage. The educated person, according to this point of view, does whatever he does in an educated way; that is to say, he makes use of the terms and the symbols of his culture in carrying on his activities.

There is no question but that education is an end in itself. However, most of us, I believe, want something more for our sons and daughters than that they be educated; we feel that we might give them the best education without doing for them all that ought to be done. We may recall here the autobiographies of Princeton seniors collected by Otto Butz (3). Almost all of these young men believed that they had had an excellent education — some thought they had had the best in the world — but this did not prevent them from displaying, in different degrees, immaturity, weakness of character, inappropriate values, and psychopathology. I have heard that some of the Princeton authorities complained about the publication of this book, as if it somehow reflected upon the good name of Princeton. This, I think, is not a reasonable view to take. I have no doubt that similar autobiographies produced by young men at any of our colleges would be no more flattering to their institutions. What these autobiographies described, simply, is how it is with some young men. Similar autobiographies collected from Harvard undergraduates twenty-five years ago (11) could hardly be distinguished from those that Butz published.

I should be inclined to agree with the young men that they had had an excellent education — perhaps as good as can be had in this country; indeed they displayed their egocentricity, failures in personality adjustment, and inappropriate value systems in a very well-educated way. Princeton need not, on the basis of these reports by Princeton men, have to worry much about the education it offers. If, however, it has other aims for young men, such as building character, making good citizens, developing the personality, and inculcating democratic values, then of course it should worry; that is to say, it should share the worries of everybody else in our society who is concerned with these latter objectives. Similarly, on a television panel discussion, one on which James B. Conant appeared to report on his studies of the high schools, someone remarked on the fact that European education, which in the main has been modeled on the German system and which in its essential features is used in Russia today, did not prevent educated Germans from becoming Nazis. Indeed, the German schools and universities, after they had ejected a few dissidents, were strongholds of Nazi ideology.

I am suggesting that in the face of this state of affairs we do not attempt to redefine education in such a way as to include all the virtues that we should like to see developed in people. I think, rather, we should stick to the narrow and formal definition of education, and say simply that there are other factors besides education that pertain to the development of individuals in our society. This will permit us to study the relations between education and other developmental objectives.

What are some of these other factors? It must be admitted that as soon as we begin talking about character development, emotional maturity, appropriate values, and the like, we enter a pretty chaotic and controversial field. Not only do we encounter a great diversity of conflicting views, but we find that our scientists have not gone very far toward defining objectives in such a way that they can be studied.

Yet there has been, in recent years, an increasing concern among psychologists and social scientists with the definition of goals of development, or with the characteristics of the healthy or mature or highly developed person. For example, Erik Erikson (4, 185–225) has set down the following as the crowning features of his "stages of development": ego-integrity, generativity, intimacy, identity, industry, initiative, autonomy, and trust. I have named them in order, from the later to the earlier. Gordon Allport (1) some time ago noted the marks of the mature personality: extension of the self, self-objectification, autonomous interests, and a unified philosophy of life. Erich Fromm (6) speaks of "productive orientation" and Kurt Goldstein (8) and Abraham Maslow (10) of the "self-actualized person." R. W. White (16), in summarizing much recent thought in the area of developmental goals, distinguishes four major trends of "natural growth": toward the stabilization of ego-identity, the deepening of interests, freedom in personal relations, and the humanizing of values.

These certainly are not all the goods that one might think of, but I do not believe anyone will deny that they are good. They can also be defined and estimated, and hence it is possible to discuss the conditions and processes of their development.

In our work at Vassar, we have undertaken to distinguish between maturity and health, and to regard both of these desiderata as conceptually independent of education. We have tried to avoid using the term maturity to stand for a variety of ethical norms such as are exemplified by White's "natural growth trends" (16); rather, we would go back to the older meaning of the term. It is, in the first place, something which distinguishes adults from adolescents and children, and most essentially it means the relative predominance of the controlling, discriminating, analyzing, and decision-making functions of the individual over the passionate, the impulsive, and, perhaps, the creative. If maturity is defined in this way, we have no difficulty in distinguishing it from positive health.

Health, in our view, is a way of meeting and dealing with life's problems. It is the capacity to manage strains, of whatever severity, in a way that permits the person to maintain himself, and that minimally impairs his capacity for dealing with future strains. The healthy person is flexible and adaptable, but at the same time stable, in a fundamental way. The most essential feature of the healthy personality is maximum intercommunication among the various parts or subsystems of the personality. In this state, optimal functioning in one area is favorable to optimal functioning in others, and when a strain occurs, as many resources as are needed may be brought to bear upon it. Similarly, where such possibilities of intercommunication among differentiated parts exist, the person is able to handle a strain with no more of his resources than are necessary. He does not, so to speak, become overcommitted on one front, thus weakening himself on other fronts or unnecessarily exposing his general position. The mature person, according to this view, may or may not be healthy. The predominance of controlling and discriminating processes that he has attained might actually in some cases interfere with the intercommunication among parts of his personality, and thus reduce his adaptability. On the other hand, there is nothing to prevent a healthy person from being mature. All he has to do is see to it that however flexible and adaptable and free he might be, his controlling and discriminating processes still have a relative predominance.

Health and maturity, defined in this way, still do not embrace all of the ethical norms or patterns of ideal development that exist and that we may wish to consider. For example, creativity is not a matter of either health or maturity, though it may involve some combination of the two.

The point that I want to emphasize is that education, maturity, and health are conceptually independent, and they may or may not be positively correlated. A person might be highly educated, even in the liberal sense, without being healthy or mature. One can act out a neurosis or be obsessionally preoccupied in the terms that he was taught at college, as well as he can in other terms. What in the untutored might be a conflict between profane and holy love, might for the educated be translated into an endless argument about free will versus determinism. Liberal education, when it really takes, actually favors the expression of the emotionally impulsive side of our nature; it might, for example, produce a poet almost all of whose internal and external conversations were carried on in terms of the higher learning, and who had to struggle in order to maintain control and discrimination on a high enough level so that he could be productive and live in the world as it is. It goes almost without saying that people can be mature and healthy, and exhibit various other virtues, without being educated.

This view in no way belittles education as a value — it only argues for the clarification of issues. The traditional educator has every right to say that he values education above health and maturity, and that he will persist in his efforts to advance it without attention to these other matters. What he cannot say is that in educating a person he is doing all for him that needs to be done. Similarly, when we set our sights on the development of the whole person and strive to attain this end, we cannot claim that we are necessarily thereby educating the person or even preparing the way for education. It might turn out that the development of the whole person were better promoted outside of educational institutions.

Fortunately, education does not necessarily conflict with the other objectives, or vice versa. In some people we may observe high levels of functioning in all of these spheres, and under some conditions progress in the one seems to favor progress in the others. But what we observe most commonly is a variety of patterns involving different degrees of the several desiderata, including education.

Let us assume that change in respect to education, maturity, health, and other developmental objectives is affected by what happens to the student in college. In trying to determine what favors, or hampers, desirable change we must pay attention to causes arising out of the general culture and social organization of the college community as well as to the policies and practices deliberately adopted and carried out by the college faculty and administration. We must consider, too, that not all the forces that are brought to bear upon the college student arise out of the unique culture and society of his college; he is responsive at the same time to diverse aspects of a much wider and more complex social and cultural matrix.

In trying to understand personality development during the college years, we should, I think, pay attention to the following aspects of the social and cultural matrix.

First, *the American ethos.* Whereas the liberal college strives to build in students an ego identity that is relatively independent of external definition, it labors in a culture that places heavy accent on *doing* — "What do you do?" — as the basis for identity.

Second, *the American society.* For example, there seems to be much confusion among students concerning what social role requirements favor, interfere with, or are necessary to one's basic identity as a woman or as a man.

Third, *the changing situation of the American society.* Compare, for example, the American students' preoccupation with the "private sphere," as reported by J. M. Gillespie and Gordon Allport (7), with the social and political orientation of Mexican or Egyptian students, whose countries are in a stage of industrial development corresponding to ours of perhaps seventy-five years ago.

Fourth, *family, community, and social class memberships.* For the student, stimuli from these quarters are still very much in the picture.

Turning to the environment of the college itself, we have to consider several aspects:

First, *the over-all culture of the college.* It appears that each college has its own unique culture, in which faculty, administration, and students all take part, which all to some extent internalize.

Second, various *subcultures.* There is a faculty-admininstration culture, and probably one major and several minor peer cultures.

Third, *the college society,* with faculty, administration, and student roles, their definitions and interrelationships.

10

The Professor Looks at the Student
The Vassar Studies

In our work at Vassar we have paid particular attention to the student culture (5). I shall elaborate on this here, without suggesting that it is necessarily more important than other aspects of the social and cultural matrix in which the student lives. By the student culture we mean a pattern of values, attitudes, ideas, ways of looking at things, rules of conduct, and the like, that exists independently of any particular student or group of students and is passed on, more or less unchanged, from one student generation to the next.

A major concern of most entering students, as we have observed them, is with acceptance by their fellows, with being included in the student society. This means that they must learn and, to an adequate degree, assimilate the prevailing student culture. For many students this process requires virtually no adjustment, since they bring a very similar culture with them from their schools; for others the process of assimilation is more or less automatic; and for still others it is a matter of some deliberate choice. Only a small minority succeed in remaining aloof, and have a sense of separateness from their peer culture. Probably for most students the assimilation of this culture is their major experience in college. One can hardly overestimate its importance to the student. It provides a major basis for a sense of identity. It shows the guideposts to a comfortable life within a complex community: how to get along with one's fellow students, how to deal with the faculty in such a way as to withstand their influence but yet keep relations pleasant, how to conceive of young men and to manage the whole business of dating. Finally, it provides valuable preparation for life after college, offering fairly realistic conceptions of future roles and statuses, inculcating the values and teaching the social skills that are well calculated to be appropriate in the anticipated future.

As for the content of the peer culture, I can mention here only some of the outstanding features. Toward each other, students must be friendly, cooperative, pleasant; toward the faculty, polite, dutiful, impersonal. The college work is to be taken seriously, but not too seriously; frivolity is discouraged; outstanding scholarly work is tolerated but not applauded — in short, here as in most other areas the accent is on moderation and leveling. If a student studies too much or dates too much, thinks too much or talks too much; if she is too ambitious or too indifferent, the peer culture has effective means for bringing her

11

into line. With respect to ideas and issues the thing is to be open-minded and noncontroversial, above all to avoid unpleasantness; if an ethical decision has to be made, the proper course is to see what the others think. This decision will then be very likely to accord with the morality that prevails in our culture as a whole.

Toward the college and its general policies and practices, the peer culture is uncritically accepting; if things come up which are unpleasant or otherwise objectionable it saves itself from involvement by saying, "Well, we're only going to be here another year or two." And similarly with respect to the affairs of the world, the peer culture does not feel called upon to have opinions: "We are only students, learning how to think, and there is so much to be said on both sides." With respect to people, the peer culture is as tolerant as it is of ideas. There is virtually no exclusion from student society on the basis of race, religion, ethnic group, or social background. Anyone can belong, so long as she does not deliberately reject the peer culture or defy its ways.

The future is seen by the peer culture with optimism and, perhaps, overrealism. There is a vision of a stable but highly complex society in which one can make a happy, that is to say, materially gratifying, life by fitting in. The techniques for fitting in are precisely those being taught by the peer culture: be friendly, cooperative, agreeable, tolerant, optimistic, moral.

Not all students, of course, accept the prevailing student culture, and we find a general tendency to move away from it in the senior year, but it seems fair to say that at any given time a majority of the students are participating more or less fully in this culture.

The observation that students largely educate each other, that the values and outlook of most students are profoundly influenced by those that prevail in the student society, is not, of course, original with us. The same observation has been made from time to time through the years concerning the British universities; and we know that those of our own colleges that have been able, largely through vigorous recruitment and selection, to create a campus society in which the highest prestige attaches to the highest scholarship, can count heavily upon social pressure to keep motivation at a high level. Our observations have been made on a student society which seems much more typical of those existing on our campuses today. These cultures share much more fully the prevalent values of our society at large; and they

12

are particularly concerned with creating and carrying forward attitudes and mores that favor comfortable adjustment to campus society and that prepare the individual for life in the world as it is. Perhaps I should say the world as students think it is; but I would not underestimate the realism of their appraisal. When they err, it is on the side of overrealism, as happens when people are somewhat anxious, and they are likely to sacrifice adequacy of long-run perspective for a certain short-run practicality. Their conceptions would seem to compare not unfavorably with those of many of us sheltered academicians, or with those of us who cannot quite believe that we are not in the 1930's.

Criticizing student culture is like criticizing American culture generally. Some philosophers, some Europeans, and some outsiders may not like the practicality, the empiricism, the ethical relativism, the egalitarianism, the accent on social skill found in student culture, and in American culture generally, but there they are. Probably no one would call it all, or even mostly, bad, but the fact remains that it is not primarily an egghead culture. And that is precisely the rub, when our concern is with motivation for serious intellectual work.

This means, and we might as well face it, that to be a serious scholar at the student level, or to be a genuine intellectual in our society, is to be exceptional. One may, if he is fortunate, belong to, or join, an exceptional subculture; but usually he must be prepared to be an exception in the group in which he lives. There is at least one thing that highly motivated, high-achieving young women tend to have in common, and that is the capacity to be exceptional, whether this is derived from strength of character, happy accident, or plain necessity.

To describe a student culture and to say that a majority of the students are participating more or less fully in it is to appear to go along with Philip Jacob's (9) rather gloomy conclusion: that the major effect of college is to socialize students — to make them more alike and to integrate them more fully with our prevailing culture (see also pp. 69–70, 87–89). It is important to remember, however, that neither Jacob's report nor what I have said does justice to the great diversity of students, to be observed among different colleges and within a given college — even one with a pervasive peer culture. College peer culture undoubtedly exerts a strong pressure toward uniformity, but it certainly does not eliminate differences with respect to sex, age, social background, current group memberships, class in college, or personality. (Such differences may, of course, be obscured simply by speaking in terms of averages for whole college populations.)

Our program of personality testing has been concerned primarily with comparing freshmen and seniors. We find a great many differences, most of which are of the kind that we, as educators, usually hope to see. Seniors are freer from the historical matrix of values, their consciences are more enlightened and humanistic, their human impulses are more fully accepted and more fully expressed in suitable ways, their capacity for discrimination and control is more highly developed. We cannot demonstrate — yet — that these differences are not merely reflections of development such as might occur in various environments, but we believe that the effects of the college have been very considerable. We suspect that alumnae, within a few years after graduation, will show a tendency to revert to patterns of attitude and value that were characteristic of them before college, but we do not believe that this reversion will be anywhere near complete.

I am speaking of average differences between freshmen and seniors. The fact that seniors on the average are less conforming than freshmen does not mean that college students in general are not more conforming than they ought to be, or that the freshman-senior difference is as great as we should like to see.

Some Implications for Policy

The generalizations that I have made concerning the impact of the student peer culture, and the influence of the prevailing culture outside of the college, have important implications for policy. It seems clear that the college or university cannot assume that each student is a mature and independent person, ready to take full advantage of the intellectual fare that is offered. We must attend to ways and means for structuring the academic environment so that the unintellectual, or anti-intellectual, pressures are somehow reduced, and so that the faculty has at least a fair chance of influencing the students. This means, I believe, that we must be prepared to consider radical changes in the organization of our institutions of higher learning. It is, after all, something of a historical accident that these institutions are modeled after the German universities, with their accent on departments, research, and early specialization, rather than after the British model that accents the tutorial and the community of scholars.

14

The Professor Looks at the Student

I suggest that we examine closely the possibilities of reverting to the British model or something like it. Some of our universities clearly have expanded to a point where some further kind of division is called for, and indeed overdue. Our practice, of course, is to subdivide in accordance with fields of specialization — that is to say, to have departments, majors, schools, something that goes directly against the ideal of liberal education. Even our departments and schools have grown so large that they no longer can be called educational communities. Students tend increasingly to find their community elsewhere, in groups organized for purposes quite different from intellectual ones — groups which tend to inculcate values that oppose what a faculty tries to do. The kind of subdivision that would seem to make most sense, as far as the education of undergraduates is concerned, would be a simple division into a number of undergraduate colleges. These colleges might well differ among themselves in respect to what was taught, but insofar as possible each college should be a community in and of itself. This could best be achieved, I think, if students who lived together also studied the same curriculum, and were taught by the same group of faculty members. We do not know precisely the conditions for establishing and maintaining an intellectual community, but I suggest that it must be small enough so that all of the students and all of the faculty know each other. I suggest also, as minimal requirements, that most of what a given person studies must be the same as what the other students he lives with are studying, and that conditions must be established according to which faculty and students can see something of each other in situations other than the classroom or the formal conference.

This seems a simple enough arrangement, but I say it is radical because it challenges directly some of our most cherished academic traditions and some of our most deeply entrenched interests. It also challenges the illusion that college students are mature people, ready and able to select their own courses. It assumes, on the contrary, that we have to make some decisions concerning what they should learn, and that we have to arrange an environment that is favorable to their development. I am well aware of the difficulties in the way of changing the structures of our institutions of higher learning, but I am also aware of the difficulties in the way of changing the personality structures found in eighteen-year-olds, particularly when what they are already is reinforced by powerful forces in our society. I should say that it is easier to change the former than to change the latter, and I should doubt that changes in the institutional structure less radical than those I suggest would make noticeable differences in the functioning of student culture, or in the attitudes and values with which students leave our colleges today.

The Individual Student

One may be able to make such generalizations as have been made here concerning the students of today, and one may be familiar with such group differences as have been indicated, but still not know any particular student very well. Indeed, when one studies a particular student intensively, it becomes apparent that all of the kinds of factors that have been discussed here — the student peer culture, pressures from the contemporary society at large, and so on—are responsible for but a small part of that student's total functioning as a person. When one looks at the student as a total person, as one is invited to do by the Princeton autobiographies collected by Otto Butz or by case studies such as we have made at Vassar, it seems that what holds the case together is not the times in which he lives, not the social situation or the social role of the moment, but the inner structure of the personality itself. And when one examines the life history, one sees that this structure has been evolving throughout the person's lifetime. It is for this reason, I think, that the Princeton autobiographies resemble Harvard autobiographies of twenty-five years ago. Times may change, but the Oedipus complex remains much the same! Differences among students, with respect to such underlying personality structures, are of course as great as the differences among people of any other group, and it may well be that predictions of what a student will do in college and of what his future life pattern will be, were more safely based upon the underlying personality structure than upon factors that are operating in the student's contemporary environment.

It is, of course, strongly to be urged that everyone who has responsibility for the development of students should familiarize himself with the variety and complexity of personal structuring that is to be found among young people in our culture. We need to develop a library of case studies that will make it possible for teachers and other educators to enlarge their understanding of the individual student.

And yet it is not the individuality of the student that stands as the best guide for action. As we have seen, administrative actions affecting students have to be based on generalizations about them, that is, on observations of what they have in common. When we come to the person who deals with the student in face-to-face situations, the teacher or the counselor or the dean, it is still true, I think, that action always depends less on what is unique in that student than on conceptions of types. Even in counseling or in psychotherapy, one proceeds according to hypotheses concerning what actions will produce what effects in what *type* of case. The study of individuals is necessary and rewarding, not so much because we can act differently with respect to each of them, but because this kind of study ensures that our generalizations will be significant and valid. Thus I would argue that in the library of case studies that we may hope to assemble, cases should be grouped according to principles, and that these principles should be those most significant for educational objectives.

Types of Students

We become most interested in students, I think, when we see them within a suitable frame of reference, and when such a frame of reference has to do with developmental patterns and phases. A student becomes interesting when we can place him with respect to some developmental course, and if, when we see him from time to time, we can note progress or regression in relation to developmental goals. Students also become interesting when we can compare them in the same significant terms with other students. All people are interesting, of course, when we get to know them well, but it is when we can see them in a framework that permits their comparison with other people that they are most fascinating.

What all this adds up to is a statement of our pressing need for significant and empirically demonstrated typologies of students.

The discovery and delineation of such types has been the major objective of our research at Vassar. Some of our efforts in this direction have already been published. For example, in one paper (12) we distinguished a group of students who were characterized by what we called impulse-expression. These were students who, as they appeared on the campus as freshmen, seemed to exhibit a general readiness to seek gratification of impulses in overt action, as well as in conscious

17

fantasies. Such students would undoubtedly seem to the educator to be in need of self-discipline, or organization and integration. They stand in contrast to those students who display, from the very beginning, a high degree of organization and structure, and who strike the educator as being in need of awakening, broadening, and opening to experience. Teaching is quite a different undertaking in the two cases.

A type, in one sense, is a fairly simple thing. It need involve, as in the present case, only one dimension. Impulse-expression, as a variable of personality, is statistically independent of authoritarianism (15). Authoritarianism, of course, can be regarded as another type. Indeed, it has been so regarded, and its implications for development in college have been shown by George Stern (13, 14) to be large. Now, since impulse-expression and authoritarianism are statistically independent, it is a simple matter to group subjects who are high on both variables, low on both variables, or high on one and low on the other. One comes out with some interesting types. For example, a person who is high on both authoritarianism and impulse-expression is likely to be a fairly unpleasant person, whose punitive attitudes are likely to be carried into action; whereas a person who is high on impulse-expression but low on authoritarianism is likely to be perceived as a true Bohemian. Of course, as one introduces more variables into his typology, he finds that the type characterizes fewer subjects. The question of how inclusive in respect to variables the most useful typologies will be can only be answered through experience.

Donald Brown, in his contribution to our report in the *Journal of Social Issues* (2), developed an educational typology based on our studies of alumnae. He distinguished the *high achievers* who were outstanding both in capacity and in performance; the *over-achievers* who worked hard and did well without acquiring any serious appreciation of the intellectual life; the *under-achievers* who enjoyed college and grew intellectually while there without becoming seriously involved in work; a group whose college years were marked primarily by *social activity* and *orientation toward the peer group*; and, finally, the *seekers of identity,* whose college experience was primarily one of radical adjustment to a social world quite different from the one they came from.

It is our impression that this scheme holds pretty well for current students. But there is one big difference between now and 1930; today's students do not fit the types so neatly; each will exhibit a predominant pattern, but at least one and probably several of the other patterns will also have a place. In 1930, it seems, people showed a stronger tendency to be one thing or another; today the inclination to try to be all things—to be a balanced person, shall we say—is strong. For better or worse, the types are blurred.

Students representing these types have much in common, but they are by no means just alike. It is always possible further to distinguish among those who exemplify a given type, to delineate subtypes, as it were. For example, among the high achievers found in our sample of interviewees was the girl who had accepted the task of living up to the high expectations of her devoted and relatively uneducated parents, who never doubted her identity or her purpose, but who had to learn that she could not take care of *all* details, as her conscience demanded, and who is still wrestling with the problem of establishing her independence of her parents.

There was the girl whose mother was a scholar and teacher and whose father was a farmer of little education; as a little girl she was very close to her father and identified with him, but once in high school she found that she shared her mother's intellectual and cultural interests; her mother was the major source of conscience, the father the source of a major identification; she suffered in college from awkwardness in taking conventional feminine roles and from alienation from her peer society. (Like most of the others, she is married now, but we are betting that she continues her intellectual interests and makes the most of her education.)

Again, there was the girl who could best be characterized as her father's daughter. He was an intellectual lawyer, the mother a housewife with a primary interest in social affairs. This girl was out to please her father, and to separate herself from her mother's value system. She was a rather unhappy science major; she complained about what she and her father called the grubby aspects of science but showed a remarkable grasp of conceptual and theoretical issues. Her biggest problem will be to find social roles in which she can use her talents. (Incidentally, it would appear that this type of girl will be found more often in coeducational schools than in the women's colleges.)

19

Finally, there was the product of a broken home: a girl who was passed back and forth between her parents, both of whom were remarried; she rejected her mother whom she described as a member of the canasta set, but felt rejected by her father — an intellectual and an artist—who seemed to have no faith in her ability or serious purpose. For her, college was a home; it offered her her first chance to make stable identifications. She incorporated fully the values of the faculty — the women particularly — and is well on her way to becoming a scholar and teacher. The fact that her motivation for scholarship has been largely neurotic will not necessarily make her activities less valuable.

I am not suggesting that these are all the types of high achievers to be found among women, or that each of these subtypes could not be subdivided. The question is, how far in this direction ought we to go? As our type grows in complexity, embracing more different kinds of factors, there are fewer subjects who exemplify it, and pretty soon we come to the single person, in all his uniqueness. As I have said, this is certainly not too far to go in search of understanding, but it is too far for general educational planning.

One might hope that we could deal practically with types as complex as those just described. But the outlook is not very promising. The students I have described attended a superior college, and yet with all their diversity they were not only treated just alike in all important matters, but they were treated just like all the other types of students. Now and then we talk of programs for superior students — programs presumably based on what they have in common. But it is clear from the above that such programs will be better for some than for others. It is possible that those who deal with them face to face can still take into account some of the differences among them.

Conclusion

The professor, as he looks carefully at the students, has to admit that he really does not know very much about these very interesting people. This is not to belittle the practical experience and wisdom that have been acquired through the years, or the studies that have been carried out in the past. Most of these latter have had to be carried out without benefit of the advances in the psychological and social sciences that have been made in the last ten or fifteen years. What we most want to know, as I suggested at the beginning, is what kinds of practices affecting what kinds of structures in the entering materials will bring about changes in the direction of specified objectives.

In our studies of students, we must find a suitable balance between, on the one hand, our interest in generalizations which hold, more or less, for all students, and upon which we may base general policy— what works best for most students — and, on the other hand, our interest in group and individual differences — what works best for the principal kinds of students.

We must also strike the right balance between persistence and change; or, more precisely, we must discover the articulation of durable trends in the personality and influences of the college environment, in the determination of the student's behavior.

A young woman, of our sample of interviewees, broke away from the student culture during her junior year in college, and thereupon there took place marked changes in her attitudes, interests, and values. This is not the most usual occurrence, and one naturally asks why, and how. In this particular case the event was striking because the young woman came from a highly conventional upper-middle-class home, and seemed to have been a fairly typical peer-oriented high school girl and college freshman. She cited as the chief reason for her change of outlook the influence of a young professor of political science, who had aroused in her a deep interest in international relations. We were inclined to accept this, but to attach importance also to the influence of a rather intellectual and offbeat roommate with whom she chanced to be thrown.

However, study of her life history revealed that she had shown some capacity for nonconformity, and for having unusual interests, as a high school student. Despite the disapproval of her parents and friends, she persisted in going steady with a boy from the other side of the tracks; when it became necessary, she saw him unbeknownst to her parents, and she actually suffered ejection from her sorority because she would not give him up. She said later it was mostly because she was sorry for the boy.

The question is, how do we account for her development of independence and wide-ranging interests in college? Was it primarily because of the teacher and the roommate, or was it that the processes making for these outcomes were set in motion long before she entered college? We may well suspect a connection between her interest in international relations and her earlier interest in the "foreigner," the boy from across the tracks. Study of her case reveals other antecedents of this trend in her personality and experience, going all the way back to childhood. It would be ridiculous to derive an interest in international relations from certain childhood experiences and dispositions; yet perhaps it would not be much sounder to suppose that the efforts of a teacher or the influence of a roommate could be so effective were not some state of readiness already present in the personality.

The kind of formulation we need might be somewhat as follows: the ongoing processes of the personality have determined certain general directions of, and probably set some limits to, development, by the time a student enters college. But many partings of the ways remain; and the more precise direction may be largely determined by influences that now intervene. What happens will be consistent, in some fundamental way, with what has gone before, but probably in no case will it be merely a playing out of such predispositions.

Thus we are not justified in accenting either fixity or change as general principles; rather should we accent change of certain possible kinds in certain structures under certain conditions.

Our tendency in planning for undergraduate and graduate education has been, I think, to overaccent the element of persistence in the personality structure. Our preoccupation with prediction, in the sense of forecasting, has been permitted to interfere with our task of understanding. We should be less concerned with what students are *likely* to do, and more concerned with what they *might* do — given an understanding of the situations that will bring out their best.

A professor of psychology, returning to his department after being absent during the fall semester, was approached by a first-year graduate student who wanted to work with him. The student explained that he had been having some trouble, that he seemed to have got off on the wrong foot, and that some of the professors perhaps did not regard him very highly. A half hour's conference revealed that he had a sort of rebel complex which drove him to provoke his teachers in order to see whether they would not reject him, so that he would have some justification for the vague hostility he felt. This was pointed out to him, and after further discussion he signed up for a seminar and for individual work. He turned out to be an excellent student, full of good ideas and willing to work. During the final examination period that semester, this student went to his professor and, in a state of great distress, announced that he had been dismissed from the department. There had been a department meeting to review the statuses of graduate students and our professor, who may have been something of a rebel himself, had not attended. Since there was no one there to speak of the student's current work, he was dismissed on the basis of his record for the first semester. Well, it was possible to get him reinstated, but the damage had already been done. He was still enough of a rebel — or had enough pride — to choose to go elsewhere.

I submit that our graduate schools and departments lose a great many students, under circumstances not unlike those just described, every year. Consider: these schools and departments select pretty carefully and, I believe, pretty effectively; there is very little reason to doubt the ability of their students to do the work. Yet of every entering class a significant number will drop out, a fairly large proportion will barely get through, and few will be highly satisfactory graduates. What makes the difference? I suggest that it has much to do with whether or not the student can integrate himself with the social structure of the school or department, whether or not his personality needs can find expression in the social roles that he is required to take.

If the situation is far less than satisfactory in the graduate schools, it is no doubt worse in the undergraduate departments, where the drop-out rate is higher than we care to contemplate and where failure to benefit from the college experience is all too common.

The state of affairs cannot be corrected by individual counseling, however beneficial this might be. The students I am talking about are enmeshed in a social structure; the difficulty lies in their interrelationships with organized other people; the therapy has to be directed to that structure itself.

Now, in the recent flurry of discussion of higher education there has been virtually no criticism of what the colleges and universities are doing. The general assumption seems to be that there is nothing wrong that higher salaries for teachers cannot cure. I am, of course, willing to participate in this conspiracy — up to a point — but as a social scientist I cannot remain as blind to the situation as might be expedient.

The newspapers tell us that our generals, our scientist-politicians, our human engineers, and many ordinary wrong-headed citizens, are going to solve our educational problems by better selection, and by earlier identification and fuller reward of talent. They propose to turn these able youngsters loose — if they survive the ravages of high school — in our presumably impeccable colleges and universities, and let nature take its course, or the devil take the hindmost.

I doubt whether anything very good will come of this. Selection can be improved, of course, but not very much; and, as for the bright youngsters who don't go to college, let the generals and their cohorts consider this: present programs for identifying and rewarding talent will hardly make a dent in the number of talented youngsters who do not go to college; the only thing that will make a sizable dent is social and economic reconstruction, involving those huge segments of our population that are economically underprivileged or socially marginal.

I should not think the college would want to invest much more in efforts to corral the best students. Instead, they should concentrate on making the most of the students they admit. Talent has to be nurtured; and talents of high order can be spoiled in college. Every drop-out, every failure to achieve reasonable objectives, is not just a criticism of the selection committee, or the high schools, or the society of today, or of our stars; it is also a criticism of the educational policies and practices of the particular college or university involved. Precisely at this point is a science of development in college most needed. Of course, such a science would require that we go on studying our students; but it would also require that we take a hard look at ourselves, as groups, as the constituents of institutional structures, and as individual occupants of social roles.

REFERENCES

1. Allport, Gordon W. *Personality*. New York: Henry Holt & Company, Inc., 1937.
2. Brown, D. "Some Educational Patterns," in Nevitt Sanford, ed. "Personality Development during the College Years." *Journal of Social Issues*, 12:44–60, 1956.
3. Butz, Otto, ed. *The Unsilent Generation*. New York: Rinehart & Company, Inc., 1958.
4. Erikson, Erik H. "Growth and Crises of the 'Healthy Personality.'" In Clyde Kluckohn and H. A. Murray, eds. *Personality in Nature, Society and Culture*, 2nd ed., rev. New York: Alfred A. Knopf, Inc., 1953.
5. Freedman, M. "The Passage through College," in Nevitt Sanford, ed. "Personality Development during the College Years." *Journal of Social Issues*, 12:13–28, 1956.
6. Fromm, Erich. *Man for Himself*. New York: Rinehart & Company, Inc., 1947.
7. Gillespie, J. M., and Gordon W. Allport. *Youth's Outlook on the Future*. New York: Doubleday & Company, Inc., 1955.

8. Goldstein, Kurt. *The Organism*. New York: American Book Company, 1939.
9. Jacob, Philip E. *Changing Values in College*. New York: Harper and Brothers, 1957.
10. Maslow, Abraham H. *Motivation and Personality*. New York: Harper and Brothers, 1954.
11. Murray, H. A., and others. *Explorations in Personality*. New York: Oxford University Press, 1938.
12. Sanford, Nevitt, Harold Webster, and Mervin Freedman. "Impulse Expression as a Variable of Personality." *Psychological Monographs*, 71:1–21, No. 11, 1957.
13. Stern, G. G. "Personality-Centered Research and Psychological Education." *American Psychologist*, 8:8, 1953 (abstract).
14. ———, and A. H. Cope. "Differences in Educability between Stereopaths, Non-Stereopaths, and Rationals." *American Psychologist*, 11:8, 1956.
15. Webster, H. "The VC Attitude Inventory and the VC Figure Preference Test: Research Manual." Vassar College, Mellon Foundation, 1957 (mimeographed).
16. White, R. W. *Lives in Progress*. New York: Dryden Press, Inc., 1952.

Mr. Sanford is at the University of California in Berkeley.

◆§ WILBERT J. McKEACHIE

How Do Students Learn?

W<small>HAT</small> happens between the time a student enrolls in a course and the time he receives his grade? The student has come to class; he has read assignments; he has taken some tests; he may even have written a term paper. These activities have become traditional because they are presumed to contribute to learning. But do they? What evidence do we have that any of the things that society pays college professors to do actually makes any difference?

When you stop to think of it, there isn't much evidence! We sometimes say that our real objective is not just the teaching of facts but the development of attitudes and values. Yet Philip Jacob's book, *Changing Values in College* (4) summarizes a number of studies showing no change in attitudes or values associated with taking a course. For that matter Jacob's book suggests that most colleges have relatively little lasting effect on students over the whole four-year period. (See also pp. 69–70, 87–89.)

It's no wonder that educational research hasn't flourished. It's too discouraging! (As a comforting aside, let me point out that evidence on the effectiveness of the church, prisons, psychotherapy, and other social institutions is just as negative.) But people do change. Even students change sometimes. Learning does take place. What sorts of learning occur? What can we professors do to influence learning? How do college students learn?

A look at our statements of the goals of our courses indicates the sort of learning we hope will take place. As a minimum we would hope (a) that students would learn some facts. In addition we would expect them (b) to develop some concepts and principles, and we would like them to learn to use these concepts and principles to solve problems they haven't previously encountered. Further, we hope (c) that they'll learn to appreciate and value scholarly activity, especially in the area in which we're teaching. Most of us have other objectives as well. Nevertheless, the basic categories I've suggested may be helpful in pointing to some principles of learning.

Motivation

Let us look first simply at the processes by which students learn and remember facts and principles. Here, psychology has done a good deal of relevant research. For example, we know that students' learning is closely tied to their *motivation*. Students will learn what they want to learn and will have great difficulty learning material they're not interested in. Much as we would like to teach only those who are eager to learn, most of us have to recognize that not all students are deeply interested in everything we like to teach.

One of our primary problems, then, is motivating students. Usually the learning psychologist stops at this point, for we don't have a well-developed taxonomy of motives and situations. But I'd like to go on. We know, for example, that most of our students want to be successful and will learn whatever they believe is necessary to make them successful. Unfortunately, they often consider that extracurricular and social activities contribute more to success than courses.

We know, too, that most of our students want to be liked. But this motive may work against us as well as for us. Our friendly approval can be an important reward for learning, but groups of students, like groups of workers, have fairly clear standards of the proper amount of work to do. The "average-raiser"—like the "rate-buster"—finds that he loses friends every time he performs better than the acceptable standard. (For more on Everett Hughes' industrial analogy, see p. 44.) Students who want to be accepted by their classmates may have to avoid any conspicuous display of academic achievement. One of the symptoms of this sort of conflict about getting good grades is the ostentatious neglect of study by some bright students and their apparent surprise when they get good grades. This ploy is so well known that its techniques have been analyzed carefully by Stephen Potter in his scholarly volume, *One-upmanship*.

Many of our students have other conflicting motives. In the age group we're dealing with, one common conflict is between independence and dependence. This means that students are likely to resent the teacher who directs their activities closely but they are also unhappy when given independence; so that we have to perform the neat trick of finding ways of simultaneously satisfying both needs. As a result of this conflict some students disagree with the instructor not on any rational grounds but simply as a way of expressing emotions.

I'm sure any college teacher could supply a longer list of important motives. My point here is simply that these provide the tools by which we get learning to take place, and as far as retention or speed of learning is concerned, it doesn't seem to matter much which motives you use — the important thing is that motivation exist and that conflicts not be activated.

If this be so, let us consider the case of our most important motivational device—grades. Whatever a student's motivation for being in college, grades are important to him. If he is really interested in learning, grades represent an expert's appraisal of his success; if he's interested in getting into a professional school, good grades are the key that will unlock graduate school doors; if he wants to play football, grades are necessary for maintaining eligibility. In short, most students are motivated to get passing grades, and much as we resent the registrar's demands, the grades for which we're responsible are a powerful motivational tool for teaching.

Most of us are a little embarrassed by this. We regard grades as one of the necessary evils of teaching. We try to discount grades in our discussion of the organization of the course, and try to arrive at grades in such a way that we can avoid trouble with disappointed students. But we frequently fail to use grades to bring about the sort of learning we want.

Because grades are important to students, they will learn whatever is necessary to get the grades they desire. Students eagerly grasp at any clues available, and their best clues are examinations. If we base our examinations on memorization of details in the textbook, students will memorize the text. If they believe our grades are based upon their ability to integrate and apply principles, they'll attempt to do this.

I said that, as far as speed of learning goes, it doesn't matter what motives you use, but this doesn't mean that the *type* of motivation used is unimportant. A good deal of evidence has accumulated to suggest that negative and positive motives affect behavior differently. Fear of sarcasm is an example of negative motivation. Hope of the instructor's approval is an example of positive motivation. In teaching we usually use mixtures of positive and negative motives. When negative motives predominate, students will work hard, but only if this is the only way to avoid unpleasant consequences. If there are ways out of the situation, they'll take them. The result frequently is that students do the least they can get away with.

Negative motives are not so effective outside the threatening situation as are positive motives because the motivating power of fear becomes weak if the danger is not close. Thus the professor who motivates his students by fear of bad grades needs to use frequent tests if his threats are to be effective.

The striking difference between the behavior of students motivated by fear and the behavior of students motivated by hope is illustrated during examinations. Studies by J. W. Atkinson and G. H. Litwin (1), and by myself (7), showed that students who were high in anxiety about tests tended to do more poorly on the final examination than in their work during the course. Why? One clue comes from behavior during the exam period. The students who complete the exam first and leave are the most anxious students; the exam situation was so painful for them that they just couldn't stay. Students with positive motivation to succeed tended to stay in the examination room longer. This also illustrates another important point. Students differ in motivation, and a situation producing good achievement for some may actually hurt the achievement of others.

To sum up my argument thus far, motivation is important in learning. We can use students' needs for success, approval, and the like to produce learning. Grades are important for many kinds of motivation. Thus it's important to make sure that grades not be separate from the kind of learning we want to occur. However, using grades chiefly as a threat may produce avoidance rather than interest, and may be particularly harmful to the most anxious students.

Organization

Now let's turn to another learning principle. A teacher's job isn't finished when he interests his class, for the amount they learn depends upon the amount he teaches, and this is not so simple as it may at first appear. It may well be that the *more* we teach the *less* our students learn! Several years ago some of our teaching fellows were arguing furiously about how to teach the nervous system. One group argued that since students wouldn't remember all of the details, we might better omit them and teach only the basic essentials we wanted everyone to learn. Another group argued that students would forget much of what they learned; "But," they said, "if they're going to forget a large percentage anyway, we need to teach much more than we expect them to remember. Otherwise they're likely to forget even the important things."

To a group of psychologists such an argument is simply an invitation to an experiment. Consequently the combatants agreed that they'd try out their ideas in their own classes, and compare the results on the final examination questions covering the nervous system. Would you like to bet on the outcome? It was clear-cut. The students whose instructors had omitted details were clearly superior to those whose instructors had given them the whole story.

This result would not have been surprising to David Katz, a Swedish psychologist who devised a number of unique experiments demonstrating that beyond a certain point, adding to the elements in an intellectual task causes confusion and inefficiency (6). Katz called this phenomenon "mental dazzle" and judging from the bluebooks I read, mental dazzle affects some of my students pretty frequently.

Fortunately, teaching is a situation in which you can have your cake and eat it too, for it is possible to teach more details and have them remembered better. The magic formula is *organization*. As George Katona (5) demonstrated in a series of experiments on organization and memory, we can learn and remember much more when our learning fits into an organization. If I give you a series of numbers chosen at random—73850472—and ask you what the fourth number was, you'll probably have difficulty remembering; but if I give you the numbers 87654321, you can remember immediately what the fourth number was. In both cases the number is 5. The difference in ease of remembering is a function of organization. By remembering the principle of organization you can recapture the details.

Teaching that helps students find a framework to fit new facts into is likely to be much more effective than teaching that simply communicates masses of material in which the student can see no organization. I should guess that the most successful organization is one in which the students themselves can achieve an insight just before the instructor makes it explicit. If you'd like to see some excellent models of this sort of teaching, reread Plato's dialogues.

Thus *motivation* and *organization* are two key concepts which should guide our efforts at reaching our first objective of communicating knowledge.

Experience vs. Words

The concept of organization leads us to the heart of the second objective we try to achieve. How can we help students develop principles and concepts which they can apply more broadly than answering a true-false examination question which quotes a sentence from the textbook? I suppose all of us have been disheartened by having a student answer a question of fact perfectly and then fail to use the same fact in solving a problem where it is relevant. This problem of transfer of training is one of the classic research areas in psychology, and organization is clearly one of the solutions. When students understand general concepts and principles they are much more likely to be able to use their learning in new situations than they are if they have learned only a mass of specific details.

But the problem of making use of learning is much more complicated than this. We all know students who can remember general principles perfectly, but who are totally unable to see their relevance to a concrete problem.

The learning-by-doing philosophy of education was an attempt to make learning real and applicable. The theory was that if a student learned something in the situation in which he had to apply it, he wouldn't have to take the extra step of learning when to apply it. This is perfectly reasonable: there is good psychological evidence that active participation promotes retention and that in training for a specific use it is frequently efficient to give the training on the job rather than simply talking about it. But this solution is not so beautiful as it may first appear. The joker is that the number of situations in which we must use learning is infinite. Can you imagine where the human race would be if each of us had to learn everything by doing it himself? We wouldn't even have reached the Neolithic Age. Civilization is based on the fact that man can use words to short-cut the long process of learning by trial and error. Direct experience is useful at certain stages of learning. If we are to learn to apply a principle in new situations, we need to experience specific instances of the principle in varying situations. But *verbalization* can help us identify the common elements in these situations and can greatly shorten the learning process as well as improve the ability to apply what has been learned.

Feedback

If we expect students to learn skills in applying principles, they have to practice. But practice doesn't make perfect. Practice works when the learner *knows the results* of his practice — when he gets feedback. For example, discussion techniques may help develop critical thinking because students do the thinking. But one of the dangers of so-called student-centered or nondirective discussions is that the *results* are not apparent. Students may make comments, express opinions, and participate actively, but this doesn't guarantee that their opinions are any more informed at the end of a semester than they were at the beginning. Not all feedback has to come from the instructor; students can learn much from other students, but in order to learn, they need to test out their ideas in a situation in which they can get the results of the test.

This criticism of student-centered teaching shouldn't lead you to dismiss it. Several years ago we ran an experiment in elementary psychology classes, comparing the effectiveness of discussion with recitation-drill, and with a modified tutorial method of teaching (3). The results were disappointing to those of us who were pulling for discussion. Not only did the autocratic recitation-drill method produce better performance on the final examination, but what really surprised us was that the more we quizzed them, the better the students liked it. These good results on examinations, of course, fit in with our belief that knowledge of results aids learning. These students had been taking tests every week, and they'd learned the results.

Developing Motivation for Intellectual Activity

But we weren't satisfied. Our students who had recited and been drilled had learned lots of facts, but we weren't convinced that this kind of teaching had achieved objectives. Consequently, in our next experiment (2, 7), we tried to measure ability to apply. In this experiment we had two kinds of classes — student-centered discussion and instructor-centered discussion. Our measure was an unusual one. We showed a filmed case history and then recorded the class discussion that followed the film. We then asked two clinical psychologists who knew nothing about the classes to give us their judgments about the discussion. You can guess how it came out!

Students in our instructor-centered classes were all too typical of beginning psychology students. They were happy to avoid the problems posed in the film by pinning labels on the heroine's symptoms. Both our judges, however, doubted that the other discussion had come from an elementary psychology class. Our judges reported that the student-centered class showed real understanding of the case presented. Despite the fact that the classes made similar scores on our final exam, the student-centered group had learned to apply their learning in a classroom discussion, and the instructor-centered class hadn't.

To account for these results we have to go a step beyond our principle that students learn what they practice with knowledge of results. It's not always easy to get students to practice critical thinking. After all, why stick my neck out? If I sit quietly, I avoid the risks of having someone disagree with me. No one will criticize my ideas if I don't say anything. And consequently, many students won't try to express their own thoughts, but simply keep quiet or try to tell the instructor what he wants to hear. To develop critical thinking, the student must learn to *want* to think critically, and must learn to do so in some way that will give him feedback. This brings us to our third category of goals of education — developing interests, creating motivation, valuing intellectual activity. There are many ways to do this. If we want to develop an interest in critical thinking we have to make it satisfying. A smile, a nod of encouragement, an excited "Good! Let's follow that idea through" — these are the tools that we can use, not only to provide knowledge of results, but also to develop the motivation to continue intellectual activity.

We need to pose problems that are within the range of our students' abilities. Studies of the development of achievement in children indicate that parents develop this motivation by encouraging the child to do well and by setting standards which the child can meet. Other parents who orient their child toward achievement fail because they set unreasonably high goals. So for the purposes of both motivating students for critical thinking and developing the ability to think critically, experience in solving problems within the student's ken is essential. This, by no means implies that the student should never experience failure or criticism, but it does mean that he should be faced with problems which will more often than not be soluble.

One of the misconceptions of educators who have recognized the importance of motivation is that they've stopped with the motives students already have. Teachers have assumed that students will learn only those things in which they're already interested; so they minimize uninteresting content. But a student's motives are not fixed. We can create new motives. We can teach students to enjoy learning for its own sake. While we must make use of existing motives to create initial satisfactions in learning, we need not be limited by them.

Summary

We can make the following generalizations about students' learning processes: (a) Learning depends upon motivation. (b) Many of our students have conflicting motives in this area. (c) Grades are goals for many important motives; therefore students learn what is necessary to get the grades they desire. (d) Anxiety is likely to cause avoidance of situations where failure may occur and thus produce poor performances. (e) Organization facilitates retention and application. (f) Practice with knowledge of results is necessary in learning to think critically as well as in developing other skills. (g) Intellectual motivation can be learned by making initial intellectual activities satisfying.

In short, college students do learn, and they can learn not only facts but ways of thinking. Most important, we can help them learn to like learning and thinking!

REFERENCES

1. Atkinson, J. W., and G. H. Litwin. "An Experimental Study of Need-Achievement and Examination Anxiety." Paper presented at Psi Chi Colloquium, Bowling Green, Ohio, March 8, 1958.
2. Bovard, E. W., Jr. "The Psychology of Classroom Interaction." *Journal of Educational Research*, 45:215–24, 1951.
3. Guetzkow, H., E. L. Kelly, and W. J. McKeachie. "An Experimental Comparison of Recitation, Discussion, and Tutorial Methods in College Teaching." *Journal of Educational Psychology*, 45:193–207, 1954.
4. Jacob, Philip E. *Changing Values in College.* New York: Harper and Brothers, 1957.

5. Katona, George. *Organizing and Memorizing.* New York: Columbia University Press, 1940.
6. Katz, D. *Gestalt Psychology.* New York: Ronald Press, 1950.
7. McKeachie, W. J. "Anxiety in the College Classroom." *Journal of Educational Research,* 45:153–60, 1951.

MR. MCKEACHIE is in the department of psychology at the University of Michigan.

~§ WILBERT J. McKEACHIE

Motivating Students' Interest

ONE of my colleagues says that his classes are only for those students who are eager to learn. The title of this chapter indicates that we don't all have such students. Yet a very good case could be made for the statement that all students *are* eager to learn. The learning they desire, however, does not always coincide with the learning we desire for them. The trick of teaching is to transfer the student's motivation to the learning desired by the instructor.

How Do We Create Motivation?

From studies of motivation we know that there are two methods of developing motivation for learning. One of these involves making learning instrumental for motives a person already has. Using this approach we try to show students how our courses will contribute to their goals in life. This approach leads to emphasis upon practical aspects of college courses — which can be a valuable tool in creating interest. But when we teach psychology or English or physics — practical subjects — we are teaching values. I'm not sure that we want to teach our students that the most important values are the practical ones of getting a job and succeeding in business. Nevertheless, we need to continually keep before ourselves and our students the goals toward which we are working and the relation of students' behavior to these goals.

The second approach to motivation involves developing new motives for learning. I would suggest that one of our goals in a liberal education is to teach our students to be interested in intellectual activity for its own sake. How can we do this?

The first step is to make learning satisfying. Paradoxically, this means that we must use the motives our students already have, so we may want to help a student see that his learning is really useful to him. But the difference between this approach and the first approach is that we can't stop here. We must also reward learning which is not directly useful. Instead of trying to justify the usefulness of each detail, we need to make rewards contingent upon longer and longer stretches of learning and higher and higher levels of intellectual activity. The teacher can use not only grades but also his own approval and warmth as rewards. By our own enthusiasm for our subject matter we make our students conscious of the possibilities of joy in learning. As one discussion group put it, "We not only want to keep the student awake *in* class; we want to keep him awake *out of* class."

Probably most of us think of ourselves as using this second approach. Let me remind you that it has to begin with the student's motives as they are, and that we have to begin by providing satisfactions for the motives our student already has. Both of our approaches depend upon a knowledge of students' existing motives — such as motivation for achievement, motivation for affiliation, and motivation for power and prestige. Knowing that such motives are common, and knowing that students have fears as well as hopes about them, we can better choose teaching techniques which will increase students' motivation for learning. We can choose when to use one approach and when the other.

Individual Differences in Motivation

Knowing *general* student motives, however, is only a first step in facilitating motivation for learning, because individual students differ. Techniques that fire some with enthusiasm may push others into sullen inactivity. For example, we have some evidence that a student high in need for achievement works well alone. Given a challenging task to do by himself he works hard and effectively. On the other hand, we have some evidence that the anxious student is relatively unhappy and ineffective when turned loose to work on an important task by himself. He feels lost, and wants the teacher's advice about how to proceed. He much prefers the comfortable routine of a conventional teacher-directed class.

Using a variety of teaching methods is another technique of arousing interest. For most students this is effective. But here again the anxious student is affected differently. He functions best, we believe, in a situation where he knows what to expect. When an instructor tries something new, the anxious student is thrown off stride. He has learned to take notes, read assignments, and cope with the everyday routine of most courses, but he is thrown off stride when the teacher changes pace. Any teacher who has tried a new method of teaching has run into unexplainable hostility and resentment. The reason is that new methods threaten students' well-learned habits of achieving. I suspect that one of the reasons we teachers settle into ruts is that the students won't let us out. I've tried to show that there's good reason for this — change is motivating, but too much change arouses anxiety; how much is too much depends upon the students.

Participation in classroom discussion is a technique which not only gives students an opportunity to check their ideas, but helps them to find answers to questions in which they're interested. Thus discussion may be a way of adjusting our teaching to some of the individual differences in motivation. But here again we run into problems caused by differences in motivation. Let's look, for example, at the student who is high in need for affiliation. He likes to participate and to influence other people and he's sensitive to the reactions of others. But this may put him in a difficult situation in the classroom. Obviously it's important to be liked by the teacher, so he is likely to volunteer often and to try to give the instructor what he wants. But at the same time our student wants to be liked by other students and there is a danger that other students will resent overparticipation and apple-polishing. Such students are likely to be more highly regarded by instructors than by their classmates; so that conflict occurs even in the student who most enjoys participation and social interaction. In the seat beside the student high in need for affiliation may be a student who fears rejection. If the instructor is occasionally sarcastic, or if some other students are argumentative, the student who fears rejection passes each hour in mortal dread of the moment when he'll be expected to participate.

How Can We Tell Whether Students Are Motivated?

In attempting to motivate students one must be able to recognize whether or not he is succeeding. Fortunately there are many clues — questions, involvement in discussion, performance on examinations, work on term papers or special projects; all provide evidence of motivation. In addition there are the visual cues of nods, smiles, and keen attention. Using these, the teacher can adjust his motivational techniques to his class.

Unsolved Problems

It is clear that motivating student interest is not a simple topic. We do not have definitive answers to any of the following questions: What motives are the most important for learning? How do students differ in motivation? What motivational techniques are best adapted to each type of student? How can we best handle individual differences in motivation? Are there certain motivational techniques which are effective for all students in our culture?

What I've said probably sounds discouraging, for it implies that teachers can't win, that any teaching method that will motivate some students will scare others. This is not quite true: the instructor's enthusiasm, I'd guess, would help increase motivation for most students. But recognizing that individual differences exist, we can more wisely balance our motivational techniques to teach students that learning is fun!

THIS chapter, prepared by Mr. McKeachie, reflects the discussion of a group of which John Neumaier of Hibbing Junior College and Ruth Eckert of the College of Education, University of Minnesota, were chairmen; and James I. Brown, St. Paul Campus, University of Minnesota, and Brother L. Michael, F.S.C., St. Mary's College, were recorders.

Challenging the Gifted Student

Of one thing I am very sure. There are very few universally accepted and certain answers to the problem of adequately challenging the gifted student. Eight or nine years ago, when I was associate dean of arts and sciences at another large state university, a freshman came into the college office a day or two after Easter vacation with a question. She said that she was troubled. She had been graduated the previous May from one of the best high schools in the state. Most of her friends had gone to eastern liberal arts colleges with highly selective admission. She had been proud of the straight A grades she had made in the fall semester and of the fact that she was on the college honors list. Her friends had thoroughly deflated her satisfaction with her performance, however, by commenting that everyone knows that an A at the state university is really only equivalent to a C at such-and-such colleges. Her question was Is this true?

During the next several years some of us worked hard to try to find out what the quality of our best students was and the extent to which they were working up to their potential. We also worked hard to revivify the traditional upper-division honors programs. We learned that very little information was easily available about the efforts of other universities in dealing with gifted students. By comparison with the efforts that had gone into experiments with general education, for example, or into remedial programs of one kind or another, colleges seemed to have given negligible attention to the gifted.

In 1955 and 1956 I was fortunate in receiving from the Carnegie Corporation a travel grant which permitted me to visit some twenty-five colleges and universities in an effort to find out some of the best measures that are being used to guarantee adequate challenge to gifted students in colleges and universities. More recently, in addition to an experimental program for the gifted in arts and sciences at the University of Kansas, I have also been involved in an effort called the Inter-University Committee on Superior Students. This organization performs a most valuable service in distributing each month a newsletter devoted to information on programs for the superior student in American colleges and universities. Except for occasional interesting reports on special projects at individual colleges, such as that describing the undergraduate research program in mathematics at Carleton College (2), and brief notes on a variety of programs, such as those supplied in the *ACLS Newsletter* (4), there is little information available concerning programs for the gifted student at the college level except through the ICSS newsletter, *The Superior Student*. J. W. Cohen of the University of Colorado is editor-in-chief of this publication.

Some Issues and Assumptions about the Gifted Student

I shall try, first, to raise some of the general issues and question some of the assumptions that circulate concerning the gifted student in higher education. Later, I should like to focus in slightly more detail on the problems of the gifted freshman. Of the general issues, seven or eight deserve attention.

First, let's worry a little less about the impending tidal wave of students (a very much overworked phrase) during the next decade. The prospectus of this conference states the over-all purpose of the conference in a significant way: "With the heavy influx of students during the next decade, the procurement of buildings and finance will be a serious problem, but the most critical concern of all is what happens to the individual student in the classroom. Will the quality of teaching be held high?" We do not usually believe in looking backward in these practical matters, but here, for me at least, a backward glance is instructive. In the university in which I teach the total enrollment in 1940 was about four thousand. Now, eighteen years later, it is nine thousand three hundred. We estimate that in the next eighteen years the enrollment may rise to fifteen or sixteen thousand. In the last eighteen years enrollment has somewhat more than doubled; the numbers of the faculty have tripled. The enrollment increases will come through small increments each year. It is wrong for us to envisage the increase as a sudden tidal wave like that of the GI bulge of 1946–47.

Because I am sure that the GI bulge did damage to our methods of teaching undergraduates (damage that was not repaired when the number declined), I do not like to see us — in a group concerned with the adequacy of our challenge to gifted students — thinking in terms merely of maintaining the present quality of our teaching.

Second, in a period when there is endless criticism of the quality of teaching in the secondary schools, two important facts are neglected: (a) there is much more active concern and experimentation in the high schools with adequate programs for the gifted than there is in higher education, and (b) the problems that confront every college that does not have a very high degree of selective admission are similar to those of the high school. In addition, the colleges have both the function of providing leadership for the secondary schools and the responsibility, especially at the freshman level, of making sure that the gifted student is not forced to duplicate in college a good part of what he has already covered in high school. One has only to examine the accelerated program for the gifted in a high school like those in Oak Park, Illinois, Omaha, and Cincinnati to realize how grave this danger is for a gifted freshman. Incidentally, when a liberal arts college has a challenging and rigorous honors program, the student who completes it with distinction and then goes on to a large graduate school faces the same danger of wasting a good part of his first year.

Third, the same teaching methods cannot be applied to all students, particularly to the gifted. I sat in the back row of a class in literature last year in a major eastern university and watched a distinguished professor of Augustan literature lecture to a highly selected and highly motivated honors group of freshmen. The minimum IQ was 130. The professor had not taught lower-division students for many years and was obviously using his standard approach to juniors and seniors. He would make a generalization, pause for a moment, and then repeat it in a paraphrase. From my vantage point I could see the students listen carefully to the first statement and then relax as their attention wandered and they patiently waited for the professor to get around to the communication of another idea. The most striking characteristics of gifted students are their quickness of mind, their ability to handle theoretical material and abstract ideas, their ability to pull together from all their experience any information or theory relevant to a point at issue, and their real delight in ideas. These students do not need lectures that water down and simplify what they have already mastered from reading assigned materials. They come to delight in seminar-style classes in which they are expected to participate actively.

Fourth, let us recognize, as did Nevitt Sanford in his chapter, that attention must be paid to the nature of THE contemporary undergraduate. The adequate challenging of the gifted must, first of all, recognize that undergraduates do not follow a pattern in many important respects; even the gifted differ immensely in personality, intellectual style, and the like. I have not forgotten an interview I had some years ago with a straight-A second-semester sophomore girl, in which I invited her to make application for a junior-senior departmental honors program, then chiefly made up of independent study. Shyly, she said she had two questions: who would lecture to her and might she have time to ask her mother for permission. Last week I talked with a very bright boy who had a different kind of personality. He volunteered before he left the campus this spring to help reorganize the department he is majoring in— to assist me and the chairman in remedying weaknesses of personnel and curriculum. These extreme cases should not be taken as contradictions of the known fact that gifted students, on the whole, are precocious intellectually, physically, and socially. Yet these students are individuals and must be treated as individuals.

Fifth, as was pointed out by Wilbert McKeachie in his chapters, it is necessary to consider the relevant psychological bases for learning. These facts and principles are important and I will not repeat them. What is often overlooked, particularly in higher education, is that there is also a sociology of higher education. In many respects an adequate challenge to the gifted, I think, depends equally upon awareness of these sociological factors. Here I will draw largely upon material by Everett Hughes of the University of Chicago (1), although some of the ideas are similar to those of his former associate David Riesman (5).

Hughes is much interested in the rhythm of effort. He speaks of a state university in which the intellectual or academic style of the student is to take life easy up to the last ten days of the semester and then burn the midnight oil in preparation for final examinations. He speaks of another university where instructors "keep the student busy at little daily-assigned chores [*so*] that they have no time to develop

43

or pursue a program of study. . . . In the effort to get some reasonable level of accomplishment and effort in his own course, each instructor . . . resorted to the device of assigning a quota of daily chores. The student gives each teacher his due, claiming in return the right not to be held responsible several months from now for debts for which he already has a receipt."

Hughes goes on to ask who sets the standards of student performance. "From studies in industry we know that levels of production are set by many factors other than the wishes of management, ability of individuals to perform tasks at a certain rate and by the formal rewards of wages, promotion and security. . . . Any group of workingmen possessed of any solidarity whatsoever, and with some common image of themselves and their situation, will not easily yield to any authority full control over the amount of work they do or over the strenuousness of the effort they put forth." Hughes speculates that there may be more individualism among students, and, depending upon the size of the college, less uniformity; that is, there may be a diversity of student worlds or student cultures. These student worlds or student cultures, however, are bound to be a significant factor influencing goals and achievements of gifted students. Eliminating some marginal students by selective admission has an inconsequential effect upon this basic problem of motivating and challenging the gifted. Similarly, treating the gifted student solely as an individual (the "encouragement of individual rate-busting" is the industrial term Hughes uses) is also unlikely to be successful. Every college has small groups of students with great intellectual drive. The cultivation and stimulation by faculty and administration of these groups, diverse as they may be, seem likely in the long run to be most productive of full challenge to the gifted. Faculty control and efforts can never be all-determining, but these student worlds or cultures are in part shaped and created by faculty and administration.

Sixth — shifting disciplines — it is worth thinking for a moment of some of the challenging ideas which are now in general circulation but which I first heard in 1955 from Sidney Pressey of Ohio State University. He pointed out that the United States has been notably successful in the cultivating of giftedness in only two areas—athletics and music. When we turn our attention to the cultivation of intellectual giftedness, he suggests that we might do well to consider the successful techniques practiced by our departments of athletics. Some of these techniques shock me, especially when I consider transferring them to the academic area. On the other hand, although I worry about the overemphasis on athletics in some of our colleges and universities, I am not easily frightened by the possibility of an overemphasis in the university on intellectual concerns. In our own Kansas experiment with the gifted — the program I know best — there has been some alarm on the part of a few parents, especially mothers, and a few personnel workers that we may be stressing academic concerns to the neglect of the well-rounded and socially adjusted graduate they envision.

Athletic departments and sports pages use the term *recruiting* for the process of attracting gifted athletes to our colleges. Should we show equal concern for the intellectually gifted? An all-state football player knows that colleges value his talents. Is a National Merit Scholar aware of the same degree of interest on our part? When a seven-foot Philadelphia high school basketball player decided several years ago to come to the University of Kansas, I noted that our basketball coach went to Philadelphia and rode out with the boy on the train, I suppose to make sure he did not get off the train in Indiana or Illinois. Two months or so ago, just after the announcement in our local newspaper of the finalists in this year's National Merit Scholarship competition, our local high school principal, reminding me of my interest in gifted students, asked me why it was that, by contrast with the athletic department which had long since got in touch with all outstanding senior athletes, no one at the university had paid any particular attention to his academically talented seniors.

In the *training* of boys who are athletically gifted, I note that our tennis coach does not train his freshman team in the regular freshman physical education classes in tennis. He separates them and works them to the extent of their capacity. There appears to be, too, a maximum amount of competition in the careers of the athletically gifted. And the publicity given to the gifted athlete seems limitless — even greater than that given to beauty queens.

As a final portion of this general statement, let me raise a number of questions. Is it true that much of our attention in academic areas is centered on the marginal student and the minimum standards he must meet, not upon the gifted student and ideal, maximum accomplishment? Most of our college requirements are stated in terms of minimums. In a grade-point system of the sort we use, we say that a student must accumulate at least 120 grade points for graduation. How many points should a good student or a gifted student accumulate by the time he graduates? We note that the minimum graduation requirement in semester hours is 124; how many hours should a gifted student complete?

Should a gifted student be encouraged to graduate in three years? One of the students in the experiment we began three years ago, a student who I knew had planned to graduate in three years but whom I had not seen for some months, made an appointment just after April 1 and came in to see me. Unconsciously assuming that all students who came into the college office have problems, I supposed this boy might be deciding not to finish this spring, and I was not surprised to hear the student begin by saying he had a problem: he had received the offer of a Woodrow Wilson scholarship at Minnesota, a National Science Foundation scholarship which could be used in several places, and a Harvard scholarship of two thousand dollars. His problem was which to accept.

Harold W. Stoke of New York University disposed of the problem of gifted students in short order a year or two ago in an article in the *Educational Record* (6). He said that the gifted student can take care of himself, and that it is undoubtedly wise simply to let him do so. I think Stoke has only a half-truth here and that the answer is not simple. Stoke is a graduate dean and graduate schools put a great deal of responsibility upon individual students. At the same time it is also true — equally true — that graduate professors expect a great deal from graduate students and often give them great amounts of rigorous attention. I suspect this is exactly the treatment that the gifted undergraduate needs and profits from.

The Gifted Freshman

Most large universities make available departmental honors programs at the junior-senior level. Many of these programs exist only on paper, in the university catalogue. At best, one finds only a few departments in which the program is fully alive and in which most of the eligible students participate. The reason for the dormant state of these upper-division honors programs is lack of vigorous student interest in them. This lack, I think, grows largely out of the student's experiences during his first two years of college. If the upper-division honors programs are to flourish, the student's first two years must be of a kind to bring him to the beginning of his junior year both prepared and motivated to volunteer for the independent study and extra work that the departmental honors programs require.

The Advanced Placement Program of the College Entrance Examination Board has called attention to the danger of repetition during the freshman year of work already done by the gifted student in high school. The first years of college are the years, too, when the greatest attrition occurs in the student body and when, obviously, the range of ability in classes is widest. New freshmen of high ability expect the university to differ sharply from high school. It is probable that outstanding freshmen for whom no special provision is made will find the freshman year little more stimulating or demanding than high school.

For several years the National Merit Scholarship Corporation has tested outstanding seniors in most of the country's high schools and has honored those in the upper one or two percentiles of ability by the award of National Merit scholarships and Certificates of Merit. Every college receives a booklet from the corporation listing all of these outstanding students. Hence, according to this one process of identification anyway, every college, whether or not it requires college boards, may easily be certain of its potentially outstanding students in advance of the opening of the freshman year.

One large university used this device toward the end of the fall semester of 1957–58 in order to check its freshman class. Those freshmen on the National Merit list were interviewed. The students were asked how many hours a week they were devoting to study. The shocking fact emerged that, on the average, this group was spending only two and a half to three hours a week in outside preparation for their classes. Further questioning elicited the additional disturbing fact that the serious reading of these students apart from their classwork was negligible.

The critical time for the student is his freshman year — the most neglected time in the university so far as the gifted student is concerned. At this level there is great concern over the marginal student: remedial courses are numerous; administrative staff and advisers, even teachers, devote most of their attention to the student who lacks ade-

47

quate ability and preparation. Although large numbers of scholarships are awarded by almost all universities on the basis of academic potential, nevertheless, when it comes to the academic program, no special effort is made to see that the gifted student is given a program that will challenge him to make full use of his intellectual powers, a program different from that of the average student. It is somehow assumed that for a year or two he must establish his academic superiority in the standard pattern of courses, after which — perhaps in the junior year — there may be honors programs open to him.

Two aspects of the sad plight of the gifted student in the lower division of the large university deserve attention. One of these has to do with counseling and academic regulations; the other with the courses in which the student enrolls.

Apart from other devices for recognizing outstanding potential ability in freshmen, there is the obvious one of using the lists supplied by the National Merit Scholarship Corporation. It is easy to check these lists, particularly in a state university, against the roster of a freshman class. A survey of eight large universities last year showed, first, that there were appreciable numbers of these gifted students in the freshman class of each of these universities; and, second, that none of the deans or associate deans responsible for the counseling and program-planning of freshmen had available the names or even the total numbers of these capable students. In all of these universities no special attention, either by the academic adviser or in the academic program, was given to these students. In one large state university no academic adviser was supplied to any student in arts and sciences until his fifth quarter in the university.

In another university each academic adviser supervised the program-planning of from two hundred to three hundred students. In a third university — where reasonably careful testing of the ability of freshmen took place during orientation week — none of this information was supplied to the adviser on the grounds that it might prejudice him against the student in one way or another and that somehow it might be harmful if the student himself learned his own scores on the various tests.

Clearly, there is a need to identify the freshman of outstanding ability as he begins his university work. Various outside agencies like the National Merit Scholarship Corporation are of great help. The task is actually done already in most universities through well-established scholarship programs, neglected though this information usually is by the academic division of the university. Lastly, anyone missed by these other devices can be identified through careful scrutiny of both high school records and the usual orientation tests which almost all universities give. Really outstanding students identified in any of these ways then deserve outstanding academic advisers — advisers who are given the authority to waive the usual regulations to the extent necessary in order to place the gifted student in a program of courses that challenge his full ability. These steps must be taken as the freshman enters the university; not after he has a semester or a year to adjust to the conventional pace of the average student.

The second matter of concern is the quality and rigor of the courses the gifted freshman takes. Most colleges have traditionally supplied a variety of remedial courses to the marginal student, particularly in English, mathematics, and foreign languages. Only a few have set up honors sections even in English for the student of high ability. Usually, the highly gifted freshman who is beginning the study of a particular foreign language in college — though he may have studied two other languages in high school and may have great talent linguistically — will be placed in the same beginning class as the student of the lowest ability and least interest in language. In freshman courses in biology or American history, or in sophomore courses in physics, all students are likely to be placed in the same classes regardless of ability and regardless of whether or not they have studied the subject in high school.

The obvious solution to the supplying of fully challenging courses at the freshman level is the creation of honors sections. Most of the freshman courses are multisectional. Just as marginal students are placed in remedial sections, students at the far opposite end of the spectrum of ability, preparation, and motivation should be placed in honors sections, where the pace of the work is fast, the emphasis on the analytical and theoretical rather than the merely descriptive, and the competition strenuous.

A few universities have been very active in setting up special advisory systems and special honors sections for highly gifted freshmen. In the college of arts and sciences at the University of Kansas a program for freshmen and sophomores of the kind described above is in its fourth year. During the 1957–58 academic year there were honors sections in the elementary courses of fourteen departments. For 1958–59 certain additions have been made, for all practical purposes completing the program of offerings in the college departments. These sections are usually open to both freshmen and sophomores who have been on the dean's honor roll (a list limited to ten per cent of the class) the previous semester and to the students in the experimental advisory program for gifted students (a group composed of entering students who have shown by ability test scores that they are in the upper two per cent of the nation's college freshmen). Out of a freshman class of approximately one thousand in the fall of 1955, thirty students of this level were identified. In the fall of 1956 the number increased to forty; in the fall of 1957 it jumped to seventy. These figures are cited to suggest the effect on the makeup of a freshman class of an emphasis upon adequate opportunity for students of high ability.

Colleges and universities are misdirecting their energies if they focus their attention upon the marginal student either in the traditional terms of providing every sort of remedial course for him while neglecting the able student; or in concentrating upon plans of selective admission aimed solely at eliminating the weakest students. The institution as a whole, and all of the students in it, will profit if much attention is given to providing the best advice and instruction for the gifted student. The effort to maintain a serious, academic, and vigorous intellectual tone in the campus community will be much more successful if this kind of attention is given to the gifted student in the freshman class rather than if the maximum effort is devoted to the problems of the marginal student.

REFERENCES

1. Hughes, Everett C. Unpublished talk for the College Entrance Examination Board, Arden House, October 26, 1956.
2. May, Kenneth. "Undergraduate Research in Mathematics." *American Mathematical Monthly*, 65:241–46, April 1958.
3. Pressey, Sidney L. "Concerning the Nature and Nurture of Genius." *Scientific Monthly*, 81:123–29, September 1955.
4. "Regional Associates." *ACLS Newsletter*, 9:4–8, April 1958.
5. Riesman, David. *Constraint and Variety in American Education.* Lincoln: University of Nebraska Press, 1956.
6. Stoke, Harold W. "Some Observations on the Education of Gifted Students." *Educational Record*, 38:133–35, April 1957.

7. Waggoner, G. R. "The Gifted Student in the State University." *Journal of Higher Education*, 28:414–24, 467, November 1957.
8. ———. "A Program for Gifted Freshmen and Sophomores in the College of Arts and Sciences at the University of Kansas." *University of Kansas Bulletin of Education*, 12:1–15, November 1957.
9. ———. "Starting the Program Early." *The Superior Student*. 1:11–12, May 1958.

MR. WAGGONER is dean of the College of Arts and Sciences at the University of Kansas. This chapter, prepared by him, reflects the discussion of a group of which Scott Elledge of Carleton College and Kenneth Bjork of St. Olaf College were chairmen, and Anne M. Collopy of the College of St. Catherine and Leonard R. Davis of Rochester Junior College were recorders.

Using Examinations to Promote Learning

T<small>HE</small> *appropriate* use of *good* examinations *can* promote learning in
at least four ways: first, by stimulating teachers to clarify their objectives; second, by motivating students to apply themselves to the learning task; third, by directing the efforts of students and teachers toward
the attainment of essential achievements; and fourth, by providing
effective learning exercises. This chapter will be devoted mainly to a
discussion of these four uses of examinations.

Before proceeding, however, it should be recognized that the discussion assumes that examinations *can* be used to promote learning. Not
all professors would grant this assumption willingly. Some would hold
that examinations actually impede learning, preventing students and
teachers from cooperating effectively. Others would argue that the
time spent in preparing for, taking, and grading examinations could
be more profitably spent in other educational activities. Quite obviously the validity of these objections depends at least partly on the
quality of the examinations used. Bad examinations — or any examinations badly used — can certainly be harmful. On this point there
need be no disagreement. But it would be wrong to apply this conclusion to *any* use of *any* examination. Good examinations, properly used,
can contribute substantially to the educational enterprise.

What is a good examination? For the professor who uses it to measure the achievement of his students, a good examination is one that
measures as directly as possible as many as possible of the ultimate
objectives of achievement in his course. To measure ultimate achievement directly it must require the student to demonstrate command of
the knowledge he possesses — to show that he can use it to solve problems, reach decisions, support recommendations, or make evaluations.
The examination must not reward the student for mere possession of

knowledge, or for ability only to recall words that he has read or heard.

The proper use of classroom examinations by the professor is to promote learning. How this can be done is the subject of this discussion. Let us consider the first use mentioned — that of stimulating teachers to define their objectives for students' achievement more clearly.

Defining Objectives

Most college professors tend to be somewhat impatient with requests from educationists that they state their course objectives explicitly. A chemistry professor I know told me once that his introductory course had only one objective — to teach the students some chemistry. A zoologist said that the purpose of his first course was to prepare for the second; of the second to prepare for the next; and so on until the student graduated. The assumption of these specialized scholars was that the essential objectives of their courses are so clearly inherent in the subject matter itself that attempts to abstract them verbally result only in a waste of time.

There is something to be said for this position. Certainly many definitions of educational objectives for elementary and secondary schools have consisted mainly of verbal platitudes or semantic confusions. In spite of the vast amounts of time and effort that have gone into these definitions, it is difficult to point to specific educational advances which have resulted from many of them. One of the problems is that the concrete outcomes of learning in any course are multitudinous and diverse. Any statement that pretends to encompass all of them is inescapably abstract and general. Another problem is that most of these statements are the products of committees composed of competent, and therefore individualistic, persons. To reach agreement they must propose statements which cannot be interpreted too clearly as supporting one point of view at the expense of others. The production of acceptably ambiguous phraseology which sounds impressively emphatic is a fine art. Some committees of educators rival political orators in the practice of this art.

The fact remains that all teaching is guided by the purposes of the teacher and of those to whom he is responsible. Not all teaching is equally effective. Part of the difference between good and poor teaching certainly originates in differences between the objectives which guide the teaching: between purposeful and aimless teaching; between essential and trivial learning; between specific and indefinite goals of achievement. The professor who disdains concern for the objectives of the course he offers is deceiving either himself or his employers.

If, as has been suggested, a good examination is one which measures the degree of attainment of the ultimate objectives of the course, then it is obviously impossible to prepare a good examination without careful consideration of objectives (1, 3, 4, 5). Conversely — and this truth is often overlooked — the examination in its finished form provides a detailed, concrete, operational definition of the objectives.

At this point some professors, especially those in the humanities, retreat to previously prepared and impressively fortified positions in the misty realm of intangibility. There are, they proclaim, important outcomes of instruction in their courses which cannot be revealed adequately by any examination, and certainly not by the despised objective examination. Precisely what these intangible outcomes are is seldom specified. Belief that they really exist, and are not simply verbal inventions, is an act of pure faith, or else it is the product of a semantic confusion between complexity and intangibility. Many manifestations of human behavior are highly complex — difficult to observe under controlled conditions, difficult to quantify on even the most primitive scales. But being manifestations of behavior they are tangible, observable, and to some extent measurable. A truly intangible outcome of education would never make an observable difference in the behavior of the individual possessing it. Despite all the sage nods of assent among some groups of professors when the importance of intangible outcomes of education is mentioned, the concept itself has less substance than a will-o'-the-wisp. Its survival among specialists in intellectual development does them no credit. With so many essential and tangible outcomes of education unrealized by many of our students, it is a great pity to waste our educational resources in the pursuit of intangibles. The real goals of achievement in the course are indicated by the tasks presented in the examination used to measure achievement. Guided by advance knowledge of the nature of these tasks, the efforts of teacher and student can be made more purposeful and hence more productive. The guidance will be as good as the test, and far better than can be obtained from any condensed general statement of abstract goals.

Using Examinations to Promote Learning

What I have said on this point implies local construction of achievement examinations to fit the objectives of a particular instructor. This is entirely proper. But the primary importance attached to classroom tests built by individual instructors should not preclude the use of externally constructed examinations, such as those sold by commercial distributors or employed in wide-scale testing programs. Externally constructed examinations provide valuable supplements to locally constructed classroom tests. They exemplify generally approved course objectives. They provide external standards of achievement. Usually they are products of careful, expert test construction. Many college courses that are going to seed could be revitalized if the attention of instructors and students were directed to externally supported goals of achievement, and to externally established standards.

Motivating Students

A second way in which examinations can promote learning is by motivating students to apply themselves to the learning task. Examinations provide powerful incentives to study. What a student studies is largely determined by what he expects to be tested on. How he studies is influenced by the kind of a test he expects. How hard he works depends in part on how soon he expects to be tested.

The motivating power of examinations is indicated by the cramming students do in the days and hours immediately preceding an examination. Cramming is generally disapproved, as it should be. Here again, however, it is not the use of examinations that should be blamed for undesirable cramming. The fault lies with the kind of examination that encourages cramming by rewarding it. If the examination requires detailed recall of limited areas of study, it will encourage and reward cramming. But if it requires the student to demonstrate command of useful knowledge by presenting him with novel questions or problem situations — tasks which require analytic and constructive thought as well as memory — cramming will be a waste of time. No student will be able to make a few hours or days of intensive review compensate for weeks of indifferent idleness. The motivating influence of frequent tests has been the subject of numerous research investigations with somewhat equivocal findings (9, 10). Broadly speaking, these findings support the general principle that the educational influence of examinations depends on their quality and on the way in which they are used. If the examinations set up appropriate and reasonable goals for attainment, and if the student's performance on these examinations makes a real difference in his future opportunities, then the examinations *do* tend to stimulate effective learning.

Directing Efforts toward Essential Achievements

A third use of classroom tests to promote learning is in directing the efforts of students and teachers toward the attainment of essential achievements. If the test which will be used to measure achievement is prepared before the course begins, and if the students are informed early about the kinds of achievement it will require of them, then the test will have a significant effect in directing the activities of students and teacher. Sometimes a test similar to the final test is used as a pre-test. This not only provides measures of initial status but also makes the students quite familiar with the general nature of the final test. Using the final test itself as a pre-test is *not* recommended, since it will tend to focus students' attention on only a limited sample of the tasks which they should be prepared to handle. A test can direct students' learning, but it does not provide a complete set of specifications for all that should be learned.

No one questions the fact that students tend to study the things they expect to be tested on, nor the fact that teachers responsible for preparing students to take an externally constructed examination try to anticipate and stress the things their students will be expected to know. But many do question the educational value of this directive influence. They fear it will narrow the field of educational development, divert attention from important but not easily measured achievements, and impose a deadening standardization on educational programs and products.

There is some basis for these fears, but again the degree of potential harm depends on the quality of the tests, and the way in which they are used. Tests can be used to widen the field of desired educational achievements. Teachers in many elementary and secondary schools have been encouraged to add instruction in the use of references and libraries by tests of study skills. Tests themselves do not set standards or impose requirements. Unless the scores on them are used blindly and mechanically, there is little danger of excessive standardization.

The kind of examination also exercises a directive influence on educational efforts. Research offers ample evidence that students do study differently in preparation for different kinds of examinations (8, 13). Many of these studies were conducted a quarter of a century ago when the art of objective testing was in its infancy. Some of them suggested that essay tests did a better job of stimulating careful, thorough study than the objective tests then in use. But the best modern objective tests, which require the student to demonstrate the ability to use his knowledge in dealing with problems, have a far different and much more salutary influence on study than the old-time objective tests which simply emphasized the recall of factual details. A good essay test can be a very effective stimulant to thoughtful study. Unfortunately, many of the essay tests ordinarily used test only the student's ability to present statements of recalled facts or to reproduce expositions from textbooks or lectures.

In this connection it is appropriate to point out that general differences in value among different types of objective test items — multiple-choice, true-false, matching, completion, and others — are less important than differences in the quality of items of the same type. True-false questions can be thought-provoking, unambiguous, and highly discriminating. That they often are not is more a fault of the writer of the item than of the form of the item. Experience has shown that multiple-choice items are more versatile and easier to use well than many other forms, but there are situations in which each of the other forms has important advantages. A general hierarchy of value among the various types of objective test items is difficult to establish or to defend.

Most teachers agree that an examination designed to reveal whether or not a student can *use* the knowledge he possesses is better than one which simply reveals whether or not he possesses it. Memory and recall are important, but selective recall and application are even more important. One good way of emphasizing the importance of ability to use knowledge is to give an open-book examination. The teacher who prepares such a test will tend to ask different — and better — questions than one who prepares the more conventional memory test. Students preparing for an open-book test will study differently — and more effectively — than they do when preparing for conventional tests. Open-book examinations deserve much wider use than they have enjoyed thus far.

Providing Effective Learning Exercises

A fourth way in which examinations promote learning is by providing effective learning exercises. The process of taking a good examination is itself a valuable educational experience. Stroud (12) has suggested that the contribution made to the student's store of knowledge by the taking of an examination is as great, minute for minute, as any other enterprise he engages in. This will not be surprising to anyone who has observed the intense concentration of students taking an examination, in contrast to their relaxed and often semi-attentive attitudes during other phases of instruction.

The value of an examination as an instructional experience is enhanced if the questions are discussed after the examination has been marked. From the point of view of the psychology of learning, it is even better if the students can be informed as soon as they have marked a response whether or not it is the correct one. A number of devices such as the Science Research Associates Self-Scorer and the Neville Trainer-Tester have been used effectively for this purpose.

A similar but far more elaborate and fundamental approach to learning has been made by B. F. Skinner of Harvard (11). He has developed a teaching machine to facilitate the occurrence of correct responses and to provide immediate reinforcement of them. Skinner points out that far greater progress has been made in the application of principles of learning to the conditioning of animals than to the education of human beings.

The Skinner machine presents a simple initial question or problem and requires the student to respond to it. It is intended to be simple enough so that he will almost certainly give the correct response. If he does, the machine moves on to the next problem, which involves a slight extension of the idea involved in the first. Step by step, and with little direct involvement of a human teacher, the student extends the scope of his concepts and abilities. It is no simple task to organize the materials of instruction into a series of steps which the learner can follow with little or no outside assistance. But a great deal of progress has been made, and experimental work is continuing actively. The implications of this approach for the improvement of educational processes may be even greater than those associated with the use of television.

It has sometimes been suggested that test questions could be used as the starting point of fruitful class discussion (6). The best items for this purpose would seem to be those which require reasoned application of knowledge to novel problem situations. But an examination of objective tests currently available, even those which have had the benefit of expert development, reveals a relatively small proportion of items which test for more than factual information or vocabulary knowledge. The contrast between these two types is illustrated in the sample multiple-choice questions on page 60.*

There are several important differences between factual and reasoning questions. Factual questions tend to be simpler to state, easier to answer, and less controversial when correct answers are announced. Reasoning questions, since they are designed to provoke thought, sometimes also provoke arguments. Critics of objective tests, including students who have just taken one, frequently find flaws such as these: (a) the best answer is not a completely correct answer; (b) some of the distracters provide answers just as good as the "correct" answer; (c) the problem situation is not described fully enough to prevent diverse interpretations leading to different answers.

The best answer to these criticisms is to present evidence that competent experts have agreed that the correct answer is clearly better than any other alternative offered, and that when the item is scored with this as the correct answer it discriminates clearly between students of high and low achievement. This evidence should not be used by a writer of test items as grounds for opposing changes in wording which improve the item by making the problem situation clearer, the best answer more nearly correct, or the distracters more clearly wrong — without destroying the ability of the item to discriminate. But this evidence *can* be used to defend thought-provoking items which require the examinee to make reasonable inferences about complex but concisely described problem situations. Loopholes for unwarranted assumptions and unconventional interpretations exist in almost all reasoning items. It is practically impossible to eliminate them without making the item excessively verbose. So long as experts can agree on a best answer, and so long as the item discriminates well between good and poor students, these alleged flaws in reasoning items need not be regarded as serious. They make the item somewhat less ob-

* The correct answers to these questions are 1. (B), 2. (C), 3. (A), 4. (B), 5. (C), 6. (C), 7. (D), 8. (B), 9. (B), 10. (A).

MULTIPLE-CHOICE QUESTIONS

Factual Questions

1. What is the technical definition of the term *production*?
   (A) Any natural process producing food or other raw materials.
   (B) The creation of economic value.
   (C) The manufacture of finished products.
   (D) The operation of a profit-making enterprise.

3. Whose name is given to the principle which helps to explain the behavior of floating bodies?
   (A) Archimedes.
   (B) Aristotle.
   (C) Buoyant.
   (D) Newton.

5. What is the product of 5 times 3?
   (A) 1⅔.
   (B) 8.
   (C) 15.
   (D) 35.

7. The poem "Hiawatha" was written by the author of
   (A) "Leaves of Grass."
   (B) "Thanatopsis."
   (C) "Israfel."
   (D) "The Village Blacksmith."

9. What cools an electric refrigerator?
   (A) A current of air circulating inside the refrigerator.
   (B) An expanding gas.
   (C) An insulated metal coil.
   (D) The flow of electricity through a low-resistance wire.

Reasoning Questions

2. Should merchants and middlemen be classified as producers or nonproducers? Why?
   (A) As nonproducers, because they make their living off producers and consumers.
   (B) As producers, because they regulate and determine price.
   (C) As producers, because they aid in the distribution of goods and bring producer and consumer together.
   (D) As producers, because they assist in the circulation of money.

4. In a beaker almost full of water a cork is nearly submerged by the pull of a spring. If the beaker is allowed to fall free, what will happen to the cork during the period of free fall?
   (A) It will stay nearly submerged.
   (B) It will submerge completely.
   (C) It will float higher in the water.
   (D) It will alternately submerge and rise out of the water.

6. If jelly beans come in five colors, how many beans must a child buy in order to be certain of getting three beans of the same color?
   (A) 3.
   (B) 7.
   (C) 11.
   (D) 15.

8. Which of the following quotations has most of the characteristics of conventional poetry?
   (A) Mary had a little lamb.
       Its fleece was white as snow.
   (B) Content to let the North wind roar
       In baffled rage at pane and door.
   (C) I'm wild again, beguiled again,
       A whimpering, simpering child again.
   (D) If at first you don't succeed,
       Try, try again!

10. If an electric refrigerator is operated with the door open in a perfectly insulated, sealed room, what will happen to the temperature of the room?
   (A) It will rise slowly.
   (B) It will remain constant.
   (C) It will drop slowly.
   (D) It will drop rapidly.

jective but more valid as an indication of important achievement. Objectivity is highly desirable, but it is not the most important quality of a test item. Validity should never be sacrificed to gain objectivity.

What has been said about the values of reasoning questions as learning exercises and as measures of achievement should not be taken to mean that a test should be composed exclusively of such questions. Important factual questions are also essential to give proper balance to all objectives of instruction. But too many teachers overemphasize factual questions in their tests and neglect the reasoning questions which, while more difficult to prepare and defend, provide essential evidence of useful achievement. In general, the kinds of questions which provide the best basis for classroom discussion are also those which provide the best indications of the degree of attainment of the ultimate objectives of instruction in a course. Our tests should be redesigned to include more items of this type.

The preoccupation of this discussion with some of the more important *direct* values of examinations in the promotion of learning should not be taken to imply a disregard for important indirect and long-term values of examinations when they are properly used for guidance, selection, placement, and evaluation. This contradicts the view sometimes expressed that unless an examination has a direct and immediate influence in the improvement of learning it is a waste of time. The emphasis here on the direct contributions of examinations to learning should not be taken as a minimization of our interest in or appreciation of other appropriate uses of examinations in the educational enterprise. (2, 7)

Two causes are primarily responsible for the considerable cultural lag in applying what we know about examining to the improvement of education. One is the conditioned antipathy of many people toward examinations. The taking of even a good examination is seldom regarded as a pleasant pastime. Most of us have been exposed to so many poor examinations, which provided invalid indications of achievement and formed a basis for unfair decisions, that our tendency to dislike them is easy to rationalize. This attitude can best be overcome by the development of skill in making better examinations, and in making wiser use of them.

The second factor responsible for this lag is the folklore prevalent among college instructors that anyone who knows enough about a subject can teach it. This leads them to regard the special training in techniques of education provided by teachers' colleges and graduate schools of education as unnecessary or even positively harmful. Unfortunately, there is a good deal of fluff in many of the courses and curriculums designed for the preparation of teachers. But this should not drive any reasonable person to the unreasonable conclusion that one can become a skilled teacher without studying how to teach. Doctors study the practice of medicine and surgery as well as biochemistry and anatomy. Lawyers study the practice of law and courtroom techniques as well as the corpus of the law. Dentists, more perhaps than either of the other groups, concentrate on developing skill in the practice of their special branch of knowledge. Someday, we may hope, a similar recognition will be given to the importance of specifically preparing college teachers to practice the techniques of their craft, and truly respectable programs for the training of college teachers will be adopted.

REFERENCES

1. Bloom, Benjamin S., ed. *Taxonomy of Educational Objectives*. New York: Longmans, Green & Company, 1956.
2. Committees on Test Standards, American Educational Research Association and National Council on Measurements Used in Education. *Technical Recommendations for Achievement Tests*. Washington, D.C.: American Educational Research Association, 1955.
3. French, Will. *Behavioral Goals of General Education in High School*. New York: Russell Sage Foundation, 1957.
4. Gasking, Douglas Aidan Trist. *Examinations and the Aims of Education*. Melbourne: Melbourne University Press, 1945.
5. Kearney, Nolan C. *Elementary School Objectives*. New York: Russell Sage Foundation, 1953.
6. Koester, George A. "Using Instructor-Made Tests for Instructional Purposes." *Educational Research Bulletin*, 36:207–8, September 1957.
7. Lindquist, E. F., and others. *Educational Measurement*. Washington, D.C.: American Council on Education, 1950.
8. Meyer, George. "An Experimental Study of the Old and New Types of Examinations." *Journal of Educational Psychology*, 25:641–61, December 1934, and 26:30–40, January 1935.
9. Noll, Victor H. "The Effect of Written Tests upon Achievement in College Classes: An Experiment and a Summary of Evidence." *Journal of Educational Research*, 32:345–58, January 1939.
10. Ross, Clay C. "An Experiment in Motivation." *Journal of Educational Psychology*, 18:337–46, May 1927.
11. Skinner, B. F. "The Science of Learning and the Art of Teaching." *Harvard Education Review*, 24:86–97, Spring 1954.

12. Stroud, James B. *Psychology in Education.* New York: Longmans, Green & Company, 1946.
13. Terry, Paul W. "How Students Study for Three Types of Objective Tests." *Journal of Educational Research,* 27:333–43, January 1934.

MR. EBEL is with the Educational Testing Service in Princeton, New Jersey. This paper, prepared by him, reflects the discussion of a group of which Joseph Kise of Moorhead State College and E. Van Norstrand of St. Cloud State College were chairmen, and Carl L. Bailey of Concordia College and Marvin E. Trautwein of Augsburg College were recorders.

~§ HARALD BAKKEN

Achieving Better Student-Teacher Relations

To BEGIN with, I'd like to state clearly the perspective from which I write. I left my undergraduate institution only a year and a half ago, and I've spent the intervening time visiting a great many campuses under the auspices of the United States National Student Association. The short interval since my undergraduate experience perhaps limits my perspective, and makes it impossible for me to draw many comparisons, but this very shortness allows me to deal with the problems of student-faculty relations with a certain sense of immediacy, and with a memory of undergraduate attitudes and problems which has not been filtered through too much subsequent experience.

However much one may disagree with the statistical validity of Philip Jacob's (2) findings or find Otto Butz's (1) students unrepresentative, these authors probably point up the sad fact that the number of students whose motivations are affected by faculty members is very small. Most students, I am afraid, rarely have any significant relations with faculty members, and do not find the prospect of such relations pleasant, for reasons I will attempt to analyze later. All too many students complete their four or five years in college without having come to know a faculty mind or indeed without feeling much excitement about intellectual endeavor.

Lest I be accused of painting too black a picture, let me hasten to add that I think those students who *do* find something of the excitement of intellectual interest are usually first influenced by one or more teachers who, themselves committed to the love of learning, were somehow able to communicate this love to their students. This was true in my own case, and I think I am fairly typical in this respect.

When such communication takes place, it is a rare and wonderful thing for the student. The real problem, then, is to determine the conditions under which such communication is possible. Jacob cites (a) intimate contact between students and faculty in the curriculum, (b) student-centered faculty who "derive a real sense of satisfaction and value from teaching their particular students (regardless of their intellectual level, social background or outlook)," (c) relatively large responsibility on the part of faculty (and perhaps students) in the educational program of the institution, (d) self-consciousness and purposefulness in its educational mission on the part of the whole institution, (e) wide diversity in the background, personality, and values of the students.

It is important to note that Jacob says nothing about the academic status of faculty members, or about their abilities in particular disciplines, or about the number of their publications. What seems important is a commitment to the values of intellectual activity and an ability to communicate these values.

I am not arguing for lowered academic requirements for teaching, but simply for an increased realization that subject-matter competency is not enough. Real stimulation of interest demands that the teacher be continually aware of the fact that he is communicating values above and beyond subject matter. It demands, too, that he make efforts to involve the student in a more than passive way in the learning process, that he be willing to listen to the student's views and deal with them with respect. The student is not asking that he be recognized on the basis of common competency in subject matter, but he does want to be recognized as having a common and sincere interest.

At present, it may be argued that a faculty member simply does not have time for close contacts with students. Not only does he have to prepare materials for his classes, but he must keep abreast of developments in his field, he must concern himself with research and publication, and he must take part in committee meetings and perform other staff functions.

In addition — and this problem will doubtless be more serious as enrollment increases — there are too few faculty members in relation to the number of students. Larger classes, including teaching by film and television, depersonalize the learning experience and decrease the faculty's influence on students.

The instructor must weigh the value of meetings with individual students against the possibility of using his time in preparing materials for the whole class. While I would not argue for his ceasing to revise his class notes, nonetheless limiting his efforts solely to the classroom is at best a scatter-shot technique. Students vary in the kinds of experiences that influence their attitudes, and the faculty member must be prepared to vary his approach.

These problems are largely problems of deployment of energies and relative utilization of financial and personnel resources. And the need for more teachers and more money is too apparent for further discussion here. There are other influences, largely a matter of students' and faculty members' attitudes, that seem to determine the impact of instruction in ways as significant.

What are students' attitudes toward association with faculty members? Teachers say that students shy away from them, and this is accurate to a certain extent, particularly insofar as students are affected by their peers. A student is unlikely to seek out a faculty member if this will be looked upon by his associates as apple-polishing.

Then too, there is what David Riesman (3) calls the "guardiness" of the current generation of students. Among other avoidances, they seek not to be disturbed by faculty members. It is my experience, however, that there are many more students who sincerely want to get to know faculty members than are presently able to do so. They find the sight of a busy faculty member, engrossed in university concerns and devoted to problems beyond their competence, a forbidding one. They are uncertain how to proceed, uncertain how they will be received, and they do not initiate the relation. If the faculty member expects all students to be passionately interested in intellectual subjects he will, of course, be disappointed. He must aim at those who can be reached — and such exist.

One final problem of faculty attitudes needs to be mentioned here. That is the uncertainty which I suspect some faculty members have regarding how even well-meant attempts at student contact may be viewed by students. The thought of entering a group of students in the lunchroom may be as forbidding to the faculty member as the thought of bothering a busy faculty member sometimes is to students. The crucial question here, too, seems to me to be attitude. If, in approaching students in groups or individually, the faculty member appears to be sincerely interested in contact, and, most important, to view such contact as a chance for him to gain as well as to give, my experience is that he will be well received by student groups.

The faculty member too, as Jacob (2) points out, may be reluctant to leave the security of his academic concerns in order to deal with students' problems. And his peers on the faculty offer little encouragement; professional advancement apparently depends very little on the quality of a man's relations with his students. Dedication to a discipline and research in it seem to be more promising ways of getting ahead. Fellow faculty members don't always notice the amount of time spent with students, and the impact of such meetings is difficult to measure.

Another factor is the difference between the goals of the faculty and the goals of the students. I have no way of knowing whether this difference in outlook is greater than it used to be. But it is obvious that faculty members frequently fail to hit students where they live, that teachers' ideals and motivations are so different from their students' that communication is considerably impeded. This means that a good deal more research must be conducted to analyze and understand the motivation of this generation of students. We need to know which factors most significantly affect values and why certain kinds of experience are more effective than others.

I do not want to leave the impression that effective student-faculty interaction never happens, or that there are no instructors who are sincerely dedicated to teaching and who do reach their students. There are such teachers, and they are the ones students remember. Unfortunately pressure of time and problems of attitude make their number too small and their influence not so large as it should be.

I have no clear-cut solution to the problems I have raised. Perhaps increased use of undergraduate students in teaching positions, as suggested by Lewis Mayhew (pp. 262–72), would produce some results. It certainly should provide stimulation for the students who assume the positions, and it might go a long way toward influencing student culture to respect intellectual activity.

What most students want, though, is understanding of their outlook. They ask that their opinions be listened to with respect and that they be treated as more than passive receptacles for knowledge.

They would ask also that those concerned with promotions would make good teaching and student contact an important criterion —

probably the most important — for professional advancement, thus giving faculty members an incentive to associate with students.

Finally, they want more than peripheral contact with faculty members; they want individual and personal relations with them.

REFERENCES

1. Butz, Otto, ed. *The Unsilent Generation.* New York: Rinehart & Company, Inc., 1958.
2. Jacob, Philip E. *Changing Values in College.* New York: Harper and Brothers, 1957.
3. Riesman, David. Speech before the Problems and Policies Committee of the American Council on Education, June 26-27, 1957.

THIS chapter, prepared by Mr. Bakken, who is with the National Student Association, formed the basis for discussion by a group of which Keith McFarland, St. Paul Campus, University of Minnesota, and Hugo Thompson, Macalester College, were chairmen, and Lawrence E. Kaupp, Itasca Junior College, Coleraine, and Sister Enid, O.S.B., College of St. Benedict, were recorders.

•§ MORRIS I. STEIN

Toward Developing More Imaginative Creativity in Students

Thinking about how we might develop more imaginative creativity in our students led me to wonder how effective college teaching is in general; that is, how effective is college teaching, not in imparting information, but in changing the attitudes and values of college students?

In answer to this question, Philip Jacob (2) has the following to say (see also pp. 13–14, 87–89):

1. "The impact of the college experience is . . . to *socialize* the individual, to refine, polish, or 'shape up' his values, so that he can comfortably fit into the ranks of American college alumni" (p. 4).

2. "This study has not discerned significant changes in student values which can be attributed directly either to the character of the curriculum or to the basic courses in social science which students take as part of their general education" (p. 5).

3. "It does *not* justify the conclusion that a student acquires a greater maturity of judgment on issues of social policy or a more sensitive regard for the more humane values because he had a larger dose of liberal or general education" (p. 5).

4. "Even fundamental revisions of the formal content of the curriculum designed to confront students more forcefully with problems of personal and social conduct and to involve them in a searching examination of value-issues rarely appear to have brought about a marked difference in students' beliefs and judgments, let alone their actual patterns of conduct. Nor is there solid evidence of a delayed reaction or 'sleeper effect.' The alumnus of several years exhibits no unusual trademarks identifying the character of his undergraduate curriculum." (p. 5.)

69

5. "Equally disturbing is evidence that the quality of teaching has relatively little effect upon the value-outcomes of general education — in the social science or in the other fields — as far as the great mass of students is concerned" (p. 7).

6. "The personality, skill and devotion of teachers to their students and their subject varies tremendously within and among institutions. So do their personal and education philosophies, the intensity of their value-commitment and the degree to which they deliberately pursue value-goals in class and outside" (p. 7).

7. "The method of instruction seems to have only a minor influence on students' value judgment" (p. 8).

Although there are colleges that are strikingly different from the national pattern and which stand out from the crowd, this is a rather discouraging picture on the mass level. If college teaching has been as ineffective as Jacob describes it, then what can we expect from it as we turn to creativity? The problem is a difficult and challenging one. Its solution will require much effort, thought, and willingness to explore on the part of both college faculty and college administration.

The Creative Process

Almost all of the research on the characteristics of the creative man has been devoted to studies of persons already acknowledged as creative by society. Unfortunately, little, if any, work has been done in predicting how creative students will be after they have completed their education and found employment in their professional and scientific fields. Without delving into the problems that confront such prediction studies and pending the final research findings, I suggest that the available research data and methods be utilized for improving the guidance and counseling procedures that are presently in use. Many such procedures place much emphasis on intellectual factors and interest inventories, yet the literature suggests that these procedures alone are insufficient. To them must be added a study of the personality of the student — his needs, his value system, the pattern of his social relations, and the like. Creativity is most likely to be manifest in an area where a person can obtain deep personal gratification. It is obvious that professional and scientific areas differ as to the problems they investigate, their level of abstraction, their operational procedures. It therefore follows that the individuals who are to be most proficient, effective, and creative in their fields must possess personalities that predispose them positively to the demands of the various fields.

D. E. Super and P. B. Bachrach (5) have recently summarized the literature on the personality characteristics of natural scientists, mathematicians, and engineers. G. G. Stern, M. I. Stein, and B. S. Bloom (4) have presented data on the differences among students in physics, theology, and teaching programs. Proper use of the data and techniques of these and other studies should be invaluable in helping students to develop career patterns in which they will find the excitement and deep-seated satisfaction that are a prerequisite for the dedicated effort characteristic of creative work.

In talking about creativity, we often attend to the final product and assess the extent to which the new idea or invention differs from earlier ideas and inventions — overlooking the fact that creation is a process. It is a process of forming ideas or hypotheses, testing hypotheses, and communicating the results (3). The research literature to date does not tell us what specific personality characteristics are necessary to fulfill all the requirements of this process. Nevertheless, some of the characteristics that have been suggested are a sensitivity to the gaps in the environment, a capacity to tolerate ambiguity, a feeling of autonomy and independence, an attitude of high self-regard, a relative lack of rigid defense against anxieties, a flexibility in perception, and a capacity to integrate observations. While most of the methods for determining the existence of these psychological factors are still in the experimental stages and while studies on the predictive value of these methods is yet to be attempted, it may nevertheless be of value to bear these factors in mind in the selection of students for specially designed or advanced programs.

Knowledge of these characteristics has additional value in alerting us to some of the difficulties that a student might have in manifesting or fulfilling his creative potential. Some students have a fear of probing the unknown, of facing ambiguous situations, of asking questions, and of seeking answers on their own. Much relearning may be necessary to overcome the fear of leaving structured situations and many students may be helped, with appropriate counseling procedures, to gain insight into the irrational bases of their conflicts and so gain confidence in their capacities and throw light on their latent potential.

71

In addition to being a process, creativity is also a function of the transactional relations between the individual and his environment. The environment of the college student for our purposes is multidimensional. He is subject to the influences of his family, his peer group, and the attitudes in American society today, in addition to the influence of his college environment. As only one of several factors that influence our student, the impact of the college environment may be minimal unless it is reinforced by the attitudes and values of the other social groups with which the student has contact. If these groups place a higher value on conformity than on individuality, if these groups evaluate a man more in terms of the size of his car and his house than in terms of his knowledge and creative contribution, then the college faculty may find itself frustrated in its attempts to increase or foster the imaginative creativity of the student body. The point I wish to emphasize here is that creativity is society's problem — not just the problem of the schools and colleges. Recent international events have unjustly and unfortunately focused concentrated attention solely on the educational system. Although the intentions and efforts of the educational system may be of the best, they will be of relatively little moment unless they are bolstered by the community at large.

An Environment for Creativity

Assuming that the college's efforts and goals will be supported by the broader society, what can the college faculty do to foster creativity?

One of the things that a college can do is to provide an opportunity for the student to manifest his creative potential. Indeed, creativity cannot be manifest without a knowledge of the facts and procedures in any specific field. A student cannot be creative in mathematics, physics, chemistry, or the arts without training in these disciplines; but by the same token, he cannot be creative if all he is expected to do is to memorize the facts that have been accumulated in his field. If all his time is taken up with what is already known and if he has no time and opportunity for thinking about and testing ideas in the laboratory or in discussion groups, he will not experience the joy and excitement that comes from finding out answers to problems for himself. He will not seek to explore the unknown but limit himself to what others have learned — if he does that.

Toward Developing More Imaginative Creativity

A second characteristic of a creative environment is that it is not hostile, critical, or evaluative. A student's creativity flourishes where he can share ideas with others, without fear that every time he says or does something, he is going to be evaluated, graded, criticized. It will not flourish where he has to defend his position even before he has had a chance to test his ideas. It will not flourish where the only correct answers are assumed to be those that society has always accepted. The creative student is likely to be an autonomous and independent student, but even his spirit may be broken by an instructor who is all too ready to point out the flaws in his argument, the errors in his method, and the fallacies of his assumptions. Some of the student's ideas may lead up blind alleys; the instructor's role is to point out potential pitfalls and obstacles but at the same time to support the student in his curiosity and enthusiasm.

A third characteristic of a creative environment is that it puts a high value on creativity. The important people in this environment — the people who are looked up to and admired — are those who have made significant creative contributions. The creative college environment is one where the creative student is highly regarded rather than looked upon as a deviate who exists in the shadow of his more athletic classmate or his classmate who is more adept in social activities and school politics.

The creative college environment provides a challenging curriculum. Colleges have taken on many of the functions previously performed by the family and added to their curriculums life-adjustment classes and other classes to prepare the student for fulfilling social functions. These have become the snap courses for which a student may obtain college credit. While many of the students who take these courses may not have much potential for creativity, the courses may also tempt the creative student or limit his opportunity to foster his professional and scientific interests.

A fifth characteristic of a creative environment is that it provides models whom the student can emulate as he develops his career. In the college environment, this role is filled by the faculty. Unless it is composed of persons who are creative or capable of exciting the imagination and curiosity of the students, there is relatively little hope of uncovering and fostering creative potential. P. F. Brandwein, describing his experiences in stimulating the creativity of high school students, regards the teacher as the key to the success of his programs. He could not fail to observe that his best teachers were those who "were in the relation of the 'father' or 'mother' image to the youngsters who were interviewed. These teachers were, in short, not only admired or respected as teachers of subject matter, but as teachers in the ways of life. They were guides, counselors, friends, guardians, father-confessors." (1, p. 67.) Because these teachers were models for their students, they could exert a positive influence upon them. Where a faculty member does not feel up to serving as a model for creativity, he can still perform a significant function by bringing the student into contact with other men in the community who *are* creative or by discussing with the student how creative people in the past solved their problems.

Since the faculty is so vital to a program designed to foster creativity, I should like to suggest that more attention be paid to the criteria for selecting teachers and other faculty members. Research on teacher-trainees (4) suggests that it is possible to develop methods that would facilitate the selection of effective teachers, and some of these might well be used. Furthermore, because of the faculty's important role, college administrators might do well to attend more carefully to faculty morale. Where morale is low, it is unlikely that the faculty will devote its energies wholeheartedly to the development of its students' creativity. For a long time now, industry has been aware of the negative effects that low morale may have on its employees' productivity, has sought the aid of consultants to gauge the morale of its employees, and has often found the sources of discontent and the methods of solving its problems. Colleges might profit from the same course of action. A morale survey that oriented itself to learning how the faculty feels about its teaching load, how the faculty perceives the administration and the student body, how the administration perceives its faculty and students, how satisfied the students are with what they are being taught, might bring to light difficulties that need to be dealt with so that the faculty's energies might be devoted more completely to teaching for creativity.

These, then, are some suggestions for developing the college student's creative imagination. While they do not cover all possibilities, they provide us with a point of departure.

REFERENCES

1. Brandwein, P. F. *The Gifted Student as Future Scientist*. New York: Harcourt, Brace & Company, Inc., 1955.
2. Jacob, Philip. *Changing Values in College*. New York: Harper and Brothers, 1957.
3. Stein, M. I. "Creativity and Culture." *Journal of Psychology*, 36:311–22, 1953.
4. Stern, G. G., M. I. Stein, and B. S. Bloom. *Methods in Personality Assessment*. Glencoe, Illinois: The Free Press, 1956.
5. Super, D. E., and P. B. Bachrach. *Scientific Careers and Vocational Development Theory*. New York: Bureau of Publications, Teachers College, Columbia University, 1957.

THIS chapter, prepared by Mr. Stein, who is at the University of Chicago, reflects the discussion of a group of which Elisabeth Nydegger of the College of St. Theresa and Sister Annette of the College of St. Catherine were chairmen, and Ruth Stenerson, Bemidji State College, and Clifford E. Larson, Bethel College, were recorders.

Helping Students to Think Critically

Oɴᴇ of the characteristics of man, at least as we know him now, is his constant effort to understand his behavior and to cope with his environment. He tries continually to make sense out of his experience and observations. Besides getting this philosophical overview he always faces the more practical problems — the day-to-day decisions and actions. These needs are the reasons for critical thinking. The process is one of asking a question, surveying and evaluating a number of alternative solutions, and making a choice — at least a temporary one. I shall not deal with a specific solution to a particular problem but rather with the process in general; I shall attempt to tell why such an approach to thinking is vital, and how it is possible to stimulate critical and independent thinking by students.

Definition of Critical Thinking

Critical thinking has been variously defined. Some of the definitions are broadly inclusive, encompassing or comparable to reflective thinking, problem-solving, and creative thinking. Others are narrowly conceived, usually implying that critical thinking means being critical — that is, fault-finding and little more. I am choosing the broader definition of David Russell (13) and Paul Dressel and Walker Hill (4): the purpose of critical thinking is to solve problems.

If such is the case, then we may ask whether there is a way to go about this problem-solving process, a formula to follow. Is this a one-stage process or does it involve a series of steps? Again I have made a choice, dictated partly by the opinions of others and partly by my own predilection. I am not accepting the flash of insight nor the ready answer as critical thinking. Instead I will hold that critical thinking is searching for solutions and testing them.

76

How many steps should there be in the process — twelve or six or three? Obviously, with a limited number of steps the process within a given step is broadened and perhaps offers an opportunity for greater flexibility. I have chosen to limit my approach to four steps: (a) defining the problem, (b) forming hypotheses and gathering evidence, (c) testing hypotheses and evaluating evidence, and (d) coming to a conclusion. Even limited in this way, it is quite possible that the process might be completed in fewer steps or with steps in varying arrangements. In order that we all understand the stages in the process, I am going to attempt to round out their meaning with some observations.

In defining the problem, care should be taken that the students not only understand what question is being asked but that they are eager to know the answer. Neither of these is possible if students come to the process uninformed about the area the question covers. Background knowledge is essential for formulating adequate questions. However, there is a danger of knowing too well what has gone before and dismissing all opportunities for original research with a "Who am I that I could do better?", thus accepting the alternative of memorizing answers supplied in texts.

Given the conditions of the student's having some knowledge of the area in question and having at least a glimmer of a need to know, the problem can then be phrased. Certain precautions should be taken here, too. Definitions are needed, and limitations must be placed on the too-broad problem. For example, students can be introduced to Percy Bridgman's (1) concept of the operational definition. Rigid limitations are not advisable, however, at least at the outset of the search. Serendipity, the gift of finding valuable things not sought for, will yield the greatest rewards when opportunities for relatively free exploration are built into the problem.

The next step, forming hypotheses, might be termed the creative or original part of the process. At this stage it is important that no evaluating be done, that ample time be allowed for idea-tracking, and that even relatively implausible and far-afield relations be explored. For defining the problem, prior knowledge of the area was pointed out as necessary. Only by having this knowledge of what has gone before can the student reformulate old answers and try out new ones. He will learn that iconoclasm is part of the game — but only, we can hope, after he knows what rules he is breaking.

77

Testing these hypotheses follows. It may be that the facts will not fit the favorite theory. In such a case, Bacon's definition of a tragedy as a theory killed by a fact may apply. Or facts may not agree. Students will learn that books are written by real people and that people make errors — deliberate and otherwise. All of this will give more meaning to one of their pet slogans, "Don't confuse me with the facts, my mind is made up." They may find that even scientists work within a framework of biases and sometimes unconsciously distort their results. Somehow the Yale rats never behave quite like those in California; they will need to ask if this can be explained satisfactorily on the basis of different strains of rats. Ligon (5) reports that during the Depression two trained interviewers, one an ardent prohibitionist and the other an equally ardent socialist, saw a number of destitute men in New York City. Their goal was to determine the cause of the men's downfall. The prohibitionist's data indicated that sixty-two per cent of the destitution was due to liquor and only seven per cent to industrial conditions. The socialist reported that sixty per cent were degraded by industrial conditions and only eleven per cent by liquor.

Finally, as a concluding step in critical thinking, an appropriate conclusion or hypothesis must be chosen. The answer is not always readily found, and delaying the decision may be necessary. This may mean that more evidence will have to be collected which will increase the complexity of the problem. Tolerance for such complexity (often it seems to be just messiness) and for unsettled business is essential. But even more essential is reaching some kind of conclusion, even a tentative one. Critical thinking is not, in its most complete form, just finding out all the things that will not work. It is not the completely negative point of view that always rejects and objects but never proposes a course of action of its own. Any answer, or course, is only an approximation of truth and but one step in a sequence of repeated quests. Knowledge is always partial, and to mistake progress for arrival is to be ensnared. Some searches, the students must understand, are so broadly formulated that the quest may continue for most of a lifetime. Einstein spent his last forty years searching for a unified field theory that would supplant the wave and quantum theories' apparently contradictory descriptions of matter.

Students must also know that there is a moral and ethical aspect to making judgments and reporting conclusions. They must realize that an experiment should not be reported as yielding significant results if there are too few cases or if appropriate statistical measures are not made. They should be suspicious of profound observations put forth by the unqualified — for example the educational advice given by laymen who have nothing to recommend them but their unbridled prejudices. They should also be aware of the distortion that individual and cultural biases give to "objective" reporting.

The Need for Critical Thinking

We should also ask, when the concern is for adequate critical thinking, whether the matter under consideration is worth the effort. For example, in the case of critical thinking itself, is there a need to bother with instructing students in such a complex process? Here, I believe, the answer is unequivocal. Never has our world been so complex. Burgeoning population and shrinking distances have magnified the problems of human relations. Ersatz moons and rocks and weather are only a prelude to the manmade problems that will arise in nature. As J. N. Rush (12) indicates, man's power over his environment is increasing precipitately and dangerously. He must take time to think carefully and responsibly about how he uses it. Not only is knowledge expanding rapidly — man added as much that was new in the past twenty-five years as in the two thousand that preceded — but facts are changing kaleidoscopically. The cry of traditionalists who advocate drill on subject-matter specifics seems a primordial echo under such circumstances: memorizing today's facts for tomorrow's world cannot be the answer.

Mature and responsible adults are needed more desperately than ever before in the era of man — adults who are sufficiently autonomous to do the independent thinking necessary to solve problems. A few seem to have reached such an estate, and some psychologists and social scientists are beginning to study these adults and to try to understand why and how they have developed. Abraham Maslow (8) sees them as self-actualizing, with an efficient perception of reality and a genuine desire to help the human race. David Riesman (9) calls them autonomous and heuristic people, willing to investigate further by themselves. Independent thinking, as a trait of maturity and a much-needed characteristic in our society, is also discussed by Ann Roe (10) and Alfred North Whitehead (15). Carl Rogers (11) has accepted a similar ideal as an adequate concept of maturity and has suggested certain associated inner conditions: openness to experience and an internal locus of evaluation.

The needs of our complex and overburdened world are apparent. The development of people who perceive reality more clearly, reason more ably, and are cognitively more efficient also seems possible, as the above-mentioned writers suggest. For the maximum stimulation of critical thinking, we must not only offer adequate knowledge of *how* to do it, but make an effort to produce people who are emotionally and intellectually *able* to do it. Two questions arise in this connection: (a) What general conditions will foster such development? and (b) What specific qualities are most necessary and how are these developed?

Conditions and Qualities for Critical Thinking

I think that the question of underlying conditions has been answered most adequately by Rogers (11), who has pointed out the need for psychological safety and psychological freedom. Psychological safety is established by an environment which (a) accepts the individual as of unconditional worth, (b) provides a climate in which external evaluation is absent, and (c) understands empathically. Psychological freedom is not softness or indulgence: it is permission to be free and carries with it responsibility for one's acts.

However, beyond this atmosphere of acceptance and this permission to be free, critical thinking needs further facilitation. Stimulation and encouragement must come both from society at large and from the home. Somewhere between lie the school and its influence. I am going to deal largely with the influence of the school, and especially of the teacher.

The teacher is of undeniable importance in setting the stage for critical thinking. Agnes DeMille (3) states succinctly and forcibly that exceptional people can perhaps be educated through reading, plays, television, and correspondence courses but that "for most of us education is a matter of inspiration. Books influence greatly, but few shape lives. . . . I believe teachers do."

Critical thinking cannot be done without information. My opinion is that it is most likely to occur when the teacher is well informed, always knowing more than he teaches. He must have a sense of the past, the urgent present, and the imminent future. Only in this way can he give the student a glimpse of upper reaches and distantly sighted horizons. Out of this knowledge can come the hypotheses that lead to more original and insightful judgments. But knowing his subject is not enough: the teacher must thoroughly enjoy it and, more, he must enjoy the act of teaching. In general, the evocative and enthusiastic teachers are best able to communicate a joy in speculating, searching, and making decisions. This joy is not without discipline, though; for, at least in certain stages of the critical thinking process, ears must be attuned to detect foolishness and trivialities, and eyes must be opened to pitfalls. I believe such attitudes — the love of learning and the dedication to its pursuit — are contagious.

The teacher must remember not only that students need challenge but that this concept of challenge can be disastrously misinterpreted. Misguided attempts can become mere busywork. Increasing the number of pages assigned or assigning more and more reports to be prepared from an encyclopedia may not be the answer. As yet, studies in learning have not given a formula for a safe balance between the unknown to be presented and the known to the student, between the interest to be aroused and the interest already held. Nor can we always know when challenge becomes frustration. Undoubtedly frustration tolerance varies with individuals. But it is fairly clear that the experience of success is necessary, and that given freedom, students choose to do those things which they hope and think will turn out well.

It is not only necessary that the teacher know his subject and enjoy teaching, but it is imperative that he like young people. Otherwise, he cannot convey a feeling that they are of unconditional worth, an attitude basic to the encouragement of free inquiry. He must show and the students must learn that intellectuality and humaneness are not mutually exclusive.

The teacher often cannot arrive at this position or hold it independently: support from the public, from the college, and from other faculty members is necessary. His own experience as a college student should have provided a suitable model. The public and the administration must vigorously protect the teacher's freedom, even when he makes mistakes. To paraphrase William Jennings Bryan, teachers have a right to make their own mistakes. They should be no more censured than M.D.'s who misuse sulfa and other antibiotics and hide behind

81

professional ethics. Administrators can add further support by recognizing scholarship, the essence of which is critical thinking, when they hire staff members. A recent situation in a local high school regarding the choice of a single person to be both coach and history teacher is so often repeated as to cause no surprise. In this case, there were three candidates: two history majors who were outstanding intellectually and moderately fit physically, and one physical education major with five letters of Big Ten caliber and letter grades of a different caliber (D's and F's) in his minor, history. The administration chose and history once again was being taught by the uninterested and the uninformed.

Another complaint of teachers indicates a general feeling that status and financial rewards go to administrators, not scholars; that scholarship is held in low esteem in the very citadels of learning. Even faculty meetings are not immune to this unconcern for thinking and for important issues. Instead of offering an opportunity for intellectual give-and-take, meetings can easily become exchanges among filing cabinets — among super-clerks equipped with built-in gripes.

Other problems plague the teacher who wants to develop critical thinking in his classroom. Large class sections make free discussion difficult. The term system may limit the number of meetings and thus preclude exploratory discussions which could lead to critical thinking. Required courses enlist certain students who are reluctant learners, and even more who are disinclined to think. In these courses, varying intellectual levels and diverse areas of interest may also militate against common discussions out of which critical thinking might emerge.

A further development — perhaps a step beyond group problem-solving where all are somewhat buoyed up by the enthusiasm of the group — is independent study. This approach necessitates administrative action and provisions for some faculty time. However, such a program has much to recommend it: challenge and opportunities to explore beyond the boundaries of the course; allowances for scholarly initiative, responsibility, and freedom not usually possible in undergraduate work; and perhaps greater effectiveness and efficiency. R. H. Bonthius (2) reports that independent study may advance the student more rapidly toward the goal of independent thinking than other approaches.

The qualities needed by the teacher, or anyone who is to engage in critical thinking, are both intellectual and emotional. Perhaps most important of all is intellectual drive and its emotional concomitants — an intense need to know and a delight in the process of finding out. This drive is an impulsion toward competence and mastery. Problems do not get a So what? response from scholars who have this drive. They listen to the query or the explanation and say, "I see" — meaning that they have had a revelation and it was wonderful; not "I see, and let's move on to something else." A necessary condition is that the person feel that he can choose freely, that he neither has to rely on luck nor be the victim of fate, but can influence his destiny or the course of events by his own decision.

A quality mentioned earlier that is indispensable in the development of critical thinking is the tolerance of complexity. Teachers and students alike will need to think across subject-matter boundaries. Often it is only in this way that they will accumulate enough responses to enable them to make wise judgments. They will need to acknowledge that an idea about psychology may be sound even when it is not suggested by a psychologist. They will need to accept alien ideas and be able to use the language of other disciplines, and they must become adept at contrapuntal thinking: in testing hypotheses, several themes must be kept in mind simultaneously and played against one another. Another aspect of accepting complexity, as mentioned earlier, is the ability to live with loose ends and unsettled business — a capacity to defer decisions and to endure ambiguity. This is as necessary as the drive toward ultimate order. Only when the disorder of temporary disintegration is tolerated is it possible to reach a higher level of integration and a more satisfactory goal. Such perceptual openness has both inner and outer facilitating conditions. As I said before, the teacher must be both scholar and evocator, but even more important he must provide a classroom atmosphere which offers both safety and security. Dealing with endless shades of gray is not easy for an insecure person in a world which most people see as two-tone.

An appropriate teacher model who maintains a safe climate for both delayed decisions and spontaneity can go far in fostering originality among students. In such an atmosphere it is possible for the student to suggest the idiosyncratic hypothesis and venture the novel insight. It is also safe to dissent. The stereotyped answer, derived a thousand times before by conventional proof, can be discarded. Students can feel secure in taking a risk, at least a calculated one. Such security and sense of worth can increase their receptiveness to ideas and allow the sensitive ear to function. This openness may often border on credulity, as pointed out by Ernest Jones (5), but only in this way can the novel solution be brought to consciousness.

Motivation for thinking — the will to use one's abilities to the hilt — does not come from just knowing the ground rules, in this case the steps in critical thinking. It may not even be enough to have a teacher (a significant other person with whom the student can identify) who is interested in the pursuit of ideas. Both motivation and an ideal with whom to identify are tremendously important, but the climate of society is perhaps even more basic. Does the society encourage and reward and esteem work with ideas? The ranks of scholarship may be thin if not. More important, scholarship cannot move forward if critical thought is discouraged. *Time* (14) recently reviewed John Keats's *Schools without Scholars.* In this book only two alternative kinds of education are mentioned: the old-fashioned, facts-and-mental-discipline sort and "life adjustment" education — the kind that will "make children unselfish and interested in others." The importance of becoming scholars by practicing the methods of inquiry — of studying because a problem festers within one and tantalizes him — is not mentioned. Open-book tests are scorned; yet what scholar worth the name has ever proceeded without checking the facts in many open books again and again? Perhaps *Time*'s assumption is that the open-book test means only copying an answer from a particular page rather than approaching a problem critically and using many sources. I hope that even the reporters for *Time,* a group at least in the broad base of Russell Lynes' (7) intellectual pyramid, *think* about memorized facts and occasionally check them for accuracy in open books.

Finally, two general problems in the development of critical thinking must be faced by both teacher and student. One is an allegiance to truth, both immediate and ultimate. Critical thinking is pure sham without this. In day-to-day situations, a teacher's honesty and integrity shows in many ways. Grading policies must be open and aboveboard. We discount the importance of school marks, yet we give our rewards on the basis of grades. In the teaching process, little acts of immorality do not escape the student — the implacable claim to possession of the right answer, when it is at best an opinion; the questions asked with the teacher's book open and the students' closed. Closely allied in students' minds with the ethics of daily classroom dealings are the ethics of society as a whole. In the classroom it is possible, through precept and encouragement, to bring students to a point of concern with world issues and human needs as well as with scientific and technical problems. It is not enough to think critically: it is imperative that student and teacher alike be concerned with significant issues, and that these issues be submitted to searching inquiry to determine probable truths.

REFERENCES

1. Bridgman, Percy. *The Logic of Modern Physics.* New York: The Macmillan Company, 1927.
2. Bonthius, R. H., and others. *The Independent Study Program in the United States.* New York: Columbia University Press, 1957.
3. DeMille, Agnes. "The Valor of Teaching." *Atlantic,* June 1955.
4. Dressel, Paul, and Walker Hill. *Critical Thinking, A Guide to Instruction and Evaluation.* Board of Examiners, Michigan State University, September 1955.
5. Jones, Ernest. "How to Tell Your Friends from Geniuses." *Saturday Review,* 40: 9–11, August 10, 1957.
6. Ligon, Ernest M. *Dimensions of Character.* New York: The Macmillan Company, 1956.
7. Lynes, Russell. *A Surfeit of Honey.* New York: Harper and Brothers, 1954.
8. Maslow, Abraham. *Motivation and Personality.* New York: Harper and Brothers, 1954.
9. Riesman, David. *Individualism Reconsidered.* Glencoe, Illinois: The Free Press, 1954.
10. Roe, Ann. *The Making of a Scientist.* New York: Dodd, Mead & Company, Inc., 1954.
11. Rogers, Carl. "Toward a Theory of Creativity." *A Review of General Semantics,* 11:249–60, No. 4.
12. Rush, J. N. "The Next 10,000 Years." *Saturday Review,* January 25, 1958.
13. Russell, David. *Children's Thinking.* Boston: Ginn and Company, 1956.
14. *Time,* April 14, 1958, p. 77.
15. Whitehead, A. N. *Dialogues of Alfred North Whitehead,* Lucien Price, ed. Boston: Little, Brown & Company, 1954.

THIS chapter, prepared by Mrs. Drews, who is in the College of Education at Michigan State University, reflects the discussion of a group of which Gerhard Alexis of Gustavus Adolphus College and Theodore Nydahl of Mankato State College were chairmen, and Father Vincent Tegeder, O.S.B., of St. John's University and Richard O. Sielaff, Duluth Branch, University of Minnesota, were recorders.

◄§ MARJORIE CARPENTER

Stimulating Students to Make Critical Value Judgments

IT MIGHT be comfortable for us to say to our colleagues at the University of Minnesota that the first hundred years are the hardest; but our complacency has been seriously challenged. Disraeli tells us that "every man has a right to be conceited until he is successful." The University of Minnesota is recognizing that the very fact that it has one hundred years of successful higher education behind it imposes an obligation on it to consider better ways of meeting the challenging days ahead. The general public is crying out that we educators may be higher but we need to go deeper. We must admit that we are vulnerable. Francis Quarles, a seventeenth-century English poet, says that "physicians are of all men the most happy; what good success they have, the world proclaimeth, and what faults they commit, the earth covereth." We might claim that educators are of all men the most unhappy; what success they have is attributed to other causes, and what faults they commit walk around proclaiming themselves over the earth.

A queer sort of battle is going on within the educational institutions themselves. On the one hand, we hear from those who maintain that science is basic to our survival and deserving of vast increases in financial support. On the other hand, some insist that all our troubles stem from the fact that science has already outrun man's wisdom in using its products; therefore we must encourage and support the humanities. Along with this verbal and fiscal war with its false dichotomies, an older struggle continues. This is the opposition between the strictly academic education and the one that takes account also of growth in the student who must constantly make choices which depend on his system of values. It is easy to forget the philological truth that the verb *to teach* takes two accusatives: the person taught and the subject taught. It is easy to forget another philological truth: there is an important root meaning in the word *intelligent*. The intelligent student makes choices (interlegere). Instruction (a building in) is "never without outcomes and growth beyond attainment of academic knowledge, but unless they are planned and controlled as far as possible, the outcomes may be fortuitous, undesirable, or ineffective" (6, p. 30).

We have some evidence in recent research that just this sort of failure has occurred. Philip Jacob (4) reports that for the most part the value systems of our college students remain unaffected by their collegiate experiences. (He defines value patterns as the criteria for making choices; the conference group preferred to include the concept of appraisal of conflicting ideas as basic to value judgments.) Jacob finds (see also pp. 13–14, 69–70) an amazing similarity in the values held by college students in the United States. The following is true of seventy to eighty per cent.

1. The college student is unabashedly self-centered and materialistic. He intends to provide for himself and his family as well as possible without consideration of the other fellow; and he expects others to do the same. He is very contented.

2. He is tolerant; he expects to live harmoniously with people of other races and creeds; BUT he wants no part in any crusade to improve conditions for minority groups.

3. He has a respect for the traditional virtues of honesty and loyalty; BUT he also expects many exceptions to be made — provided the lapses are socially acceptable.

4. He has a respect for formal religion and the institution of the church; BUT religion as a force in business and social life is not considered; it is not supposed to have any influence on practical matters.

5. He has a respect for the government; he expects to obey the laws, to pay his taxes, and to fight our wars; BUT he does it with no sense of being committed to a cause, and with no sense of participation in the decisions which create taxes and make wars.

6. He is sure that there will be another world war within ten years; he would rather have peace; he believes that some supra-national organization or control would be good; BUT he is ignorant about the United Nations and its possibilities.

7. He puts great stock in a college education; BUT his reasons are

nonintellectual. He values the prestige which goes with a college education, the friends who will be helpful to him, and the increased opportunities which college will offer for his vocation. His intellectual curiosity is so low as to be practically nonexistent.

Jacob goes on to state: "This study has not discerned significant changes in student values which can be attributed directly either to the character of the curriculum or to the basic courses in social science. . . . The quality of the teaching has relatively little effect upon the value-outcomes of general education. . . . The method of instruction seems to have only a minor influence on students' value judgments." The chief response of students, Jacob concludes, is to the cultural or moral climate of the institution.

Some of the findings of Jacob's study need to be supplemented with such studies as those of the Mellon Foundation. Whereas Jacob points out that seniors are even more homogeneous than freshmen in their pattern of values, the research of the Mellon Foundation reports more variation among seniors than freshmen (see pp. 12, 14). Also, there are serious questions about the type of changes which are not revealed by the various questionnaires Jacob summarized. However, one must face the challenge in Jacob's report.

Among the several disturbing features of these findings, two stand out. First of all, the prevalence of privatism in a contracting world points up the Greek root for our word *idiot*. Idiotes is the Greek word for a private citizen, one who tends to seek what he wants, without a sense of responsible sharing of public responsibilities. A second fact is still more symptomatic of failure to educate for the development of intelligence. A complete lack of critical judgment is demonstrated in the hopelessly contradictory sections of each statement of philosophy we have quoted. By anyone's definition, an emphasis on critical thinking should point up the fallacies in simultaneously wanting to stay out of war and wanting to stay out of policy-making.

Nor is it a cause for optimism to state that the youth of today merely reflect our national cultural pattern. If we tend merely to socialize the individual so that he readily conforms to the norm of college graduates then we may be guilty of what Adlai Stevenson calls M.I.T.'s "efforts to humanize the scientist" as over against Harvard's attempts to "Simonize the humanist."

I should like to assume that integrity of thinking is a value of basic importance. If we are going to stimulate students to make critical value judgments we have to be realistic about the goals of the student and then try to move the goal post. Without making a scholarly survey of the reasons which entering students have for going to college, it seems clear that there is a widespread opinion held by parents and their children that going to college is the thing to do if you can afford it. Students want to get ahead. To induce a change of attitude will require much stimulation toward growth in intellect and in appreciation. The goad or stimulus may vary from campus to campus, teacher to teacher, but certain common denominators suggest the way to better chances of success.

Jacob himself refers to some institutions which have a different climate; he does not analyze the difference, but he does infer that the classroom, especially in the social sciences, has little to do with it. It is worth our while to examine some courses that do have an effect on students' values; and it is important to see what we can learn from various experiments which are being conducted with a genuine concern for the student's growth, and in recognition of his pattern of values and his desire for change. Instructors in many disciplines have written descriptions of courses in which they have reason to think such changes are taking place. Some of these experiments might well be considered. (Much of the following material is from letters and unpublished manuscripts recently sent to me.)

Supplementing a series of formal courses offered the first two years, there is at Boston University a six-week unit in Utopian Planning. The students use literary texts and work in groups to plan and draft a utopia; they are challenged to integrate the subject matter of the courses in psychology, social relations, science, communications, and the humanities. As they examine the utopian literature for the solutions presented in the areas of economics, esthetics, ethics, science, psychology, and religion, they are forced to become aware of the interrelationship and interdependence of value systems. Groups of five to seven students write their utopias and prepare for an oral examination, in which they defend their vision. From the viewpoint of students' interest and involvement, the experiment is a success; some of the results provide interesting and challenging paths for research. For example, students readily drop their belief in competition and free enterprise, but apparently cling more tightly to the rest of their value structures. (1, 2.)

At Michigan State University (8), the course in communications has been used to help the student to see in himself the basis for prejudice. This is an approach to the improvement of personal relations; but the goal is not pursued theoretically. The first assignment asked for a statement of reasons for not liking another student. The reasons had to be as specific as possible. It was then announced that one project for the term was that each person become better acquainted with the person whom he had described. At the end of the term, a re-evaluation was asked for. The members of the class were asked to describe the process used in becoming better acquainted; they were to describe facts learned about the student; and they were to state whether or not they now liked the person. It was made clear, however, that the grade for this paper would depend on the quality of expression and not on the extent or direction of the change in attitude. This written assignment proved difficult. Neither instructor nor student felt that the skills involved in English composition had been neglected. Twenty-six of twenty-eight students indicated varying degrees of change. One student, after attempting the first paper, commented to the instructor that after thinking about the student whom he disliked, he was convinced that the cause of his dislike lay entirely within himself. His final evaluation was a self-evaluation. Voluntary comments were added to many papers. Typically they read: "This assignment was worthwhile; we need to do more of this."

The psychologist has a kind of subject matter which provides a natural approach to the development of self-understanding. A course taught by Wilbert J. McKeachie at the University of Michigan, called Psychology and Religion, recognizes a culture-wide concern with the relation between these two fields, a concern with religious and psychological ways of approaching man's nature and man's disharmony with himself and others. In this course, religious behavior is examined, then approached with the methods and theories of psychology. Students are asked to examine their own and other religions in terms of psychological concepts and theories. In small discussion groups they raise such questions as Does unconscious guilt exist? and What effect does religious training have on a person's values? Students reported that the course developed in them a critical and objective attitude toward their beliefs. Neither students nor instructor felt that the principles of psychology had been neglected.

A senior synthesis course, called Ideological Foundations of Western Civilization, is taught by Kerney Adams and James R. Flynn at Eastern Kentucky State College. It attempts to provide an opportunity for students to read some great books in the Western heritage and at the same time makes an effort to stimulate the students to relate specialized knowledge to broader human purposes. The popular name reveals the objective: it is referred to as the IF course, since the primary concern is that each person see the logical consequences of his beliefs and attitudes. He is first led to see which of his values and beliefs contradict one another, then to discriminate between the beliefs which he really holds and those which he thinks he holds. The discussion method is the heart of the consideration of the philosophical problems, for the instructor feels that a student who would normally absorb merely the content of a lecture, is stung to a real response by a comment of a fellow student which seems to him absurd or false. Once he becomes involved in a discussion, at least the precondition for his examination of his values is established when he is forced to state and defend his opinion.

Teachers of science find it difficult to cover in the alloted time the skills and facts expected of the specialist in science, and it is understandable that they have made few experiments in considering values in connection with their formal courses. An interesting exception is a course offered at Johns Hopkins University. John Woodburn reports that content and method are adapted in such a way that the instructor may give an added attention to the philosophical objectives of science. He begins with a brief description of the patterns of thinking which are identifiable in the history of civilization. He would answer the colleague who objects: "But I am not a philosopher!" by maintaining that "It is not well that natural science should be assigned exclusively to one class of persons, called scientists, and philosophy to another class, called philosophers." He adds: "A man who has never reflected on the principles of his work, has not achieved a grown-up man's attitude toward it." The second part of his project is the presentation of such basic topics as magnetism, heredity, diastrophism. Students are assigned the task of searching the array of explanations of the three phenomena to see if they recognize a pattern of thinking. In evaluating the experiment, they agreed that this approach was more effective in stimulating thought than a lecture on the details of currently accepted information. The evolutionary nature of scientific explanations became vivid for them. The professor came to agree with Abraham Maslow that "there should not be any questions—even in the area of the un-known, the chaotic, the dimly-seen, the unmanageable, the mysterious, the 'not-yet well-phrased'—which we dare not ask" (7, p. 330).

It could even be that courses in the sciences are among those best suited as an approach for examining a pattern of values. As Dean Thomas S. Hall of Washington University commented in a letter to me, "Our general biology course has specifically concerned itself with value development and value awareness—our principal effort has been to dramatize the almost religious ethics of the scientific spirit; and a second approach has been to answer, through the methods available in the sciences, basic questions about man—*what are we? whence came we? whither go we?*"

Certainly one might expect from courses in philosophy and religion the most obvious and direct approach to teaching values. However, this is not the case, for many teachers of such courses seem to fear becoming nonacademic. The emphasis on subject matter for its own sake, the desire to cover the ground, has a tight hold on philosophy instructors. Perhaps they are aware that they deal with what Maslow calls the dimly-seen, the unmanageable, the mysterious; perhaps they have been scorned as dangerous mystics; in any case, the fact remains that only a few philosophy courses are planned with a conscious objective of having students examine their own values.

Needless to say, this has been a far from complete report of the many efforts which are being made in formal courses to affect student attitudes and values. Even so, certain common characteristics or trends can be observed. The instructor in each experiment believes that it is important to state the objective explicitly. He does not just take it for granted that if the valuable content of the subject matter in social studies, humanities, psychology, science, or even philosophy and religion is presented in clear lectures which the student absorbs, the student will thereby necessarily be helped in examining his own values. Secondly, these experiments have put a notable emphasis on the kind of thinking which makes for valid judgments. There is also a marked tendency to use materials from many departments, and a universal dependence on discussion as a method needed to supplement lectures if the student is to be personally involved. Various devices are used for stimulating oral and written articulation of the pattern of values currently held by the student. Papers are often required both at the beginning and at the end of the course. Propagandizing is universally avoided; the development of a person who is in conscious control of his decisions is the common objective.

The claims of the various instructors whose courses have been mentioned in this chapter are not extreme. Some of the evidence may be open to question. Discussion with instructors in various disciplines reveals agreement on the principle that clear thinking is a value of major importance and that it is important for the student to examine his own preconceptions and assumptions before he can think clearly. Instructors recognize that some students come to college with serious limitations of background. They are at an age when they are ripe for an approach that encourages rebellion against former ideas. They soon come to see that the teacher makes implicit value judgments in his choice of material and his treatment of it; they can be led to see that textbooks make implicit value judgments. To bring these basic assumptions of teacher and writer to the surface is one way of assisting the student in independent judgment and thinking.

Teachers of all subject-matter areas agree that the student can be led to see the consequences and implications of the beliefs he professes. Whether we like it or not, students will always weigh the significance of the facts we teach. For me, it is impossible to imagine instruction without some results over and above academic knowledge. The point is the value of our values instruction; it is better at the conscious level; it should be related to issues of importance. We dare not trust to chance. The only realistic approach to formal courses is one which takes values into account; otherwise, facts are dead and the carrion smell pollutes the learning process.

A few principles have become clear to me in my own teaching. If we take as a conscious central objective the training of young people to entertain a new idea, we have a natural ally in stimulating students towards critical thinking in the area of value judgments. Almost every young person likes to think that he is more modern than his teacher. Actually, the majority of seventeen- or eighteen-year-olds are very conservative and have never really thought out their points of view. They have either accepted what their parents thought or rebelled against their parents' opinions, without any discrimination. In either case, they need and can be led to consider a new approach. On the one hand, they can see that it fits in with their desire to be a success in business and an interesting person. On the other hand, it meets an emotional or deep-felt urge to form independent judgments. It is a common denominator for teacher and student. The instructor does not have to sell out to a purely vocational goal.

Furthermore, inducing students to entertain new ideas seemingly by-passes the problem of general education as an opposite to vocational education; actually, it gets at the very core of the problem. Some freshmen would like to feel that they know what everybody else knows, and that there are no areas of knowledge closed to them. Most of them, however, have already decided that several areas are definitely not for them and not worth exploring. The educator's definition of general education usually springs from a desire to introduce the young to some experience with all the big divisions of knowledge. The educator thinks first of subject matter; and a sharp dichotomy is at once set up between his objectives and those of the student. It becomes a different matter when the process of making intelligent judgments is the goal. The ability to *use* materials in various areas is a part of life which an eighteen-year-old can understand even though he does not of his own volition submit easily to the discipline of learning many detailed facts in a lot of subjects. This does not mean that facts are not used in the process of entertaining new ideas; it does mean that for many students the facts are not in themselves the goals. He can later decide to take more advanced courses; his goals will change.

Moreover, the approach which concentrates on entertaining a new idea is in itself stimulating, and stimulation and motivation are close allies. Too often the classroom procedure follows the lines suggested by a story told by President Sarah Blanding of Vassar, who was teaching a class of teachers-to-be. When she had finished her presentation of a unit on motivation, one young teacher in training said: "I see what you mean; you try to kindle a spark and then water it." Entertaining a new idea, by the way, does not mean bowing to it and passing on. When we entertain people, we spend some time with them; we listen to them, we do not do all the talking; usually we feed them; we intro-

94

duce them to other people — but we do not necessarily accept them as lifelong bosom friends.

The stimulus of entertaining a new idea, with the objective of making intelligent judgments, involves time spent in the presence of more than one idea; it involves open-minded consideration of principles which cut across narrow subject-matter fields; it involves feeding the idea with many other ideas, and trying it out until, after careful consideration, we make a judgment as to the degree of truth we have found for our own lives.

If, then, we are trying to motivate students toward intellectual achievement, there are advantages in taking as our central objective the process of making intelligent judgments: we appeal to the natural desire of the young to make independent decisions; we present a tenable reason for an approach to the various areas of knowledge; and we have, inherent in the objective, a stimulating procedure. There are, of course, disadvantages: thinking is hard work; teaching people to think is harder; evaluating the success of the process is harder still.

My own experience has been with the kind of course that uses the arts to concentrate on man as a creative being. The insights the arts give us about ourselves, our own age, and other people in other lands touch the heart as well as the mind. Care needs to be taken that instruction concentrates on the process of making judgments and the process of handling materials and thinking about them. The materials should be of high quality. Cheap popular reading will not do. As Randall Jarrell comments in *Poetry and the Age*: "Since the animal organism thinks, truly reasons, only when it is required to, thoughtfulness is gradually disappearing among readers of popular literature" (5). The instructor, then, is in the classroom to assist the student in attaching vital *significance* to *significant* works of literature, art, and music, and not just in attaching labels to them.

Let us assume that *Antigone* has been chosen as a play which all students are to read. "WHY?" the freshman asks (probably not out loud). "I do not want to know about Greek plays; I am going to be a salesman for Standard Oil. What does this have to do with the price of oil?" If we say, "It is a good example of Greek drama; it shows the power of tragedy to release in us pity and fear and produce a sort of catharsis," I doubt that the boy who wants to get ahead will be motivated.

What will go on in the classroom? Will the instructor lecture on Greek drama and the origins of tragedy? Are the students to answer questions pointing up the aesthetic principle of catharsis and the ethical problem of the individual versus the state? Will the questions deal with the function of the chorus in Greek drama, the costume of the actors, the appearance of the Greek stage? When the questions are given out, will the students be told that they are to be responsible for answers on a test which will cover what the lecturer has said and what they have read?

If the play is to come alive for students, the issue of the individual versus the state must be urgent in their minds. Therefore the class might profit from a fifteen-minute debate on a present-day issue in this area. Some students might like to expand that idea into a paper. There is a contemporary play by Jean Anouilh which uses the classical play as its source. Some of the class might read it, act out parts of it. Better still, if there are possibilities for acting such a play in the college playhouse, have everyone attend and then make comparisons between the two versions. If there are students especially interested in Greek literature, have some of them read *Oedipus Rex* and compare the attitude toward fate found there with that in *Antigone*. If there are any students from overseas who have themselves lived under a dictatorship, or otherwise learned of it first hand, use their experience to heighten understanding of life under a dictator. If there are students whose fathers hold responsible positions in government, have them defend the need for laws — even laws which seem unduly strict; then have members of the class apply this principle to student government. Ask that they read such books as George Orwell's *1984* or listen to a recording of Gian-Carlo Menotti's opera *The Consul*. Ask for reports and comparisons that underline the conditions of life under a dictator and the displaced person's entanglement in red tape.

We can stimulate ourselves and our students if we try to see facts and principles in the large and in the small, if we try to relate information from other subject-matter areas with our own, and if we follow our thinking to its ultimate consequences and see the criterion for each choice in the light of a total pattern.

Back to another obvious point. The classroom teacher and the counselor should both approach the problem. Preferably every classroom teacher should be a counselor, and every counselor should do some classroom teaching. The activities which go on in the so-called extracurricular program should be re-examined to make sure that information from the classroom gets used; and the classroom teacher needs to use insights which students get in their out-of-class experience.

One great difficulty in education is that theories and facts do not enter the blood stream and produce people with different attitudes and values unless the theories and facts are attached to living experience in as many ways as possible. The battle between extra-class and in-class programs is fought on too low a level and with too much defensiveness on both sides.

The residence hall is frequently the informal and unconscious testing ground for relating the knowledge learned in the classroom to current, immediate, and personal problems of living. What might happen if residence-hall personnel shaped their activities around educating the student while he is in the halls? In addition to concern for the creation of an atmosphere in which the student could study and relax, what might be important to teach? What provisions for creative educational re-creation could be established?

None of us can escape making value judgments; we must stress integrity of thinking for both classroom teacher and counselor. Courage is necessary for the honest handling of values; we must make clear to the student the basis on which we arrive at our conclusions and be as willing as he is to explore the consequences and implications of our own patterns of values. Four years' time, most instructors agree, is not long enough to measure the change in students. In takes many years to determine impact of college teaching; nor can we identify change in students with the usual ways of collecting evidence in past educational research.

Albert Camus wrote in one of his letters: "There is a dead justice and a living justice; and justice dies from the moment it becomes a comfort, when it ceases to be a burning reality, a demand upon oneself." When values are burning realities to us, demanding much from us, students know it; teaching and counseling are vital. When there is no struggle in us, no crisis to demand a re-examination of our own attitudes in the light of today's dramatic changes, then realistically we cannot expect anything to happen which seriously affects students' patterns of values. An understanding of the concepts of outer space is not as difficult as insight into the depths of inner motivation and the mainsprings of our action as individuals and groups. Both are essential today.

REFERENCES

1. Fisher, James. Personal communication about Utopian Planning unit at Boston University.
2. ———, and Peyton Richter. "Education for Citizenship." *Journal of Higher Education,* 28:220–24, No. 4, April 1957.
3. Freedman, Mervin B. Paper as analyst for Group 5, Association for Higher Education, March 1958.
4. Jacob, Philip. *Changing Values in College.* New York: Harper and Brothers, 1957.
5. Jarrell, Randall. *Poetry and the Age.* New York: Alfred A. Knopf, Inc., 1953.
6. Justman, Joseph, and Walter Mais. *College Teaching.* New York: Harper and Brothers, 1956.
7. Maslow, Abraham H. "Problem-Centering vs. Means-Centering in Science." *Philosophy of Science,* 13:326–31, October 1946.
8. Platt, James H., and Russell Jenkins. "A Class Project in Communication." *The Speech Teacher,* 2:97, March 1953.

THIS chapter, prepared by Miss Carpenter, who is at Stephens College, reflects the discussion of a group of which Ralph Ross, College of Science, Literature, and the Arts, University of Minnesota, and Richard Marsh, Hamline University, were chairmen, and G. M. Wissink, Mankato State College, and Benjamin W. Teigen, Bethany Lutheran College, were recorders.

THE TEACHING END

◆§ W. H. COWLEY

College and University Teaching, 1858-1958

A HUNDRED years ago Abraham Lincoln began his famous "house divided" address with these words: "If we could first know where we are, and whither we are tending, we could better judge what to do, and how to do it" (3, II:448). Four and a half years later he concluded his second message to Congress with this epigram: "Fellow-citizens, we cannot escape history" (3, I:537). The program committee has asked me to survey the past century of college teaching because presumably it subscribes to Lincoln's sentiments. Certainly it would not have chosen the topic if it agreed with Henry Ford's declaration that "history is bunk" (quoted in the *Chicago Tribune*, July 15, 1919), or with Hegel's that people have never learned anything from history (16, p. 6).

No one is likely to be interested, however, in having me narrate history for the sake of history. Lincoln looked to the past that he might better understand the present and more effectively prepare for the future. I write in that same spirit.

The history of college teaching extends back twenty-three centuries to Athens and the academy that Plato founded there in 387 B.C., but the most spectacular changes have come during the centenary being celebrated by this conference. Throughout the past hundred years the pace of change, including academic change, has been accelerating at a fantastic rate; and it will not lessen. Awareness of what has happened in and to American colleges and universities since Minnesota became one of the states of the Union puts to use the history from which we cannot escape and helps in reckoning where we are and whither we are tending. In any case, I shall review the major curricular and instructional changes made in American higher education during the past century.

101

THE TEACHING END

The Situation a Century Ago

One of the most publicized of all American educators declared in 1936 that "if rightly understood," education will be "the same at any time, in any place, under any political, social, or economic conditions" (18, p. 66). This has long seemed to me to be one of the most uninformed statements about education ever made, and I therefore begin by sketching the state of the world a hundred years ago. In comparison with some of the years surrounding it, nothing especially eventful happened in 1858; but a review of its occurrences not only illuminates the fallaciousness of Mr. Hutchins' pronouncement but also prepares the ground for describing what developed in American higher education during that and later years.

Probably the paramount political event of 1858 was the decision of Japan to end its long isolation and, by entering into commercial and educational relations with the United States and Europe, to modernize and Westernize. Less dramatically, the nations of Europe also made or prepared for momentous changes. Several groups of patriots were energetically preparing to weld Italy into a single nation. Bismarck was getting ready to assume the leadership of the Prussian drive for domination of the German states and for European hegemony. France, almost as unstable politically as now, suffered under the weak regime of Napoleon III. England fought successful imperialistic wars in China and India but inducted its fifth government in six years. Russia, defeated by England and France two years earlier in the Crimean War, sought to ameliorate domestic discontent by making ready to emancipate the serfs.

These circumstances would formidably affect the future of the world, but much more potent would be the results of the writing being done by a University of Berlin doctor of philosophy named Karl Marx. In 1858 he worked quietly in the British Museum on *Das Kapital*. To help support himself he wrote articles for the *New York Tribune* and the *New American Cyclopedia* (24, X:173). Not many miles away another writer who would mightily influence the shape of things and of thoughts to come received a manuscript on June 18, 1858, from a young colleague in Malaya named Alfred Russel Wallace. It impelled him, Charles Darwin, to publish his *Origin of Species* the next year. (19, p. 42.)

Americans in 1858 agonized in the midst of the most calamitous problem of our history. Six years earlier both Henry Clay and Daniel Webster had died. Their political genius had helped keep the slavery and states' rights issues from coming to a boil. That same year, 1852, Harriet Beecher Stowe's *Uncle Tom's Cabin* appeared. Then in 1857 the Dred Scott Decision greatly increased the number of abolitionists and the activity of the Underground Railroad. In March of that year James Buchanan became the fifteenth president of the United States, but he did not possess the qualities needed "to ride the whirlwind and direct the storm" that harassed the nation. The timid position he took when South Carolina seceded six weeks after Lincoln's election made civil war inevitable.

A disastrous depression also buffeted the United States in 1858. It had begun the previous July, but it did not touch bottom until eighteen months later (29, III:95). Among other things it swept away a large part of the land that the federal government had made available to the Territory of Minnesota for the endowment of this university (14, p. 5). Thus the impressive building erected in 1858 stood empty until 1867 when the preparatory department opened with a few dozen pupils. Not until 1870 would students of college grade be admitted (11, p. 48), and not until 1880 (according to the University of Minnesota calendar), would their numbers be larger than those in the preparatory department.

The political, intellectual, and economic occurrences of 1858 immeasurably overtowered those in education; yet one of the most portentous events of American higher educational history germinated that year in Congress. Three weeks before the end of 1857 Justin Smith Morrill of Vermont introduced a bill in the House of Representatives providing for the donation of public lands to support "at least one college in each state. . . . to promote the liberal and practical education of the industrial classes" (8, p. 32). President Buchanan vetoed it; but the next Congress passed it again, and President Lincoln signed it on July 2, 1862. Nothing before or since has more powerfully molded American higher education than that legislation, the first Land-Grant College Act. The University of Minnesota and sixty-eight other higher educational institutions have benefited directly from it and from supplementary enactments, and it has influenced the programs of every college and university in the nation.

The Land-Grant College Act broke the bottleneck that had prevented educational progress since the founding of the nation. The bottleneck consisted in the belief that all essential educational problems had been solved and that educators needed only to follow what President Josiah Quincy of Harvard in 1840 called "the wisdom of antiquity." "The giants of former times," he declared, had "chiselled" sound educational practices "upon works little less admirable than those of nature herself, and imperishable as her mountains." (34, II:456.)

Quincy spoke for the great majority of American educators of his day, but a handful of farseeing and courageous men fervently disagreed. Their first conspicuous success came with the passage of the Land-Grant College Act, but others would follow not only in the land-grant institutions but also — and at first chiefly — in a number of private institutions.

The Beginnings of Educational Change

A century ago the country had no universities worthy of the name; and Yale, the largest college, had (according to its 1858 catalogue) 447 undergraduates and 118 professional students. The former gave most of their time to studying Quincy's "wisdom of antiquity." They had no instruction in modern literature or in any of the modern humanities; they dallied only briefly with the social sciences; and they openly sneered at the experimental sciences. Concerning one of the latter a member of the Yale class of 1853 later wrote:

. . . one day in my senior year, looking . . . from my window in North College, I saw a student [of the Sheffield Scientific School] examining a colored liquid in a test-tube. A feeling of wonder came over me! What could it all be about? Probably not a man of us in the whole senior class had any idea of a chemical laboratory save as a sort of small kitchen back of a lecture-desk, like that in which an assistant and a colored servant prepared oxygen, hydrogen, and carbonic acid for the lectures of Professor Silliman. I was told that this new laboratory was intended for experiment, and my wonder was succeeded by disgust that any human being should give his time to pursuits so futile. (46, I:290.)

I shall return in a few minutes to comment further about the undergraduate curriculum, but first the status of graduate and professional education needs sketching. A number of attempts were made before the Civil War to establish advanced work in the arts and sciences, but most of them failed completely. Even those that succeeded amounted to little of consequence until after the opening of Johns Hopkins in 1876. Thereafter graduate work began to improve and expand. The Harvard reorganization of 1890 and also the opening of several pioneering universities propelled it into orbit: Clark University in 1889, Stanford in 1891, Chicago in 1892. During the hundred years beginning in 1815, some ten thousand Americans matriculated in German universities, and most of them returned home with the coveted Ph.D. degree (43, p. 40). After 1900, however, few needed to go abroad, because American graduate schools had achieved maturity. In 1876 they granted only forty-four Ph.D. and associated doctorates and in 1900 only three hundred forty-two. (44, pp. 19–20.) In 1956 the number zoomed to 8,903 (13, p. 5).

Professional education ripened along with graduate education, but it began with greater disadvantages because with few exceptions professional schools were conducted for profit and had no connections with universities. More than that, most professional men of all varieties got their training by means of the apprenticeship system, and only a few of those who attended professional schools had had even a single year of college work. As late as the mid-seventies the majority had such defective general education that the dean of the Harvard Medical School bitterly opposed President Charles W. Eliot's suggestion that written examinations be inaugurated because, the dean observed, his students could not write well enough (10, pp. 126–27).

Medical education comparable to that of Europe did not become available in the United States until the opening of Johns Hopkins School of Medicine in 1893. Law and engineering developed a little earlier, but the newer professions all had to wait until the twentieth century to override the objections of those who continued loyal to the doctrine of President Quincy or who protested against practical education's being admitted to the hallowed precincts of universities.

The educational reformers worked exuberantly and successfully to step up the quality and quantity of specialized education both graduate and undergraduate, but they also gave much of their attention to what most people in those days called liberal education but which President Eliot of Harvard preferred to call general education.

To begin with, the reformers very considerably extended both the range and depth of subjects taught. To break from the stranglehold that the classical languages had on the curriculum, they employed the elective principle. May I point out that I have used the term elective *principle* and not elective system. The elective principle got expressed in a variety of systems, the most discussed — the Free Elective System of Harvard — being the least significant. Only Harvard College followed it. Harvard's other undergraduate college during President Eliot's regime, the Lawrence Scientific School, did not. Further, Harvard College abandoned it in 1910.

The country at large chiefly adopted two other elective systems: what might be called the selective system, which Jefferson had developed at the University of Virginia and which all universities with multiple undergraduate colleges still follow; and the group elective system initiated by Daniel Coit Gilman first at Yale and then at Johns Hopkins. With few exceptions all the liberal arts colleges of the country as well as all university colleges of arts and science still employ it.

The elective principle opened the curriculum to the onrushing new knowledge which the old prescribed curriculum neglected or underprivileged. It also contributed strategically to changing the college professor from a drillmaster to a teacher. President Andrew Dickson White of Cornell, the member of the Yale class of 1853 whom I have already quoted, has cogently reported the kind of instruction given college students a century ago:

The worst feature of the junior year was the fact that through two terms, during five hours each week, "recitations" were heard by a tutor in "Olmstead's Natural Philosophy." The textbook was simply repeated by rote. Not one student in fifty took the least interest in it; and the man who could give the words of the text most glibly secured the best marks. . . . Almost as bad was the historical instruction given by Professor James Hadley. It consisted simply in hearing the student repeat from memory the dates from "Putz's Ancient History." . . . it amazes me to remember that during a considerable portion of our senior year no less a man than Woolsey gave instruction in history by hearing men recite the words of a textbook. (46, I: 27–28.)

A Yale sophomore of 1858 who became a great publisher, Henry Holt, observed about the then-current methods of instruction that "the most diabolical ingenuity could hardly have done more to make . . . scholarship repulsive" (17, p. 36); and a Harvard historian has reported that "almost every graduate of the period 1825–60 has left on record his detestation of the system of instruction. . . . The Faculty were not there to teach, but to see that boys got their lessons." (30, p. 260.)

Professors trained in Germany denounced and abandoned the deeply rooted recitation system and vigorously pursued new methods — the lecture, laboratory, and seminar methods in particular. They also sent students to work in the college libraries whose collections they insisted be constantly improved. Here they made slow but eventually large progress. In 1858 the Columbia College library remained open a total of nine hours a week, and it had only a minute fraction of the books available today (4, p. 7). In 1876 Harvard's much larger library included about a quarter of a million volumes in comparison with more than six million today. In 1870, the year that William Rainey Harper, later to be the prodigious first president of the University of Chicago, graduated from Muskingum College, it possessed only nine hundred books in comparison with some forty thousand today (4, pp. 88, 6).

It must be noted that at first the college librarians objected to the new emphasis put upon the *use* of their treasures. A friend of the Harvard librarian in office a century ago, for example, meeting him on the street, asked him why he looked so happy. He replied, so the story goes, "All the books are in excepting two. Professor Agassiz has those, and I am going after them." (4, p. 2.)

Unlike Agassiz and his European-trained colleagues, however, most professors did not often use the library. Believing that "the wisdom of antiquity" had resolved all essential human problems and that their textbooks and a handful of Great Books embodied it, they gave much of their time to supervising the religious and moral welfare of students. Indeed, they had considerably more interest in the souls of their students than in their minds. The log of Mark Hopkins was actually a chapel pew, each Williams College student of Hopkins' day (he retired in 1872) being required to sit in his assigned seat more hours than he attended class.

Every weekday included two chapel sessions, the first at 5 A.M. and the second at 5 P.M.; and Sunday had four. In addition to these sixteen compulsory chapel services, students were expected to attend a midweek prayer meeting. (33, p. 24.) If a student consistently stayed away, a professor or tutor would usually come to pray with him in his room. All the liberal arts colleges (called, in those days, academical colleges) similarly emphasized religion at the expense of intellectual achievement.

Not that most students had much interest in things intellectual. President Eliot, who graduated from Harvard the same year as Andrew Dickson White from Yale, estimated that during his undergraduate years a bright student could adequately prepare for his classes in a single hour each day (9, p. 54). Since the passing grade at most colleges stood at fifty per cent — at Dartmouth (35, II:548) it remained at forty per cent until 1877 — most students neglected their studies for more attractive activities including riot and rebellion. Harvard, for example, had nine major rebellions between 1766 and 1841. They included the Bread and Butter Rebellion of 1805, the Rotten Cabbage Rebellion of 1807, and the Great Rebellion of 1823. The last helped prepare the way for the major curricular and administrative reorganization of 1825.

Students also not infrequently engaged in fights with townsmen. In one such fracas occurring a hundred years ago this spring, a Yale student shot and killed a fireman (12, pp. 42–44). Chiefly, however, students directed their energies against members of the faculty — and sometimes fatally. In an 1842 riot at the University of Virginia a student shot and killed the professor of law (5, II:309), and eight years later a student in a small Mississippi college stabbed the president to death (41, IV:590).

Students brawled not only because the curriculum and methods of teaching thoroughly bored them but also because they objected to the constant snooping of members of the faculty into their personal lives. A Dartmouth historian has observed that

Teaching was not the only duty of the professor. He was also expected to be a detective, sheriff, prosecuting attorney, and judge. . . . At the beginning of the year, the village was divided geographically, and each professor was assigned a section of it. It was his duty to visit the rooms of all students located in his area at least once a term, acting partly as spy, partly as inspiration to good. (35, II:461).

During an academic year not long before the beginning of the Civil War the Dartmouth faculty held sixty-eight meetings, and "cases of discipline occupied the greater part of the time." When no disciplinary problems appeared on the agendum, the faculty went about creating some by the device of "reading the catalogue." The president would read the names of the students in alphabetical order "with a call for comments by any professor who had information concerning [*their*] 'moral delinquencies.'" (35, II:461.) Small wonder that students "considered the Faculty as their natural enemies" and proceeded to make their lives as miserable as possible (32, p. 200).

The introduction of elective systems and of improved methods of instruction helped to reduce antagonism between students and faculty; but three other developments helped even more to domesticate the animal spirits of college students: the admission of lady students, as they were called until almost the beginning of the twentieth century, the gradual replacement of clerical professors by laymen, and the rise to pre-eminence of the extracurriculum.

Concerning women students, I report only that their presence helped improve students' manners and, among other things, probably had much to do with extinguishing the male habit of incessant spitting both on the campus and indoors (21, pp. 11, 27). This abomination continued even at strait-laced Oberlin until after the Civil War. Concerning laymen superseding clerics in professorships, space permits only the observations that even in state universities clergymen held most teaching positions, that many of them had become professors because of their failure with congregations, and that American higher education took an impressive leap forward when laymen supplanted them. About the sprouting into lusty life of the extracurriculum, however, somewhat more must be said.

The Extracurriculum Becomes Dominant

The extracurriculum has been a part of student life since the time of Plato's academy, but during the sixty-odd years from the end of the Civil War to the beginning of the Great Depression it swelled into elephantine proportions on every American campus. Sports had been banned in the old-time college, but the educational reformers removed the prohibitions because, among other things, they believed that athletics would reduce the number and intensity of riots and rebellions and, in addition, lure the interest and financial support of alumni and legislators. They also believed that sports would clear students' minds and thus improve their intellectual concentration.

A crew race between Harvard and Yale in 1852 initiated intercollegiate athletics, and in 1858 four New England colleges organized the first athletic conference (42, I:208). After the Civil War baseball captured the imagination of the country and of college students, and soon thereafter football took the center of the collegiate stage. By the end of the nineteenth century intercollegiate teams in a dozen sports had been organized. Meanwhile, however, the administrators and professors who had welcomed sports perceived that they had cast out the devils of riot and rebellion only to have the new devils of commercialism and hypocrisy replace them. Undergraduate interest in intellectual activities, they also observed, had improved not a whit.

Fraternities boomed along with athletics and became no less troublesome. They had begun as literary societies, and some of them possessed libraries that shamed those owned by the colleges. Long before the advent of Dale Carnegie, however, the changing pattern of American life transmogrified them into clubs chiefly interested in training their members in the arts of winning friends and influencing people. Here the educational reformers — especially those associated with state universities — also misfired. They idealized German universities; and since German students lived around town in rented rooms, they concluded that their American counterparts should too. American undergraduates responded, however, by inventing the fraternity house.

Fraternities had much to do with the increasing emphasis upon athletics, and they also promoted extracurricular enterprises in general — student newspapers, magazines, and yearbooks; glee clubs, mandolin clubs, and dramatics; proms, houseparties, and informal dances. By the time I entered college in 1920, the extracurriculum, in the liberal arts colleges at least, had decisively triumphed over the curriculum.

That the college was an educational institution students agreed unreservedly, but they defined education quite differently than did the professors of both the old school and the new. Few students had time to read Emerson; but if they had read him, they would have agreed that "a great soul will be strong to live, as well as strong to think." Above all else they wanted to live strenuously. They were willing to pay the customs fees and tariffs demanded by the faculty in the form of admission credits, course examinations, grades, and graduation requirements because these admitted them to the joys of college life; but they had little interest in what professors taught. Indeed, most of them judged faculty scholarship to be pedantry and the professors themselves spiritless book-readers or mildewed laboratory grubbers who had chosen the academic life because of the foreknowledge that they could not succeed in business or in the professions. Scorning the intellectual diet proffered them by their teachers and yet highly valuing education as they conceived it, they organized and administered their own educational program — the extracurriculum.

Professors, deans, and presidents publicly lamented over what Woodrow Wilson in 1909 called the neglect of the main tent for the sideshows (47, p. 576); but the extracurriculum would continue to be the cynosure of most undergraduates until the economic devastations of the thirties, the Second World War, and the threats of Russia reduced it — intercollegiate athletics excepted — to more manageable proportions. During the years immediately preceding and following the First World War, however, a new generation of educational reformers appeared upon the scene. Historians have generously reported the mighty exploits of Eliot, Gilman, Harper, and their associates in opening up American colleges and universities to new knowledge and new functions; but they have almost entirely overlooked the different but equally significant accomplishments of the educational reformers who followed them. Among other things these neglected men helped cut the extracurriculum down to size. They also initiated or fostered other changes, some of which in due course I shall be citing.

This new generation of leaders included Frank Aydelotte who transformed Swarthmore from an insignificant little Quaker college into one of the most effective and influential educational institutions of our history; William T. Foster who catapulted Reed College into immediate superiority and fame; Herbert E. Hawkes who developed the nation's first successful integration courses at Columbia College and thereby set a pattern which would be widely and profitably copied; John B. Johnston here at Minnesota who conceived and nourished the General College and also remodeled and revitalized the College of Science, Literature, and the Arts; Arthur E. Morgan, himself not a college graduate, who took Antioch when it verged on bankruptcy and made it renowned from coast to coast; and above all A. Lawrence Lowell who reformed the reforms of his more famous predecessor and completely remade Harvard College.

I have named only six among the most pivotal and successful of the new leaders, and I can enlarge upon the activities of but one of them —

President Lowell, who in time, I feel certain, will be counted among the most constructive minds and personalities ever to grapple with the problems of American higher education.

President Lowell's Reforms at Harvard

Lowell had been an excellent athlete as a Harvard undergraduate, and all his life he approved of intercollegiate athletics and of the extra-curriculum in general. He deplored, however, their swallowing up the curriculum; and even before he became president in 1909 he set about the task of making serious study "respectable if not admirable" (28, p. 85). What he accomplished can be compared with a business executive's taking hold of a corporation deeply in the red and converting it in short order into a blue-chip investment. I'll try to sketch rapidly the problems he had to meet, his method of attack, and his extraordinary success.

The increasing prosperity of the country after the Civil War brought to the colleges, and especially to what people now call the Ivy League colleges, several new varieties of students: sons of men of wealth who thought of the colleges as gentlemen's clubs, youths on the make who believed that extracurricular success or association with rich class-mates would give them good starts in business, and gifted sons of immigrants who craved education as a means to establishing themselves and their families in American life. The members of the third of these new groups of students generally did not participate in college life and, in any case, were dismissed by the others as "greasy grinds" and "weirs." From the second group came the majority of athletes, extra-curricular managers, and class officers; but the first group, the play-boys, set the tone of the colleges. At Columbia, for example, they limited their class attendance to the hours between ten and one (7, p. 180); at Yale — so the story went — they never scheduled a course which met above the first floor of a college building; and at Harvard they made it clear that C constituted the "gentleman's grade" (23).

Lowell set about the tasks of wresting the control of student attitudes from the playboys and of diverting some of the energies of the extracurricular zealots into academic channels. His opportunity came seven years before his selection as president when he became a member of the faculty Committee on the Improvement of Instruction in

Harvard College, one of the most strategic faculty committees ever appointed anywhere.

The committee gathered facts which showed how little students worked outside of class, facts which aroused the faculty to take prompt remedial action. Much more important, however, were the private studies undertaken by Lowell on his own. Among other things he investigated the relation of Harvard undergraduate scholarship to inclusion in *Who's Who* and to success in the Harvard professional schools (26, p. 513). He discovered, for example, that only six per cent of those who graduated with undistinguished records took honors in the law school in comparison with sixty per cent who had made summa cum laude. As everyone knew or would soon learn from Lowell, the honor men of the law school were snapping up the best opportunities open to beginning lawyers; and this fact alone had immediate effect on the scholarship of Harvard undergraduates. Moreover, the law school honor men included a high percentage of the greasy grinds and weirs; and this fact too gave pause to the playboys and the extracurricular heelers. (27, pp. 217ff.)

Lowell's investigations made his election as president upon Eliot's retirement all but inevitable, and immediately upon taking office he set in motion a series of brilliant moves to the end — to repeat his own expression — of "making scholarship respectable if not admirable." He got the faculty to abandon Eliot's free elective system and to put in its place what he called concentration but what the rest of the country had already decided to name majoring. He removed incoming students from the influence of unredeemed upperclassmen by housing them in freshman dormitories. He talked the faculty into establishing comprehensive examinations at the end of the senior year, a tutorial system, three weeks' reading periods free from instruction before semester examinations, and a new system of academic honors. Toward the end of his twenty-four-year administration he employed the millions supplied by a Yale graduate to build new residences where groups of about three hundred undergraduates might have a common extracurricular life but where intelligent conversation at meals would not *ipso facto* be ridiculed. Finally he contributed several million dollars of his own inheritance to organize the Society of Fellows where brilliant young graduate students, selected from many colleges, could steer clear of

113

what his friend William James had called "the Ph.D. octopus" (48, pp. 523–34).

When Lowell took office, only a handful of Harvard students studied for honors. Their proportions climbed to 16.8 per cent six years later, to 37.2 per cent the year he retired, and to 42.5 per cent two years later (30, p. 448n). These statistics witness Lowell's brilliant success. They indicate, in the words of a Harvard professor of history, that Lowell so thoroughly " 'sold' education to Harvard College" that its director of athletics defended its increasing number of defeats in football by observing that "study . . . is now Harvard's principal sport" (30, p. 449).

Lowell's example encouraged such other reformers as those mentioned above but whose activities and achievement, unfortunately, I cannot describe here. Instead I must move on and discuss briefly two crucial developments of the period in which they and Lowell worked, that is, between the two world wars: first, the emergence of specialization, and second, the rise to dominance in American colleges and universities of the research function.

The Emergence of Specialization

Professors teaching single subjects did not come upon the American scene in influential numbers until toward the end of the nineteenth century. Thus Oliver March during his thirty-seven years on the faculty of Northwestern University beginning in 1862 taught botany, chemistry, geology, Greek, logic, mineralogy, physics, and zoology (45, p. 100); and Allen C. Thomas of Haverford College at one time or another from 1878 to 1912 taught American history, biblical literature, constitutional law, English history, English literature, political economy, and religion, and also served part of the time as librarian and business manager (22, p. 102). Contrast the not untypical teaching range of these professors with the following description of the fragmentation of chemistry made in 1933 by the dean of the graduate school of the University of Wisconsin:

We not only have "chemists," we have "colloid chemists." We not only have "colloid chemists," we have "inorganic colloid chemists." We not only have "inorganic colloid chemists," we have "aerosol inorganic colloid chemists [and even] "high temperature aerosol inorganic chemists," and so on indefinitely until the scientist is fractionated to a single paragraph of his doctor's thesis. (37, pp. 97–98.)

114

Professorial specialization, in coordination with the elective principle, inevitably led to undergraduate specialization or majoring. Today all students major, but a hundred years ago none did or, in fact, could. Majoring did not become a requirement at Harvard, for example, until its abandonment of its free elective system in 1910. Now nothing is more characteristic of American higher education than the practice of majoring.

Its results have been both desirable and undesirable. On the credit side stand the unmistakable improvement of the subject matter taught in advanced courses, the employment of infinitely better methods of teaching, the weeding out of the rah-rah boys, and — above all else — the contribution it has made and increasingly continues to make to meeting the knowledge-power and man-power needs of society. The debit side, however, has at least one serious entry, namely, the narrowness to which specialization so frequently leads. Contemplating the nation's need for scientists, engineers, and other specialists in 1886, Justice Oliver Wendell Holmes suggested that perhaps "we need specialists even more than we do civilized men"; but he went on to urge that "if a man is a specialist it is most desirable that he should also be civilized" (15, pp. 77–78). Holmes's plea and those of others, however, did not halt the subjugation of general education to special education either in the United States or in Europe. Thus in 1930 the Spanish philosopher José Ortega y Gasset could make the following statement in an address at the University of Madrid:

Civilization has had to await the beginning of the twentieth century, to see the astounding spectacle of how brutal, how stupid, and yet how aggressive is the man learned in one thing and fundamentally ignorant of all else. Professionalism and specialism . . . have smashed the European man in pieces. . . . The guilt of the universities is not compensated for by the prodigious and brilliant service which they have undeniably rendered to science. (31, pp. 61, 58.)

Education for specialized depth and for civilizing breadth have been in conflict in American higher educational institutions for more than half of the hundred-year period under review here, but I for one believe that they can live together in harmony. I shall enlarge upon this observation after commenting upon the elevation of research to the place of highest honor among the functions of American universities and even colleges.

THE TEACHING END

Research Overwhelms Teaching

Research has become so firmly established that today everyone takes it for granted. Few know, it seems, that it had no status at all a century ago in either the United States or England and that only during recent years has it achieved its lofty rank in the universities of both countries. Benjamin Jowett, the famous master of Balliol College, Oxford, expressed the sentiments of many American and English administrators and professors when, about 1890, he sneered: "Research! A mere excuse for idleness; it has never achieved, and will never achieve, any results of the slightest value" (40, p. 737).

Not many years before that, President Eliot of Harvard also had his doubts about research as witness the following anecdote told by one of his biographers:

. . . Professor C. L. Jackson relates that when he was a young teacher of Chemistry in the seventies he asked Eliot if he might be relieved of the duty of teaching one class in order to prosecute certain investigations. The President, in his stately manner, propounded a question to which an answer can seldom be given —"What will be the results of these investigations?" They would be published, was the reply. The President wanted to know where. Mr. Jackson named a German chemical journal. "I can't see that that will serve any useful purpose here," said Eliot, and therewith dismissed the matter. (20, II:19.)

In 1876, however, Johns Hopkins University opened, emphatically committed to research; and its success convinced Eliot and other administrators that the function could no longer be underprivileged. Thereafter it began to blossom in the private universities, but the state universities did little with it until this century. The graduate school of the University of Minnesota, for example, did not come into existence until 1905; and the regents endorsed its establishment "only on condition that it was not to cost anything" (39, p. 247). A distinguished scientist who visited Minnesota four years later reported that "the regents generally regarded research as a private fad of a professor, like collecting etchings or playing the piano, and they rarely interfered with it so long as he . . . did not ask for money" (39, p. 246).

Today money for research, in contrast, flows in ever-mounting quantities from government, industry, foundations, learned societies, and private benefactors with the result that scientific and scholarly investigations prosper as never before in history. The most potent word of mid-twentieth-century man seems unmistakably to be research; and its adherents grow in numbers, prestige, and power. By and large this has been good — very good — but some of the changes it has wrought since Jowett's sneer of seven decades ago have not been good. One of these is the depressed status of teaching.

To get ahead in the academic world it has been necessary for a long while now for professors to give their attention chiefly to what is called "productive scholarship" and "extending the boundaries of knowledge" rather than to their students. The Committee on College and University Teaching of the American Association of University Professors, for instance, included the following passage in its report of 1933: "The good teacher, even though he be conspicuously good, often has to wait his turn [*for promotion*] in order of seniority, because there is no systematic way of singling him out and recognizing him by an early advancement. Success in research, on the other hand, is bound to be observed and rewarded." (1, p. 21.)

A few years later a member of the staff of the University of California challenged a colleague in print "to name a single member of the faculty who has been promoted to an associate or full professorship . . . solely or primarily because he has been an excellent teacher or because he has had a beneficial, elevating influence on the student body" (38, p. 16). The challenge went unanswered.

The fact seems clear that large numbers of faculty members — especially younger ones striving to get established — give their primary allegiance to research and consider teaching a chore to by-pass whenever it interferes with their investigations. This has become almost inevitable even in the liberal arts colleges not only because raises in rank and salary come sooner to those who develop reputations in research but also because the good teacher has to contend with the criticisms of his in-the-saddle, research-minded colleagues who scoff at him as "a mere teacher," "a damned popularizer," "a hippodrome artist." Some strong personalities are able to rise above these limiting circumstances and to teach brilliantly, but on most campuses great teachers seem to be almost as rare as southpaw shortstops.

Now clearly both teaching and research are essential functions of American colleges and universities. We cannot escape the history that has entwined them anymore than we can escape the history that during the past century has made specialized education as imperative as general education. Somehow these three functions — general education, specialized education, and research — must be operationally blended better than they are at present. How? This in my judgment is the axial question now facing American higher education.

My assignment has been to explore the history of college and university teaching during the past hundred years, but I have never been interested in the past except as a guide to understanding the here and now and as an aid to judging what to do and how to do it in planning for tomorrow. With Thomas Jefferson, "I like the dreams of the future better than the history of the past" (25, XV:59). I hope therefore that you will bear with me while I suggest how these three mandatory functions of colleges and universities can be reconciled and, indeed, how they can enrich one another.

Analysis of Types of Teaching and Research

Ever since the end of the nineteenth century the administrative and professorial leaders of American higher education have almost universally agreed that one cannot be a good teacher unless he does research. This conception has come to dominate the thinking of academic people in all countries because it embodies the great truths that out-of-date facts and ideas foist outmoded people upon society, that only growing minds can arouse and hold the interest of students, that creativity begets creativity. These truths seem to most educators to be self-evident. They certainly do to me.

But to state such axioms forces one to ask what one means by teaching and what one means by research. I suggest that neither is a unitary activity but that, instead, different kinds of teaching and different kinds of research can be identified and, further, that each kind of teaching and each kind of research requires unique personal qualities.

Let me illustrate what I mean by recalling the only occasion on which I can remember going to sleep during a lecture of a distinguished campus visitor. The place was Ohio State University, the visitor the renowned John Dewey. He was so egregiously dull that he literally hypnotized me — and others too, I noticed — into slumber. I thought him the worst teacher under whose ponderous ministrations I had ever suffered. A few years later, however, I read a piece by Professor Irwin Edman (8a, pp. 38–43), a colleague and former student of Dewey's. Therein he sang his praises as one of the most exciting teachers he had ever had, and he went on to tell why. John Dewey, he wrote, could take advanced, well-prepared students on captivating journeys into uncharted paths, but his students had to have been prepared for him by other and different kinds of teachers.

Edman himself was such a different kind of teacher. He contributed little to extending the boundaries of knowledge, but he had the intellectual and social traits needed by those who can ferret out the conceptions of frontier thinkers like Dewey and translate them into language comprehensible to laymen. In my experience few professors have the equipment to do both of these kinds of teaching equally well since each requires its own research skills and its own teaching abilities. More about this in just a moment. First I need to point to a third kind of teaching which comes half way between the two I've just cited — teaching neither facts nor ideas per se but, rather, teaching students how to *do* something.

Courses in English composition, mathematical computation, logic, legal pleading, laboratory techniques, machine design, methods of social science research, and hundreds of others require this third kind of teaching. It differs quite distinctly from the teaching of abstractions and from interpretive teaching; and it, too, requires distinctive traits.

Clearly to distinguish these three kinds of teaching I suggest that they need to be named; and, building on some terms used by Aristotle (36, pp. 492–93) and on a suggestion made thirty years ago by a well-known Cornell chemist (2, pp. 396–97), I call the kind of instruction that deals with the frontiers of knowledge *logodemic* teaching, the kind that shows the utility of such knowledge *practidemic* teaching, and the kind that interprets the first two kinds for the nonspecialist *pandemic* teaching.

A friend of Richard Wagner's once remarked that people have poor ears for new music, and so these terms may not at first sound pleasant or desirable. I've been using them with my students and colleagues, however, for about a decade; and among them at least they have taken hold because apparently they fill a need. In any case, the stem of each is the Greek noun *demos,* meaning people; logo comes from one of the Greek words for knowledge; practi comes from *praxis* meaning prac-

119

tice; and pan means all. Thus: logodemic teaching clarifies and develops the subject itself; practidemic teaching communicates the knowledge needed by the practitioners of the art or arts associated with the subject; and pandemic teaching interprets for nonspecialists what the logodemists and practidemists do, how, and why.

Other terms exist for these three kinds of teaching, but the three that I have just named are correlative and hence have the advantage of bringing one another to mind. This, I suggest, helps to make an honorable place for each of them. Further, these terms help to differentiate two kinds of research and to indicate how they relate to teaching. The first of these varieties of research my students and I call factual research, the second kind conceptual research.

Factual research consists in adding new facts to the store of knowledge, facts which enlarge upon existing data or which open up new areas of knowledge. In the research for my doctoral dissertation, for example, I sought by means of psychological tests to discover whether or not recognized leaders in three situations differed from their followers and from one another and, if so, how. I added thereby a few snippets of new factual knowledge.

Conceptual investigations differ from factual studies in that they either appraise and reorganize facts already in hand or do the same for existing concepts. The work of Einstein constitutes a dramatic illustration of conceptual research: he never, I understand, undertook any factual investigations but, rather, worked entirely with mathematical and physical concepts. Physicists and astronomers, however, had to check his findings by means of factual studies. This must be emphasized because it makes clear the unequivocable necessity of keeping both kinds of research constantly in balance. Frequently, however, the same individuals do not undertake them since each variety demands different capacities.

This analysis leads to the proposal that colleges and universities need three kinds of teaching and two kinds of research differently combined; and, further, that general education and special education require teachers with dissimilar combinations of teaching and research abilities. Specifically, every general education teacher is engaged, as I see it, in pandemic teaching. To stay vigorously alive he needs to be constantly engaged in conceptual research which, to repeat, consists in organizing existing facts and concepts rather than in searching for new facts. Indeed, I would go further and maintain that factual investigations usually interfere with good pandemic teaching for the reason that they necessarily concentrate one's attention on small segments of knowledge and thus block out the broad view which constitutes the genius of good pandemists. Special education teachers, on the other hand, are or should be logodemists and practidemists and as such need to engage in either or both factual and conceptual research as the problems with which they deal dictate.

All of this may seem to be far removed from the topic of this chapter, and I hasten to show its relevance by means of two short anecdotes. The first is of a boy who asked his mother, "Mother, what is a penguin?" "A penguin, I think," she replied, "is some sort of an antarctic bird, but ask your father." "No thanks," said the boy, "I don't want to know that much." This story seems to me to illustrate the need of good pandemic teachers who have the ability to communicate the esoteric knowledge of the logodemists and practidemists into language understood by nonspecialists and without going into wearisome details. Pandemists, I reiterate, cannot stay fresh and vital, however, unless they constantly engage in conceptual research.

The second story is of two women talking over a back fence. One says to the other, "Never mind the gist of it, give me all the details." Students in their majors and in their occupational-training courses require, I suggest, not the gist of it which satisfies the needs of students in general education courses but, instead, all the details. Special education courses, in sum, require the skills of practidemic and logodemic teachers who keep in touch with the factual and conceptual details of their fields and who, through research, constantly add new ones.

Unhappily the graduate schools do not distinguish among these three kinds of prospective teachers, but that's a story into which I cannot go here. I must, however, say this: in my judgment the reform of the graduate school of arts and science toward the end of differentiating the preparation of logodemic, practidemic, and pandemic teachers constitutes the most urgent need of present-day American higher education.

We Are Part of a Great Continuity

In this seven-league-boot summary of college and university teaching between 1858 and 1958 I have of necessity jumped from peak to peak and hence have leaped over interesting and instructive landmarks that may seem to some to be more significant than those I have selected. One of these passed-over landmarks is the monumental 1945 report of a committee of twelve Harvard professors entitled *General Education in a Free Society*. From an article, however, written by its chairman, Paul H. Buck, I take an aphorism which expresses the point of view that I have been trying throughout this paper to document and to stress: "We are part of a great continuity" (6, p. 121). I have tried to describe that continuity as American colleges and universities have lived through the past century of it, and I have especially sought to emphasize the willingness — indeed, the eagerness — of the great bulk of students to respond to the challenge of excellence when discerning educators understand them and the needs of their times.

Today American education is under heavy attack, but I am as optimistic about the century ahead as I am proud, as an American, of the attainments of the one immediately behind us. When in particular we can resolve the conflicts between special education and general education and between teaching and research, I have no doubts at all that the attainments of the future will soon dwarf those of the past.

In the years ahead the great educational thinkers and doers of this past century will have successors worthy of them — men and women who will find the answers to our present problems and whose perceptions and deeds will be gratefully honored in 2058 by another generation of Americans meeting to celebrate the two-hundredth anniversary of Minnesota's admission to the Union.

REFERENCES

1. American Association of University Professors. *Report of the Committee on College and University Teaching.* 1933.
2. Bancroft, Wilder D. "Pandemic Chemistry." *Journal of Chemical Education,* April 1926.
3. Basler, R. P. ed. *The Collected Works of Abraham Lincoln,* 9 vols. New Brunswick: Rutgers University Press, 1953–55.
4. Brough, Kenneth J. *Scholar's Workshop: Evolving Conceptions of Library Service.* Urbana: University of Illinois Press, 1953.
5. Bruce, Philip Alexander. *History of the University of Virginia, 1819–1919; The Lengthened Shadow of One Man,* 5 vols. New York: The Macmillan Company, 1920–22.
6. Buck, Paul H. "The Role of General Education in School and College." *Educational Record,* January 1947.
7. Burgess, John W. *Reminiscences of an American Scholar, The Beginnings of Columbia University.* New York: Columbia University Press, 1934.
8. *Congressional Globe.* Thirty-Fifth Congress, First Session.

College and University Teaching, 1858–1958

8a. Edman, Irwin. *Philosopher's Holiday.* New York: Viking Press, Inc., 1938.

9. Eliot, Charles W. *Harvard Memories.* Cambridge: Harvard University Press, 1923.

10. ———. *A Late Harvest; Miscellaneous Papers Written between Eighty and Ninety.* Boston: Atlantic Monthly Press, 1924.

11. Folwell, William Watts. *Ninth Annual Report of the President of the University of Minnesota to the Board of Regents, 1874–75.*

12. French, Robert Dudley. *The Memorial Quadrangle, A Book about Yale.* New Haven: Yale University Press, 1930.

13. Gray, Dorothy. *Faculty, Students and Degrees in Institutions of Higher Education.* U.S. Office of Education Circular No. 514, February 1958.

14. Hall, Christopher W. *The University of Minnesota, An Historical Sketch.* Minneapolis, 1896.

15. Harvard University. *A Record of the Commemoration . . . on the Two Hundred and Fiftieth Anniversary of the Founding of Harvard College.* Cambridge: John Wilson and Son, University Press, 1887.

16. Hegel, G. W. F. *Lectures on the Philosophy of History,* tr. from the 3rd German edition by J. Sibree. London: George Bell & Sons, 1894.

17. Holt, Henry. *Garrulities of an Octogenarian Editor.* New York: Houghton Mifflin Company, 1923.

18. Hutchins, Robert Maynard. *The Higher Learning in America.* New Haven: Yale University Press, 1936.

19. Irvine, William. *Apes, Angels, and Victorians; The Story of Darwin, Huxley, and Evolution.* New York: McGraw-Hill Book Company, Inc., 1955.

20. James, Henry. *Charles William Eliot.* Boston and New York: Houghton Mifflin Company, 1930.

21. Jex-Blake, Sophia. *A Visit to Some American Schools and Colleges.* London: The Macmillan Company, 1867.

22. Jones, Rufus M. *Haverford College.* New York: The Macmillan Company, 1933.

23. Keppel, Frederick P. "President Lowell and His Influence." *Atlantic,* June 1933.

24. Korsch, Karl. "Karl Marx," in *Encyclopedia of the Social Sciences.* New York: The Macmillan Company, 1933.

25. Lipscomb, Andrew A., and Albert E. Bergh, eds. *The Writings of Thomas Jefferson,* 20 vols. Washington, D.C.: Thomas Jefferson Memorial Association, 1904–05.

26. Lowell, A. Lawrence. "College Rank and Distinction in Life." *Atlantic,* October 1903.

27. ———. "College Studies and the Professional School." *Educational Review,* October 1911.

28. ———. *What a University President Has Learned.* New York: The Macmillan Company, 1938.

29. Mitchell, Wesley C. "Business Cycles," in *Encyclopedia of the Social Sciences.* New York: The Macmillan Company, 1930.

30. Morison, Samuel Eliot. *Three Centuries of Harvard.* Cambridge: Harvard University Press, 1936.

31. Ortega y Gasset, José. *Mission of the University.* Howard Lee Nostrand, tr. Princeton University Press, 1944.

32. Peabody, Andrew P. *Harvard Reminiscences.* Boston: Ticknor & Co., 1888.

33. Porter, William D. *A Semi-centennial History of the Class of 1850 at Williams College.* 1900.

34. Quincy, Josiah. *The History of Harvard University.* Cambridge: John Owen, 1840.

35. Richardson, Leon Burr. *History of Dartmouth College.* Hanover: Dartmouth College, 1932.

36. Sarton, George. *A History of Science.* Cambridge: Harvard University Press, 1952.

37. Schlicter, Charles S. "Polymaths: Technicians, Specialists and Genius." *Sigma Xi Quarterly,* September 1933.

38. Schneider, Franz. *Teaching and Scholarship and the Res Publica*. Berkeley: The Pestalozzi Press, 1938.
39. Slosson, Edwin E. *Great American Universities*. New York: The Macmillan Company, 1910.
40. Smith, Logan Pearsall. "Oxford." *Atlantic*, June 1938.
41. Sprague, William Buell. *Annals of the American Pulpit*. New York: R. Carter and Bros., 1857–69.
42. Thayer, William Roscoe. "Harvard College." In *Universities and Their Sons*, Joshua L. Chamberlain, ed. Boston: R. Herndon Co., 1898.
43. Thwing, Charles Franklin. *The American and the German University*. New York: The Macmillan Company, 1928.
44. Walton, John C. *Graduate Study in Universities and Colleges in the United States*. U.S. Office of Education Bulletin, 1934, No. 20.
45. Ward, Estelle Frances. *The Story of Northwestern University*. New York: Dodd, Mead & Company, Inc., 1924.
46. White, Andrew Dickson. *Autobiography*. New York: Century, 1906.
47. Wilson, Woodrow. "What Is College For?" *Scribner's*, November 1909.
48. Yeomans, Henry Adams. *Abbott Lawrence Lowell*. Cambridge: Harvard University Press, 1948.

MR. COWLEY is at Stanford University. An earlier article, "A Century of College Teaching" (*Improving College and University Teaching*, 1:3–10, No. 3, November 1953) discusses still further the historic changes in classroom procedures.

◄§ REUBEN G. GUSTAVSON

Contemporary Civilization and Its Challenge to College Teaching

FREEDOM and science are two words that come with increasing frequency from the lips of men. Freedom has meant political freedom, with the right of free speech, and the freedom to worship as one's conscience dictates. Within the last few decades, these two basic freedoms have been related to two others, namely, the freedom from want and the freedom from fear. The people of Asia — one half of the world's population — and two hundred millions in Africa, cherish their freedom, still in its swaddling clothes, or are demanding its birth. These people are not only looking forward to a higher standard of living with freedom from want; they are demanding it. The new freedom is being sought by the underdeveloped countries at a time when the world is divided between two great ideologies: democracy and totalitarianism. The underdeveloped countries are looking to science and technology to achieve their goal. The big question today is whether these countries will work out the answer to this fundamental question within the framework of democracy or of totalitarian government.

The standard of living enjoyed by our own country today makes tremendous demands not only upon the resource base of the United States but upon the resources of countries at great distances from us. For example, with approximately seven per cent of the world's population, we are consuming about fifty per cent of the world's goods. The United States is so mechanized that it can consume about two thirds of the world's production of oil, leaving only one third for all of the other countries. Our very high consumption of the world's available resources will increasingly meet competition from many parts of the world where there is an insistent demand for a higher standard of living, which will not be denied. We have been thrust into the leadership of the world by two world wars. It is difficult to see the possibility of another leader's emerging for a long time to come — perhaps several centuries. Basically this means that we have become on a worldwide scale our brother's keeper — or shall we say democracy's guardian? This means accepting the responsibility for helping the underdeveloped countries conquer their poverty and disease within the framework of democracy. Leadership is a very simple role to discern but an awful responsibility to live up to. We did not seek the position of leadership, but it is our destiny to fulfill it.

In the world of science, man's greatest achievement has been the realization that he lives in a consistent universe; that is, if he asks nature a question by way of experiment at two different times, and if the conditions of the experiments are the same, nature will give identical answers on both occasions. The path from the concept of a universe ruled by caprice to the concept of a universe ruled by law is a long and difficult one. Gradually a body of knowledge which we now call science has been established. Niels Bohr, distinguished Danish atomic physicist, has described this body of knowledge as the result of "the finding of techniques that have enabled man to place limiting values on his preconceptions."

The important thing to notice in Bohr's statement is that it is not the preconception which is most important in science but the techniques by which man can determine the limitations for his preconception. My own professional research, for example, has been in the field of female sex hormones — chemical substances which have now been isolated in crystalline form. They are elaborated in the ovary and carried by the blood stream to distant parts of the body where they bring about growth and development of the uterus and breasts. It occurred to me that when animals become sexually mature, physical growth ceases. I therefore developed a preconception that the cessation of physical growth might be due at least in part to the elaboration of sex hormones within the body. To test out this preconception, a number of young female rats, thirty days of age, were injected for a period of three months with sex hormone dissolved in a small quantity of oil. The animals were weighed once a week and the results compared with the growth curve of animals which had been injected only with the oil. Those rats injected with the sex hormone lagged far behind in their growth rate. In other words, the preconception was validated by the technique.

Dr. Edward Doisy of Saint Louis University carried out precisely the same experiment. He had developed a preconception that the spurt in growth which seems to take place at about the time of puberty might be due to the presence of sex hormones. This preconception is the exact opposite of the one I started with. He designed and carried out an experiment almost identical with mine. To his surprise, he found that far from stimulating growth, the hormones inhibited it. You see, therefore, that the fact that we started out with different preconceptions is of no consequence. The important thing is that we arrived at the same conclusions. In one case the preconception was validated; in the other it was found false. But what counts is that the basic scientific information was the same in both cases.

Let us contrast this with a conception of art: art may be defined as a body of accomplishment obtained by realizing preconceptions. If you would paint a portrait of Abraham Lincoln you must first develop a conception of the painting. You decide whether you will paint the rail splitter, the Indian fighter, or the weary war president. You examine paintings, photographs, and various other pieces of art representing the Great Emancipator and then you start to work with brush and paint and canvas. But there is nothing in the painting process that tells you whether you are right or wrong.

Let us review some of the recent achievements of science. The outstanding discovery in the realm of physics has been the conversion of matter into energy so beautifully described by Einstein's equation, $E = mc^2$, where m is the mass of the matter destroyed and c is the velocity of light. The velocity of light is 186,000 miles per second; this number squared is 35,000,000,000. You can see from this that even if the amount of matter destroyed is very small the amount of energy liberated will be very large.

The discovery of the conversion of matter into energy rests upon a half century of basic research. At the turn of the century, studies made of the element radium revealed that it was giving off energy to its environment in the form of strong X-ray-like penetrating radiations called gamma rays, negative electrical particles called electrons, and positively charged atoms of helium called alpha rays. These helium particles were thrown off from radium at a velocity of 10,000 miles per second and represented at the time of their discovery the greatest concentration of energy known to man.

Comparison of the energy of the steam particle with the alpha particle reveals that the alpha particle contains approximately 400 million times as much energy as the steam particle. Sir Ernest Rutherford bombarded nitrogen with this high-energy alpha particle and found that hydrogen atoms were formed as a result of the bombardment. This was one of the great fundamental discoveries of the past half century. In following up this kind of experiment W. Bothe and H. Becker in Germany found that when the element beryllium was bombarded in a similar fashion, a strong penetrating radiation was given off, which they erroneously interpreted as a kind of X-ray. Sir James Chadwick in England corrected this impression by showing that the beryllium under bombardment with the alpha particle was giving off an electrically neutral particle of about the same mass as the hydrogen atom but with a velocity of approximately 10,000 miles per second.

Workers then began to bombard the elements with this neutral particle. In the course of this kind of experimentation it was discovered that when natural uranium is struck by the neutron some of the uranium atoms go to pieces and elements of smaller atomic weight are found in the debris. Matter is destroyed and tremendous quantities of energy are liberated. This is the work of Enrico Fermi in Italy and Otto Hahn in Germany. On the basis of these experiments, atomic bombs have been built — two of which have destroyed Japanese cities — and temperatures which approach those of the sun have been made possible. These experiments are also the basis of the great effort which is being made today to work out peaceful uses for this energy in the form of electrical power, space heating, and many others.

It has been known for a number of years that the energy of the stars is primarily the result of collisions at tremendous velocities of light atoms such as those of hydrogen at very, very high temperatures, resulting in the formation of helium and the destruction of a certain amount of matter in the process. There, at temperatures of ten million to twenty million degrees Centigrade, atoms of hydrogen stripped of their electrons strike each other with such force that the nuclei combine to form helium. Attempts are now being made to realize experimentally the reactions that produce heat in the sun and stars. Experiments in Russia, the United Kingdom, and the United States indicate some success in duplicating this process in the laboratory. Deuterium gas (an isotope of hydrogen having an atomic weight of 2) is held in a container under a very low pressure of four ten-thousandths of a millimeter. A current approaching 200,000 amperes which lasts only four millionths of a second is discharged through the gas; this discharge is repeated every ten seconds. Temperatures approaching five million degrees have been obtained. Under these conditions the deuterium atoms lose their electrons and the positively charged stream of nuclei is constricted away from the sides of the container. Some combination of nuclei takes place with the liberation of neutrons, and there is evidence that some helium may be formed with the liberation of energy. So far the energy liberated is a very small fraction of the energy used, but there is every reason to believe that we are witnessing the birth of a new age — that of manmade thermonuclear reactions, reactions until now known only in the sun and stars.

In 1831 Faraday demonstrated with a very simple apparatus that plunging a magnet through a coil of wire gave a momentary electric current. The electrical industry grew from this experiment. The significance of the modern experiments is that they may once again open a door to vast quantities of energy.

The standard of living enjoyed by any country is directly related to the amount of energy available to the people of that country to carry on their work. If you want to dramatize the difference between the standards of living of India and the United States, there is probably no better way than to point out that the per-capita amount of energy available to do the work of the Indian people is 6,000 large Calories per day. The per-capita daily amount of energy available to the people of the United States is roughly 120,000 large Calories per day. The advent of atomic power from the conversion of matter into energy, growing out of the experiments I have discussed, now brings about the possibility of almost unlimited power for all the nations of the earth; therefore the possibility of a higher standard of living for all the people of the world looms large today.

I say *possibility* because the establishment of an atomic energy program requires a large capital investment. Where can this capital be found? In the underdeveloped countries where ninety per cent of the people are engaged in elemental agriculture, capital grows slowly. For this reason it is possible that the gap between the highly industrialized nations of Europe and North America and a country such as India will widen with time unless ways and means are found for increasing capital from outside sources.

In this connection it is interesting to note that the *Eastern Economist* in its 1957 annual number compares the progress made by India and by China over a period of ten years. China's progress in the percapita consumption of steel, coal, cotton, and rice is phenomenal. It offers impressive proof that the standard of living in an underdeveloped country can be materially raised within the framework of totalitarian government. Surely every thoughtful person will ponder the consequences of this success and its meaning and implications for the foreign policy of our own country.

Let us take a brief look at the field of biochemistry, where the work that has been carried on with large molecules commands attention. I should like, however, to explore for just a moment the new knowledge we are receiving in connection with the highly complex large molecules called proteins. These proteins are made up of something like 20 to 25 basic units called alpha amino acids. These units are combined in different orders in different molecules and obviously if you have 20 to 25 units you can arrange them in an enormous number of different ways. As a matter of fact, if you have 18 such units you can arrange them in 10^{23} different ways. It has always seemed to the organic chemist that the problem of understanding the order in which these units are put together was so complex that man probably never would be able to unravel it; and yet within the last few years that is exactly what has been done. One of the recent Nobel prizes in chemistry went to Vincent du Vigneaud for determining the complete structure of one of the proteins of the pituitary body. Choh Hao Li of the University of California has recently indicated the order in which some 39 amino acid molecules were arranged in one of the other hormones from the pituitary body.

Some of the recent work of Wendell Stanley of the University of California in connection with viruses has suggested tremendous advances in understanding the chemical structure of these very complex bodies. In this field of large molecules we have every reason to believe the answer to the cancer problem will be found.

In biology the basic understanding of genetics, a discipline still in

130

its infancy, is opening up very rapidly. The new tools of biochemistry and biophysics are giving us the opportunity to carry out work in this field undreamed of a few years ago. As a result, new varieties of barley, for example, have been developed by irradiation, thereby producing a higher yield, stronger straw, and greater resistance to disease. In the mustard plant, changes have also been brought about genetically which have given very large increases in yield. Radiation genetics is in its infancy. As a result of these studies, science is now not only pointing to possible results that may be of benefit to mankind coming through work in this field, but it is also setting up a very definite warning against what may happen if in the age of atomic power and atomic bombs we are not careful about powerful radiations which can alter some of the genetic characteristics of man himself.

It is very important to note here that when changes are brought about in the genetic makeup of a plant — for example, by using ionizing radiation from these radioactive materials — that most of the changes will result in the death of the plant, stunted growth, or characteristics less desirable than those of the plant used in the original experiment. But every once in a while — every once in a great, *great* while — these radiations will cause a change which will give us a better variety of plant.

As an illustration of the complexity of this problem, suppose an office boy with a bean shooter is shooting beans at the typewriter of a secretary who is transcribing the speech of a well-known speaker. It is obvious to all of us that most of the time the bean striking a key would introduce a letter which would not add anything to the composition of the speech. But all of us can imagine that it might be possible for the bean shooter to strike a letter that would alter a word in such a way that the speech might be a better speech. Certainly this would be a rare occurrence, but it is a possibility. This illustrates something of the problem of getting better varieties through radiation. Of course in the plant world we have available to us thousands upon thousands of seeds for irradiation; the same is true of microscopic forms of life. And in such cases some changes for the better have been brought about. But with a limited population as is the case with animals, you can see that the chances of getting better varieties is really very small indeed.

The significant work that is going on in the physical and biological sciences today is typical of much that might be described. What are the implications for education? One thing that stands out is that all of the sciences — physics, chemistry, biology — are becoming increasingly quantitative. As information becomes quantitative it becomes subject to mathematical analysis and to description in mathematical terms. Mathematics is the language of quantitative data. This inevitably means that in our schools for those who are going into technical work, mathematics becomes more and more a necessity. Our public schools have done a remarkably fine job in teaching reading, and it is obvious now that some very fundamental work must be done in teaching arithmetic. I am not ignorant of the progress that has been made, but research must be intensified. Our social organization has been undergoing change. Numbers today for the youngster in the kindergarten and early primary years are related to television channels, radio wave lengths, telephone numbers, license numbers, house numbers — in all of which cases the number has no quantitative significance. The research that is currently being done at the University of Illinois, under a grant from the Carnegie Foundation, on the mathematical curriculum for the ninth, tenth, eleventh, and twelfth grades is indeed promising. But much more research needs to be done in the early grades, especially, I should say, from the fifth to the ninth grade, because it is during this time that the antagonism against and the distaste for mathematics seem to be born.

In the opinion of many qualified scientists, biology may well be the next discipline in which great progress will take place. Biology is a very complex field in which research problems have many unknown factors and many variables. It is a field that is ripe for great advances because new tools — biochemistry, biophysics, radiochemistry — are becoming more readily available to investigators.

Traditionally the effective tool in biology has been the microscope, with dyes as secondary tools. The emphasis has been on morphology and classification, and on ecology. The underlying theory which has guided research has been the theory of evolution. This gave a strong stimulus to the study of taxonomy, comparative anatomy, and embryology.

The new fields cover the detailed structure and chemical reactions that characterize the protoplasm of cells and tissues. Among the new tools and methods are the electron microscope, the spectroscope, and

132

ultramicrotomy (cutting biological material into sections so thin as to permit its study with the electron microscope). The radioactive isotopes are also powerful tools for metabolic studies.

Serious consideration must be given to the high school and college curriculums in biology. The high school student who has talent in mathematics, physics, and chemistry should be aware of the possibility of using these disciplines in exploring the field of biology.

Basic research has as its objective understanding the world about us — simply to *know*; it is the kind of research that grows out of pure curiosity. This kind of research has found its home very largely in Europe, but today responsibility for it falls more heavily on the United States. The tremendous recent advances made by Russia in the development of technical skills and engineering have undoubtedly precipitated a crisis in the minds of many people. I do not share their anxiety. I do think, however, that the Russian developments can be a stimulus to increase the efforts that we can and should make in these fields. These developments have many implications for education. At the elementary level curiosity must be fostered. Asking students to merely repeat experiments in cookbook fashion must be eliminated from our educational program. I think if we once begin to explore the possibilities of rewriting the textbooks and reorganizing the experiments we'll have great fun in this task.

It was my privilege to teach sixth grade students one afternoon a week for a period of three years. I never had more fun.

Let me describe one session and I think you'll see what I mean. I took a Pyrex test tube, put some ice in it, and asked the youngsters what they thought would happen if I heated it in the flame of a Bunsen burner. Almost with one voice they said: "The tube will crack." To their surprise it didn't crack; the ice melted. We wrote an equation on the board in their own language:

$$\text{ice} + \text{heat} = \text{water}$$

We then heated the water to the boiling point, noted the steam that was formed, and again we wrote an equation in their own language:

$$\text{water} + \text{heat} = \text{steam}$$

Then I asked the youngsters what they thought would happen if I heated some paraffin. From their experience with burning candles they

133

told me it would melt. We heated the wax; it did melt. We wrote the equation:

$$wax + heat = watery\ wax$$

Then followed the question: "What will happen if we heat the liquid wax?" The answer: "It will form steam wax." We heated the wax, and it did become "steam wax."

Then I placed some pieces of rolled sulfur in the test tube and said: "What do you think will happen if we heat the sulfur?" The answer: "It will form watery sulfur." We heated the rolled sulfur; it became watery sulfur. The question: "What do you think will happen if we heat the watery sulfur?" The answer: "It will become steam sulfur." We heated the liquid sulfur and to their surprise it solidified.

"Let's see that again!" they cried.

Now I am not holding myself up as a master teacher; I am merely trying to indicate what I mean by organizing experiments to stimulate curiosity.

I then asked one of the youngsters what he made of all this. I shall never forget his answer. He spoke with a kind of drawl. "Well," he said, "it seems to me what it means is that just because you know something about water or ice and wax is no sign you know anything about sulfur."

What wisdom!

Let us seek balance in our educational programs. One of our greatest dangers is our tendency to go to extremes in times of crisis. Many of us can remember the strong movement to eliminate the teaching of foreign languages in our schools during and after World War I. Today we see the folly of this attitude. Today the success of Russian scientists in putting satellites into space is giving rise to strong forces to emphasize the physical sciences and mathematics. Up to a limit this is good. We need to periodically review our work. But let us not forget the social sciences and the humanities.

I'd like to point out some examples from the work of a man who is working entirely in the realm of psychobiology, Curt P. Richter of Johns Hopkins University. Richter for many years has recognized the fact that rats are very sensitive and seem able to react in ways that increase their well-being. For example, if they are given a choice of many different fluids to drink, among them various strengths of alcohol, the rats will not touch alcohol in greater concentration than six per cent. Or if you offer a rat in which diabetes has been induced by the removal of the pancreas an assortment of isolated proteins, fats, carbohydrates, mineral salts, water, and vitamins, in a few days he will arrive at a balance just as good as the diet we human beings have been able to work out only after decades of study.

If you remove the adrenal glands from rats they develop the same symptoms as man develops when those glands are destroyed by tuberculosis. In the human this is known as Addison's disease. Among the numerous symptoms of this disease that it took us many, many years to learn is that the potassium salt content of the blood rises and the sodium salt content of the blood falls. We have learned to correct this and to make the patient more comfortable by removing foods high in potassium and emphasizing ordinary table salt in the liquids he drinks. It took us decades to learn this. If you perform this operation on a rat and give him a free choice of foods, within forty-eight hours he refuses foods high in potassium and he emphasizes the table salt content in his diet.

Now let me give one for you to think about. If you give a rat a free choice of fluids — coffee with or without sugar, with or without cream, with both; Coca Cola; various kinds of alcoholic drinks; and tomato juice — the rat will drink approximately twice as much tomato juice as any other fluid you put in front of him. Why? What is there in tomato juice which makes him choose it? Is there something lacking in his diet which is furnished by the tomato juice? I leave the problem with you.

Now I want to discuss some recent experiments in a new field that is just opening up and which is very hard to describe. Richter begins a paper presented recently before a memorial seminar in honor of the late Walter Cannon with the following statement:

"Voodoo Death" — that is the title of a paper published in 1942 by Walter Cannon. It contains many instances of mysterious, sudden, apparently psychogenic death, from all parts of the world. A Brazilian Indian, condemned and sentenced by a so-called "medicine man," is helpless against his own emotional response to this pronouncement — and dies within hours. In Africa a young Negro unknowingly eats the inviolably banned wild hen. On discovery of his "crime" he trembles, is overcome by fear, and dies in 24 hours. In New Zealand a Maori woman eats fruit that she only later learns has come from a tabooed place. Her chief has been profaned. By noon of the next day she is dead. In Australia a witch doctor points a bone at a man. Believing that nothing can save him, the man rapidly sinks in spirits and dies.

Cannon made a thorough search of reports from many primitive societies before he convinced himself of the existence of voodoo deaths.

Cannon then asked himself the question: "How can an ominous and persistent state of fear end the life of man?" Having accepted the possibility of voodoo death, Richter proceeded to set up experiments trying to place limiting values on this preconception. His experiments, in my opinion, are fundamental. He found, for example, if he trapped wild rats in a sort of leather bag which provided ample air for life but kept them trapped, they struggled for a while, then apparently gave up and died. Why did they die? Not for lack of air, not for lack of stored chemical energy in their muscles. What physiological and psychological processes were involved?

If one repeats the experiment but this time liberates the animal for a short time after it has struggled and then traps it again, it will go on a second time to complete exhaustion — making a much longer struggle than the first one. The upshot of this experiment apparently is that if the rat has reason to believe, by virtue of a single experience, that its situation is not hopeless, it makes a struggle far beyond what it would make and lives much longer than it ordinarily would under the same conditions. The implication of this kind of study for education is obvious.

Science and technology lead to engineering and large-scale production with tremendous implications for our social organization. Eventually this calls for social judgments. No better illustration of this can be given than the question of radioactive fallout, which is a difficult problem before the world today.

We recognize in radio and television marvellous instruments for the education of young and old. On one Sunday afternoon recently, we were given the opportunity of watching a fine interview with Mr. de Valera of the Irish Republic, and we were able to review some of the life of Mahatma Gandhi. On the other hand, we also know the abuses which take place through the same medium of communication. Television would lead us to believe, for example, that certain drugs will cure us when we are ill. This calls for social judgments.

Where will we develop these social judgments? In science? No.

Science is not interested and cannot be interested in making social judgments. These are value judgments. Where will you find a better dramatization of the age-old problem of how to do justice without doing an injustice than in Shakespeare's *Hamlet*? What kind of foreign policy should the United States have? Perhaps we should listen to Immanuel Kant making his plea to act, to act, to act, so that our actions may become the standards of conduct. When we are being placed as educators under pressures to teach the law of the thing in terms of the physical sciences to the neglect of the social sciences and the humanities, shall we listen to Emerson when he warned us:

> There are two laws discrete,
> Not reconciled,—
> Law for man, and law for thing;
> The last builds town and fleet,
> But it runs wild,
> And doth the man unking.

When we are under pressure by the crowd to think and work with the crowd rather than maintain our independence, should we listen to Emerson: "It is easy in the midst of the crowd to be true to the crowd's opinion; it is easy in the solitude to be true to one's own, but the great man is he who in the midst of a crowd keeps the independence of the solitude."

What to do about it? It is obvious that technology will play an ever-increasing part in our culture. The teaching profession will be given heavy responsibilities for preparing our young people to play their part in this world of change. Young people with ability in the field of mathematics must be given the opportunity to grow in this field. They must also be given the opportunity to become aware of the increasing importance of mathematics to physical and biological science. At the same time the door must not be closed to young people who have a blind spot in mathematics. History shows many examples of great creative research in physical sciences done by those who were not highly trained in mathematics. There is much research to be carried on in disciplines that are not yet quantitative, as I have tried to show.

For the teacher all of this means better preparation and this in turn means that he should have the opportunity for advanced study. Our universities must re-examine their requirements for the master's degree for teachers who have only two years' preparation in their subject-matter fields. A comradeship which has been broken during the past decade or so that existed between the university teacher and the high school teacher must be re-established. For the citizen all of this means that our teachers must be paid salaries commensurate with their responsibilities. The prestige of the teacher must be such that the profession will attract young people from all economic sectors of our society.

In concluding I shall paraphrase George Eliot: "Let us not be pessimists because educators have done a magnificent job in educating our young people to work within the framework of democracy: let us not be optimists because optimism can dull our sense of what is critical and what is significant in a changing world and lead us into a chronic state of mediocrity. Let us rather be ameliorists, that is, if things in education are not as they should be, all of us will lend our hands, our heads, and our hearts to making them so."

MR. GUSTAVSON is president of Resources for the Future, Inc., Washington, D.C.

◆§ VIRGINIA L. SENDERS

The Growth of the Educator: A Reaffirmation

IF things in education are not as they should be, all of us will lend our hands, our heads, and our hearts to making them so." These concluding words of Reuben Gustavson's address determined the climate for the small group discussions of the ways in which college teachers might cultivate their own growth and improve their artistry of teaching. Are things in education not as they should be? And if not, how can college teachers work to make them so?

The most important product of these discussions was not a collection of brand-new ideas about the growth and development of the educator. Many ideas were advanced and many suggestions probed, but most of these ideas have been advanced before, discussed, argued over, and developed fully. What was most important and most heartening was the fact that the members of the discussion groups, representing college teachers from a wide variety of colleges and a wide variety of subject-matter fields, here took occasion to reaffirm the need for growth and to evaluate anew the many ways in which growth might be achieved. The reader who searches the reports from the groups for complete novelty of approach will be disappointed, for the newness does not lie in the reports but in the minds of the individuals who gave old ideas rebirth. These men and women assumed almost without discussion that things in education were not as they should be, and as a matter of fact, never would be as they should be. They took it for granted that for the teacher growth and development must be a continuous and a never-ending process. Starting with this as their basic assumption, they sought the ways in which growth might be defined and achieved. Naturally many of the ideas voiced in the discussion groups reflected directly the nature of the subject-matter fields upon which the division into groups was based. In spite of the specific nature of some suggestions, however, all the groups found themselves seeking the nature and conditions of growth as *teachers*, as *scholars*, and as *human beings*. In addition, suggestions were made about the financial and physical facilities that could stimulate growth, as well as about the age-old problem of how to overcome the time pressures that interfere with development.

How Can We Grow as Teachers?

The improvement of teaching artistry is *not* primarily a matter of developing techniques and methods. A great teacher is great not because he uses superb tools and clever gimmicks but because he is himself a devoted scholar and a warm, wise human being. The methodology of instruction is not to be overlooked, but neither is it the first consideration in the development of teaching artistry. Whatever will make us grow as scholars and as people will automatically foster our growth as teachers. It does not follow, however, that attention to the techniques of teaching is wasted or unnecessary. A deliberate attention to method and an attempt to improve teaching artistry can be fruitful — provided the more important preconditions are met. How, then, is teaching artistry to be improved?

A first step in the process is diagnosis and learning. What is wrong with our teaching now and how can it be remedied? Many sources of information are here available to us: our students, our colleagues, the examples of great teachers, and even, when seen in proper perspective, the literature on educational methodology. Our students can teach us both by what they say and by what they are. In one sense, students are the consumers of our product — education and instruction. In another sense, the student is himself the product, since in the last analysis it is people that we teach, rather than French or mathematics. By listening to the students as consumers and looking at them as products, we can learn much about our strengths and weaknesses.

Formal evaluations of teachers by students can be extremely valuable to the teacher in spite of their obvious weaknesses. Although many doubt the worth of such forms for use by administrators, there is more enthusiasm about their use for self-diagnosis (see pp. 184–85). In private conferences and through his faculty adviser as intermediary, the student can offer opinions and make constructive suggestions for the improvement of teaching procedures.

The student regarded as the product of our educational system can supply us indirectly with information, provided we have clearly in mind our criteria for the quality of the product. To judge ourselves by the results of our teaching we must first formulate objectives with precision, then compare our actual students with what we wish they had become. This comparison requires, in turn, that we develop excellent evaluation instruments and that we see our students over a long enough period — preferably several years — to observe and measure their growth.

Our colleagues, too, though in a different way from our students, can tell us or they can show us. Where the teacher does not object to having the vaunted sanctity of his classroom violated, the criticisms of a faculty friend or a trusted graduate student can be of inestimable value. Or he can himself be the visitor who learns by watching other teachers in action. The advent of television teaching has brought with it the happy opportunity to visit in dozens of different classrooms, most of them conducted by teachers chosen for their excellence, without invading privacy or disturbing a class in action.

We learn from our colleagues by working with them and talking with them. Formal or informal conferences among department members can help to clarify course objectives; if course syllabuses and examinations are filed, so that they are also available to other department members, duplication can be avoided, gaps filled, and a more truly integrated program of studies provided. Working with a scholar in a related field on a course to be taught jointly can simultaneously promote intellectual growth and provide valuable insights into the other scholar's teaching methods. Even that much-bemoaned bane of every professor's life — committee work — can be a source of growth, as when, for example, participation on a university social science committee leads to better integration of one's own field with those of others.

Not all our ideas about our own improvement can come from others. Some must be got not from students or colleagues but from reading, study, experimentation, and soul-searching. Much is written about teaching methods, but how much of it is read by college teachers? Several groups were willing to admit that they might learn from such reading, and one group expressed its wish that there were more fellowships available from such sources as the National Science Foundation for men and women who wish to study teaching and improve their competence at it. Willingness to experiment in the classroom, and a certain optimism and freedom from preconceptions, were mentioned by one group as important. This group added several specific suggestions: changing the textbook from time to time helps the teacher to feel a newness about his work and to put himself in a position a little closer to that of the student. *Writing* a textbook was suggested as a most illuminating experience. The same group suggested that to *not* teach a course in which one had grown stale would help one return with new ideas and new enthusiasms. Whatever the experiment, whatever new methods, new techniques, or new attitudes are to be brought there, these must be ruthlessly evaluated by all the methods at our disposal, including the use of tape-recordings of class hours.

After diagnosis and learning comes action. It is not enough to learn how to teach better — we must actually do it. Suggestions for the improvement of teaching were many and varied, often reflecting the subject-matter fields of those who made them. Physical scientists spoke of the value of demonstrations, and social scientists of participation in social institutions of the community. The value of class discussions was considered, and student papers and projects were often mentioned as useful teaching devices and learning experiences.

Of more interest than the suggestions about specific techniques, however, was the stress placed by most discussion groups upon the broader aims of teaching. What are we really trying to do, and can we make techniques serve our aims rather than determine them? Though the question is broad, some of the answers were practical and specific. For example, the teachers of foreign languages felt that growth as teachers implied growth, for both themselves and their students, of "social and cultural awareness of the civilization of the country whose language we teach . . . The association of language and literature is but a traditional one; we have a right and a responsibility to deal with all materials which use that language as a means of expression. Since we must deal with the entire setting in which the language is used, our knowledge has to grow in a variety of areas — political situation, the structure of the society, and so forth. Instead of using the present departmental designations such as 'Department of French' or 'Department of Russian,' we ought perhaps to adopt such names as 'Department of French Studies' or 'Department of Russian Studies.'"

This same group gave serious consideration to the almost-universal problem of the relation between the student's level of competence and the level at which a course is taught. In foreign-language teaching, this problem arises in a very specific way: is it really possible to teach literature in a foreign language to students who are only at the intermediate level? And how much should the literature be doctored to bring it down to the student's level of comprehension? The group members agreed that to teach at a level continually beyond the student's comprehension is useless, but to require the student to reach, to strive, to stretch beyond his present development — at least part of the time — is a necessity. They concluded that literature should be introduced, not because the intermediate student can fully appreciate it at the time, but in the hope that he may come back to it and see more fully its richness of meaning.

The social scientists pointed out that whatever our decision about the relation of teaching level to student level, it is important to have a realistic appraisal of the latter. This is not as easy as it sounds, because over the years students change in the kind and amount of knowledge they bring with them at the start of a course. A study was reported which showed that today's students, entering a course on family living, have more knowledge, and more correct knowledge, than did their counterparts of a decade ago. Thus techniques for assessing the level of entering students are an important prerequisite to matching the course level to the students' competence.

Several groups expressed what others probably took for granted: the teaching of facts is not enough. The student is not truly educated in any subject matter who has not learned to question textbook conclusions, to deal at least to some extent with original sources, to understand the rationale and methodology of the subject, and to learn the historical role of human judgment in making the subject matter what it is today. The teachers of philosophy and religion had much to say on this topic. The most important function of the teacher in these areas, they felt, is to generate a problem in the learner's mind. "Wonder is natural to man. The teacher should develop the art of stimulating wonder in the student." To do this, he should draw attention to problems of which the student has not been hitherto conscious, but which are somehow in his experience; and the teacher must see these problems as real problems. For the student, thinking about problems should become more important than learning the answers, and the teacher must lead him to do this.

Finally, several discussion groups made the vital point that each instructor is unique, with his own abilities, his own motivations, his own weaknesses, strengths, and attitudes. We can learn from others, yes, but we cannot simply apply unchanged the techniques that have worked for others nor copy their manners and methods. Teaching is one of the most individualistic of all vocations, and this is as it should be. That is why, especially for the college teacher, scholarly development and personal growth will always outweigh in importance any mechanical study of educational methodology.

How Can We Grow as Scholars?

Thus phrased, the question is really too narrow. We cannot all be great scholars — the ultimate authorities in our fields — and indeed greatness in scholarship narrowly defined is not a prerequisite to, nor perhaps even a frequent concomitant of greatness in teaching. Nevertheless, the teacher who would communicate to his students the joy of intellectual activity and the zest of research must feel these emotions himself. If the function of teaching is to develop wonder, the teacher himself must *feel* wonder; and if the function of teaching is to stimulate intellectual growth, then a truly great teacher must himself be in a continuous process of intellectual growth. If scholarship be broadly defined to include intellectual growth, a zest for research and a search for understanding, rigorous thinking, and continuous joy in learning — if scholarship starts and ends with wonder — then we dare not shrink as scholars if we would grow as teachers. How is this growth to come about? What can we do to cultivate it?

Even more than artistry of teaching, intellectual growth is an individual matter. For some of us, growth will be vertical, leading to increased specialization and expertness, while for others it will be horizontal, leading to broader understanding, and greater integration of our own fields with others. For some of us, growth will come largely from social stimulation — from attendance at meetings and discussions, both formal and informal, with our colleagues and fellow scholars. For others, the primary source of stimulation will be the palette or the test tube, the printed word or solitary musing. For all of us, the classroom and the student can be a vital and important stimulus to growth.

The Growth of the Educator

The nature of intellectual growth, as well as the method of its attainment, will depend partly upon the needs of the growing individual and partly upon the field of his specialty.

Many specific suggestions were made by the various discussion groups about the ways in which college teachers might continue their own intellectual growth and development. These included continued reading of all sorts, both in one's own field and in other areas; continued instruction and public performance for the teacher of fine arts; laboratory research in the sciences; consultation for business, industry, or government in both the natural and social sciences; and the wise use of sabbatical leaves and fellowships. Teachers of foreign languages felt that for them the learning of a new language, the study of comparative literature, the study of writing techniques, and the study of some complete subject-matter field such as philosophy could be important sources of growth. All these measures can be taken by an individual teacher without support or stimulation from his colleagues.

Formal and informal contacts with other scholars were considered important in promoting intellectual development, and specific suggestions for such contacts included attendance at workshops, departmental colloquia and graduate-level seminars, faculty discussion clubs, and most valuable of all, professional meetings. It was suggested that members of a department who attend professional meetings have a responsibility to report back to those who were unable to be present. Outside speakers can be a valuable source of information and stimulation, and the physical scientists suggested that such an association as the Academy of Science might provide a valuable service by announcing through a newsletter service the forthcoming engagements of noted speakers, particularly when these are not on a university campus. Visiting professors who remain in residence for an extended period can be immensely stimulating, and it was suggested that programs for the regular exchange of faculty members on both national and international levels might be extremely valuable. Day-by-day exchanges with one's own department members and with members of other departments are important; one group spoke of the value of having a diversity of opinions within a single department, but warned that no department, and particularly no small one, can afford to become a set of armed and hostile camps.

Teaching itself can be a vital challenge to professional growth. Ways of increasing its value include the already suggested device of teaching a course jointly with a colleague, providing young instructors with a diversity of courses to teach, and cooperation among department members in the preparation and planning of the basic course.

How Can We Grow as Human Beings?

A teacher is more than a teacher and a scholar. His day has twenty-four hours in it, and some of these are spent with his family and in his community. He will have friends outside of his college and his profession, as well as more prosaic dealings with his grocer or his milkman. Since he is human, he must face human problems, and how he solves them may well have indirect but vitally important effects upon his performance as a scholar and a teacher. Growth in teaching and intellectual competence can result in growth in humanity, but the interaction can also work the other way: a better and happier man is often a better teacher. How, then, can we come to know ourselves better as people, and how can we grow as human beings?

It will come as no surprise that the group which devoted the most time to discussing this aspect of growth was composed of teachers of psychology and education. They pointed up the problem most explicitly, cited examples of the effects of the teacher's personality upon his teaching function, and sought solutions to the question of personal growth.

An example of the problem was contributed by a teacher of nursing education who reported that she and her fellow teachers had been meeting regularly each week for a discussion of cases that were to be presented to their students. During these meetings, the discussions of several cases had produced strong emotional reactions in the instructors, who were expected to be completely objective in presenting the cases to their students. The preliminary preparation in the meetings helped them to achieve the objectivity they sought, but without such preparation, the instructors' personal needs and involvements might seriously have interfered with their teaching functions. Several similar instances were reported by other members of the discussion group.

Recognizing the need for self-insight and maturity is, unfortunately, quite a different thing from achieving it. Actually, sensitivity to the possibility that one is using students to meet personal needs and that dogmatism in the classroom or impatience with students outside it can stem from emotional rather than logical causes can be a first step in eliminating these conditions. But no other suggestion seemed to the group to be very practical except this: each of us needs some time to be alone. Too often this important time is continually pushed aside in favor of the many interruptions and appointments of a busy teaching day. Time to be alone needs to be included in the schedule; it should be a time when one is fresh, and it should be kept free from all but the most unavoidable interruptions. How to use it will depend upon the individual and his needs — there was no suggestion that a daily period of self-analysis or brooding introspection was desirable. Reading, writing, or perhaps just undirected thinking may be the order of the day. The important thing is to have the time available when it may be needed.

The Prerequisites of Growth

All these aspects of growth depend largely upon the individual and his own desire and effort to grow, but they do not depend entirely upon him. The college or university, by providing proper physical facilities, can contribute greatly to its faculty. A good library, up-to-date laboratory facilities and research equipment, the availability of audio-visual and other teaching aids, can encourage both teaching and scholarship. Group after group referred in its discussions to the value of faculty coffee rooms, lounges, and clubs where the informal meetings with members of other departments, so important to intellectual and personal growth, can take place. Even a college that cannot possibly support a full-fledged faculty club can usually manage a faculty coffee room, and the returns, in terms of broadened interests and reciprocal understanding, can be immeasurable. The importance of outside support for research, and of fellowships for those interested primarily in improving their teaching, was repeatedly stressed.

None of these physical and financial aids will solve completely the perennial problem of *time*. Where is the time for growth to come from? One group suggested that this problem may not really be as bad as it seems; perhaps we rationalize when we say that we do not read or write or think because we have no time. Other groups sought ways of finding time. These included lighter teaching loads (loads of nine to fifteen hours per week were considered too heavy), budgeting time, and the use of students for such nonteaching duties as course-scheduling. Whatever the solution, all forms of growth do require time, and teachers and administrators will have to work and plan together to see that as much as possible is available.

Overview

Discussions by the various groups centered on three aspects of growth: as teacher, as scholar, and as human being. The need for growth was accepted by everyone, and the groups showed great vigor in attacking the problem of how it was to be achieved. Their enthusiasm, so difficult to communicate in a summary report, gave new breath to old ideas and made them live again in the words of the men and women who recreated them. There are obstacles to development, but these will be overcome. As long as teachers as devoted and alert as these affirm their need, the world can be satisfied that growth in all its aspects will characterize the profession of college teaching.

THIS chapter, prepared by Mrs. Senders, who is in the College of Science, Literature, and the Arts at the University of Minnesota, sums up the Friday morning discussions of nine conference groups on the subjects of growth and artistry in teaching:

biological sciences: Rodney Briggs (St. Paul Campus, University of Minnesota), chairman; Brother L. George, F.S.C. (St. Mary's College), recorder;

physical science and mathematics: Arild J. Miller (Carleton College), chairman; Rudolph Lokensgard (Winona State College), recorder;

foreign languages: Eugene Falk (College of Science, Literature, and the Arts, University of Minnesota), chairman; and Sister Mary Henry, C.J.S. (College of St. Catherine), recorder;

English literature: Father Alfred Deutsch (St. John's University), chairman; Sister Mariella, O.S.B. (College of St. Benedict), recorder;

fine and applied arts: Albert Elsen (Carleton College), chairman; Harvey R. Waugh (St. Cloud State College), recorder;

history and political science: Robert P. Fogarty (College of St. Thomas), chairman; R. Stuart Hoyt (College of Science, Literature, and the Arts, University of Minnesota), recorder;

psychology and education: Kenneth Doane (Hamline University), chairman; Sister M. Digna (College of St. Scholastica), recorder;

sociology and economics: Harlan Smith (Hamline University), chairman; Mary A. Ericson (Gustavus Adolphus College), recorder;

philosophy and religion: David White (Macalester College), chairman; Father Henri DuLac (College of St. Thomas), recorder.

HAROLD TAYLOR

The Teacher at His Best

THERE is great variety in the styles of good teachers. There are those who lecture brilliantly, bringing to the students new insights and new ways of relating facts and ideas, ways which would not occur either to the students or to other scholars and teachers in a given field.

There are others who do not lecture brilliantly, but whose presence in the classroom carries weight and significance for the students by the sheer integrity of thought and the power of the ideas expressed. John Dewey was a teacher of this kind.

There are other teachers who work best in a tutorial situation, inspiring the confidence of the student, encouraging the student into new and fresh ways of thinking, and committing him to independent study and a genuine involvement in the things he is doing.

There are other teachers who have a talent for leading discussions and for persuading those who have not thought for themselves to join discussion in uninhibited and honest ways.

The task of the university is to find the way in which the particular talents of the teacher can be given the best setting. To do this it is necessary to think of teachers as individuals, and to center the educational planning in the ideas and talents of the teacher, rather than trying always to fit the teacher into a prescribed curriculum. The trouble with a great deal of American higher education is that the system itself defeats its own purposes. That is to say, every teacher is considered to be a lecturer in every class; every class, no matter what size, is considered to be a means of disseminating information. The teacher is put in the position of transmitting what he knows to a group of listeners. This produces certain habits and attitudes on the part of teachers which they pass on to other teachers through the mechanism of the university system of departmental courses and a standard pattern of

149

subjects. In many ways, it is bad for a teacher to be asked to lecture continually since he very soon comes to like it, and to enjoy the immunity to questions which comes from standing before a classroom of listening students. The difficulty about anyone who talks continually for fifty minutes at a time is that he never does know if anyone is listening, or if listening, if the listening means anything. It is impossible to tell what a listener is thinking. Thinking most often begins in the exchange of ideas, not in the reception of information. The teacher's aim should be to induce such exchange and response, to make teaching a transaction between the materials of learning and the students in his class.

The teacher begins to move toward the enhancement of his talent as an artist in the field when he thinks of himself as an educational planner and not simply a lecturer or vehicle for disseminating knowledge. He must think at many levels about his teaching. He must ask himself questions about the readiness, aptitude, talent, and interest of his students, and about the selection of materials from the variety of things he knows which might be relevant to the student's readiness to receive the knowledge he wishes to impart. He must consider the effect of his own enthusiasm for a given body of knowledge on the receptivity of the students, and he must understand the effects on his students of their own enthusiasm for the studies they have undertaken.

The Attitude of the Teacher

I would like to say something about the attitude of the teacher as a determining fact in his success with students.

What is the teacher's purpose? It must be to involve the students directly in their own education. Until this happens, the student is either forced to imitate the ideas of the teacher or to anticipate, sometimes in a cynical or a self-seeking way, the kind of response the teacher is likely to demand to examination questions later in the year.

But it is the attitude of the teacher which controls the response of the student. If the teacher thinks of himself as an educational planner, he will find ways in which the students he is teaching will form themselves into a group who feel that they are working together toward a common aim. Once the student knows that the teacher is genuinely concerned that he learn, and once the teacher manages to communicate to his whole class an attitude of expectancy and trust, the students begin to form such a group and influence each other to become involved in the life of the class.

This attitude of expectancy is demonstrated by the way in which a teacher assigns the duties for each week. By this I mean that the teacher who is careful to make assignments which are provocative, informative, and interesting will gain a degree of respect from his students simply because he has taken the pains to search out materials which might not be readily available to any student who was not in touch with the particular class taught by this particular teacher. This makes demands upon the teacher's resources both in his private reading and in his work as a scholar. But the assignments have to be weighed not only in terms of the quality of the scholarship and information they contain, but the appropriateness of the given assignment to the student at a given point in his intellectual development.

The Teacher as Leader

The attitude of a teacher should be primarily that of an intellectual leader who, as Alexander Meiklejohn said in his inaugural address at Amherst College, should "stand before his pupils and before the community at large as the intellectual leader of his time." If the teacher thinks of himself as the intellectual leader of his students, he then finds ways in which the students can respect his opinions, can learn from his range of intellectual experience and from the knowledge which is his personal possession. I believe it is because the modern teacher often does not conceive his mission as that of an intellectual leader that so much of higher education in the United States is ineffective. Some recent research on student growth and learning has been referred to at this conference by Marjorie Carpenter and by Harald Bakken. The research suggests that the student is more affected by the values of his age group and of his society than he is by his university life or his academic courses. Philip Jacob's research results, as reported in *Changing Values in College*, indicate that, except in a small number of special colleges, there is no effect on students' values which could be attributed to any part of the curriculum, including the curriculum in the social sciences. (See pp. 69–70, 87–88.)

We might ask then, How is the value system of a college or university determined? In the long run, it is determined by the attitudes and beliefs of the teachers who make up the basis of that community. The students come and go, leaving traces of their attitudes and ideas behind them. College presidents and deans come and go. Some of them stay long enough to make some changes or to antagonize or please the faculty before they go, but by and large it is the body of faculty members on tenure, joined by others for varying lengths of time, who determine the character and values of any institution.

This is the reason why the teacher must not only be an intellectual leader, but must be an educational planner who is sensitive to his students and who must have his students' confidence if he is to be successful in his mission. I do not mean that the teacher must be popular, or that he must be entertaining, although he may be on occasion, or that he should trim his teaching to the winds of opinion and interest blowing across the young students' minds. What I do mean is that sensitivity to students is the first step toward winning their confidence and committing them to the study in hand.

The way this is done varies greatly from teacher to teacher, although there are certain basic patterns of attitude and of method which constitute the essentials of teaching in the style which I am advocating. One of these is the simple availability of the faculty member to students who wish to see him. Availability to students is of course a drain on the emotional and physical energies of the faculty. But I submit that it is impossible to persuade the students to join in the common intellectual enterprise being conducted in the university classroom and on the campus unless students feel that they can go to their teachers and that they will be assured of a welcome there. Since it may be completely impracticable to assure a welcome to a class of five hundred students, some particular means of conferring with groups of students and with individuals must be arranged.

But above all, the teacher who has from fifty to five hundred students assigned to him for instruction should assume that what he has in reality is a small college of his own in which he has the privilege of appointing his own faculty members — that is to say, to choose among the students in the class and among the graduate students who are working with him, if there are such, those who have particular aptitudes for and interests in joining him in the teaching process. If the teacher shows his confidence in his students by asking them to conduct discussion groups for members of the class, if he asks for written reports on the discussion by others, if he takes the students into his confidence by showing the way in which his course will unfold, then he has established a beginning in forming a community of students from the heterogeneous units who comprise the enrollment of his class.

Student Motivation

We are dealing here with the wide question of student motivation. I believe that the capacity of a student is measured as much by the quality of his motivation as by the formal measures of his intelligence. Without commitment and involvement in the process of study, the intelligence of the student is not put to work. Thus we find very often teachers approaching the problem of teaching from the wrong end. Rather than considering the capacity for response to the materials of the course, teachers consider the capacity for absorption of information and evaluate student progress by whether or not a given amount of information has been absorbed. Although we can have no precise tests for motivation in the sense that we can have vocabulary testing and analogical reasoning tests to designate those who are said to be intelligent, we have rough measures of motivation which should be taken into account as of greater importance than the trained capacity to report information accurately. This is not to say that the capacity to receive information and to present it at request is not a very important intellectual skill and one which demands the highest degree of intellectual discipline. However, it is to say that such capacity is developed by the student after his capacity to respond to the material has first been evoked. Those who learn to play football or tennis at a high level of skill are those who want very much to play the game well, and are willing to undergo the hardship and discipline which the game demands of anyone who wishes to play it at any more than a mediocre level. We are very familiar with the involvement of students in sports, but forget it completely when we are dealing with the enjoyment of intellectual pursuits.

One of the ways in which the dedication of the student to intellectual pursuits is achieved is by a clear indication on the part of the teacher that he has a passionate concern for ideas and for the intellectual and cultural values which exist for all scholars. Young people in America in 1958 have by and large accepted the material advantages of American culture, and have their interests centered in a world

153

in which objects, things, and external success dominate their motivations in community and academic life. The young need to be told what it means to be truly alive in one's own time. To be truly alive in one's own time is to be involved in something that really matters *to* one's own time. The young need to know that it is necessary to become committed to something, to an ideal of some kind, in order to be fully alive. This is what brings excitement to life and flavor to human experience. The college teacher has a mission in this regard. The teacher who loves to teach, who enjoys working with students, who finds his students not a series of nuisances which have to be dealt with, but a group of interesting younger colleagues who can bring a fresh eye and a different point of view to the ideas with which he is concerned, will not only command their respect but will deepen and enrich the knowledge he possesses.

Some Personal References

I would like to make some references to my own education in order to clarify the meaning of what I am saying. Education, I had been persuaded while I was undergoing it formally, was something that people did *for* you. The educators set tasks to carry out which were not too difficult for the student, and the educators spaced the tasks in such a way that they would not interfere with one's playing on the football team, or playing the clarinet, or enjoying the pleasures of companionship. It seemed a little odd, although it did not bother me a very great deal at the time, that nearly every book or idea which interested me, or caught my attention, or distracted me from the regular course of my life, was outside the college curriculum. This meant that in college I worked out ways of dealing with the assigned tasks, and thus saved myself sufficient time to develop a passion for literature by reading Virginia Woolf, T. S. Eliot, E. M. Forster, Aldous Huxley, Hemingway, and a number of other writers who were considered advanced at the time.

I had absolutely no intention of becoming a college teacher or of having anything to do with organized education.

I would advise young people who are now considering the question of entering a profession or a business to think seriously about what they want to do with their lives, not merely about what profession seems to be most promising. Again, I base the advice on personal experience. I had no notion of what was involved in university teaching until I was actually doing it, nor had I any conception beforehand of how fascinating a profession it could be. When I first came to the University of Wisconsin I found that I had begun a life which had in it elements of an intellectual excitement I had never known before.

In Canada and Great Britain, where I had grown up, there was a particular set of assumptions about what university life should be, and what kind of students were suited for it. In general, these were students who were considered to be "university material" and who were already selected from the total population of Canada and Great Britain for their aptitudes and scholastic achievements in University terms. At the University of Wisconsin, the students, many of them, had not been selected at all. They simply came to the University after graduating from high school.

This made of university life a completely different affair from the life of the European and British institutions. The students approached their university education as they approached everything else — informally, directly, freshly. I discovered that they were greatly lacking in preparation for university studies. But they were, on the other hand, ready to respond to what the teacher had to offer, provided he seemed to them to have something to teach which was worthwhile to learn. They were quite practical about it. They asked awkward and honest questions. They wanted to know why the study of philosophy was important, why philosophers raised the questions they did. Unless answers which satisfied them were given, they simply ceased the study of philosophy. This tended to eliminate the academic dullness which I had found to be so great a factor in the study of philosophy as I had known it in an undergraduate college. The students put all ideas to the test of their own experience.

Very early in my first term of teaching at the University of Wisconsin I learned what this could mean in practice. I was teaching formal logic, and was dealing one day with the Square of Opposition, whose significance I had never fully understood. This soon became clear to the class. I drew the Square of Opposition on the blackboard and so arranged matters that I misinterpreted the way the corners of the square were related to each other. I was corrected by a young man from the back of the room and suddenly I realized the whole game was lost, since he was quite right. The class then turned into a discus-

155

sion as to why I had been wrong, and then, why the Square of Opposition had any significance in the field of philosophy. Before we had finished, I had become a true advocate of the discussion method.

My conferences with Professor Otto about teaching logic and about students in general were enlightening both as to the meaning of philosophy as an element in the education of the young, and as to the approach to students a teacher of philosophy might take in order to stimulate their thinking and to provoke them to independent examination of their own beliefs. Visits to Mr. Otto's class were a revelation to me. Having become accustomed to listening to lecturers who reviewed the material already published in the text with which we were being instructed, I found startling the freshness and vitality with which Professor Otto talked, never referring to a text but always to original sources, never using a customary example but finding new analogies and examples from his own experience and from his own private reading.

Professor Otto was a true teacher and a gifted philosopher. He was impatient with philosophy and technical philosophical questions. He believed that philosophy should deal with real questions that bothered real people, and that the task of the teacher was to stir his students into intellectual action and controversy. Professor Otto was himself constantly engaged in controversy and was frequently under attack both by academic philosophers who disapproved of his gay, informal way of writing and talking, and by politicians and churchmen who disapproved of his views on religion.

But his students learned to think, and in a real sense Professor Otto's courses gave an intellectual and moral center to the university from which ideas spread to all parts of the community, carried there by his students who had started to think and who then made others think. Like William James and John Dewey, who were a part of Professor Otto's tradition, he learned as much from his students as he taught them, and as James used to do, he left his office door open so that a student could come in at any time.

Allow me to refer to a few sentences from William James to indicate the style of thinking and writing which marks this approach to teaching. James was a man who, when he wrote philosophy, wrote to everyone — students, faculty, colleagues, the world at large, *not* just to other philosophers.

The Teacher at His Best

The world to which your philosophy professor introduces you [*says James*] is simple, clean and noble. The contradictions of real life are absent from it. Its architecture is classic. Principles of reason trace its outlines, logical necessities cement its parts. Purity and dignity are what it most expresses. It is a kind of marble temple shining on a hill.

In point of fact, it is far less an account of this actual world than a clear addition built upon it, a classic sanctuary in which the rationalist fancy may take refuge from the intolerably fused and Gothic character which mere facts present. (1, p. 21.)

James goes on to say that because philosophers present the world to students and to others in this way, we find men of science "preferring to turn their backs on metaphysics as on something altogether cloistered and spectral, and practical men shaking philosophy's dust off their feet and following the call of the wild."

The Abstract and the Real

This is a teacher talking to students. It is also a philosopher talking about real things to real people. The style of James is infused with the reality of things as they are seen and of ideas as they are appreciated. James is saying here what Max Otto was saying at the University of Wisconsin, and what seems to me to be the essential point of the teacher's mission if he is to assume intellectual leadership. That is to say, the teacher as an intellectual leader makes no sharp separation between the real world where people live, and the world of the intellect where abstractions are to be employed. These are merely two aspects of a universe in which we are all involved, and the student is another learner along with the teacher, a person who learns with him.

It is here that the central task of the college professor takes shape in the work with students. Certainly we know that true teaching must be fed by true scholarship. But scholarship is enriched and deepened by the work one does with students, that is, if one works in the way in which James and Otto suggest. This can and should be a collaborative effort, with the student taking a full share in the learning and taking a full responsibility for helping the teacher to understand more fully the intellectual tasks which they both have in hand.

Most students, no matter what their interests, have not yet learned to distinguish the unimportant from the important, nor have they had a chance to put together a scale of values by which their own interests and ideas can be measured. The construction of a course, from no matter what materials, and the teaching of the course itself, give the teacher his greatest opportunity. The question is not whether the student of philosophy can be entranced by Kierkegaard, moved by Nietzsche, or excited by Descartes. These emotional and intellectual factors are subordinate to the teacher's total aim. That aim is to stimulate the student's thinking toward some ideas of his own, to give his thoughts the beginning of an order which may later harden into belief. The order will not be final, nor will it be an order which the teacher establishes for him. It will always be something which the student begins to feel to be true and begins to regard as something quite personal to himself.

If any serious learning is to take place, the ideas from the writers and philosophers must be those which the student can understand, not because they are simple and easy (there is no simple idea), but because at a particular stage in his development, with the capacity of understanding peculiar to that stage, these are the ideas and issues with which he can most adequately and successfully begin. To construct a good course in philosophy or in any other field requires from five to ten years of experiment by the teacher. Once constructed, it will continue to be the basis for experiment and continued change.

Knowledge of Students

Suppose then that the teacher does think on several of these levels at once. Suppose he does take acount of his students and their readiness for what he has to say. Suppose he is interested in the development of independent thinking through his work in the courses, in order to bring students to an understanding of themselves and their world. How does he find out what issues and ideas are most important to the young people he is called upon to teach?

He needs to confer with them in their own terms. He needs to have them write for him on the subject of their own beliefs.

I believe I have heard more people talking about this generation of students than there are members of the generation itself. This is all to the good, provided the talk is based upon understanding and direct acquaintance with the young people being talked about. This is not often the case, and the clichés, "security-minded," "conformist," "silent," "tired"— these clichés fall like rain on the heads of the young. But it is true that each student generation has its own truth and its particular reality, its private world and its own way of looking at life. If the teacher is to help the young student, and if education is to be effective, he must begin by understanding their truths. He gains this by establishing the relation to them which I have already described, and he is there, on the campus, at times when he can listen to the students talk, because he knows that they want to talk to him. We need to listen to the young as we listen to music - - sympathetically, expectantly, appreciating the individual sounds, and recognizing the total intention of the music.

There is in fact just now a new attitude in the present generation of Western youth. Having been brought up in the Western world to have no illusions, the present generation is not so much disillusioned as it is unillusioned. It accepts the world as it finds it, having been taught to do so by its teachers.

This can have one of two effects. In the case of the angry young men of England, celebrated by John Osborne, the playwright, this can have the effect of creating a tough-minded minority who attack the complacency and the closed-in quality of the life around them. Or, as in the case of American writers and students, who aren't mad at anyone, it may involve a movement away from the external issues of politics and social values, into analytical thinking and introspection.

We now have in American colleges the first generation of understood children who have been brought up by understanding parents. Being understood by parents and by educators puts a special kind of burden on the child, the burden of personal decision. In the absence of a strong line of authority, the child and the student have little to rebel against. In a world in which the young person is not ordered around but told to choose his way, he may stifle in an atmosphere of kindly, over-all approval. In such an atmosphere of acceptance and freedom from restriction, the young person often feels a deep emotional fatigue as a result of continually being forced to make his own decisions before he has had enough time and experience to feel able to do so.

The New Generation

In the previous generation what children and college students needed was a release from the constrictions of authority laid down by tradition, academic convention, parental rights, and social custom. This generation has received such release. But having been released and having also achieved a higher degree of self-understanding, combined with a higher degree of tolerance for deviations in all human behavior, they now wish to be relieved of some of the burden of self-responsibility. As a result, we often find college students bored by discussions, tired of asking questions, and just saying, "Give us the word. You know more than I do. What's the answer?" Or on the other hand, students will ask, "What is the point in so much student self-government? We had all that in high school. Let's get on to the more interesting things. I don't have time for this young people's activity."

In some of the colleges in the East this past year we have had trouble finding students willing to run for student office. Many colleges find the machinery of student government running down because responsible students do not wish to hold office in it. This is for a very good reason, as far as they are concerned. They would prefer an orderly arrangement of student life, run by someone who had had a lot of experience, to a life organized by inexperienced students who waste a good deal of time doing it. Having been given their freedom, students find that the freedom works well but is a bore to administer.

There are other qualities in the lives of the young in college today with which educators must be familiar if they are to understand them. I give you the following statement by a young man who seems to me to have come close to defining the attitude of the more astute in his college generation. "We are the generation of the third eye, the eye of self-consciousness, the eye of self-criticism. The characteristic fear of our generation is our horror of finding ourselves ludicrous."

This I find to be a characteristic fear among many of the young. They want to look around them before acting, in case by acting impulsively and sincerely they may be considered naïve or silly. I have also noticed that among the young who are beginning to find themselves, the person who acts sincerely, boldly, enthusiastically, can be brought down in full flight by a sneer or a cynical smile. At a time when negative qualities dominate our cultural life, it is always easier not to risk one's own self-confidence by a show of public enthusiasm and idealism. It is wiser just to be quiet. Young people prefer to sit back, to watch, to understand — not to act. Thus we get a monotone of feeling, with few wishing to risk the larger emotions of joy, anger, dramatic action, and most preferring the gentler pleasures of approval and adaptation. The level of idealism is thereby lowered, and the young, having been taught by their environment to be careful, do not choose to involve themselves in controversy, nor to deal with big and significant issues. They are absorbed in what has been called a fun morality in a period of material prosperity.

Another student, a member of the group at Princeton referred to in a recent volume as the unsilent generation, states a common ideal for the young when he says in response to a question as to his own ideals: "Success for me would mean a job that I could leave after eight hours and that would provide for self-fulfillment within a framework of inconspicuous luxury."

I believe that this young man has caught the spirit of many in his age group. This is surely a modest demand, and surely much less of a demand than the young in our colleges should be making. This young man was taught his style of expression and this way of living by his life in America; he holds a set of values which his university life has not altered. When we ask What can teachers ask of their students?, I reply that we can ask much more than this. I do not think that because this generation has failed to respond to challenge, or has not been challenged, that this means that they are less idealistic than their predecessors. It seems to me that this generation is more talented, better educated, and better able to handle its problems than any other we have had. This generation has been taught to recognize the advantages of material and personal security, but not the means of translating idealism into productive action.

Teaching This Generation

The real question is not what is wrong with this generation, since the question of what is wrong with it is much less important than what is true of it. The real question is, given the character of this generation, what kind of teaching can we carry out in our colleges to do what must be done in every age — to raise the level of human ideals and the level of human achievement. I believe that if we think of students as people who will respond to challenges of an intellectual and moral kind which go beyond mere teaching of subject matter, then we are on the way to helping the modern student achieve his self-hood. Education in college is the means by which the student may achieve his self-hood. To achieve the flavor of individuality, for a person or an institution, it is necessary to be one's self, and not simply a cluster

161

of approved characteristics. It is necessary to give up wanting to be liked or wanting to have everything arranged in a smooth and easy fashion. It is necessary to discover what is really true, and to discover this by one's self. No one can make this discovery except by his own effort. No true teacher at his best can teach well unless he has made these discoveries for himself. Life in the college of liberal arts or life in the big university must be organized in all its component parts in such a way that the student is continually thrust into situations of an intellectual and personal kind out of which he must extricate himself by his own efforts. Otherwise his education will be that of a passive person receiving what is given.

The educational destinies of the student and of the teacher are linked. Where teaching is cautious, noncommittal and inhibited, learning is timid and ineffectual.

The Qualities of the Teacher

I return again to my central theme that it is the richness and depth of the inner life of the teacher and the qualities he holds as a man of character and commitment that determine his students' response to his teaching. We therefore need to do everything in our power to arrange the community life of our college campuses in such a way that its elements conspire to produce stimulating and provocative effects in the intellectual and personal growth of teachers. Those who administer educational institutions — department chairmen, deans, or college presidents — must realize that if the rules of the game call for continued publication of articles and monographs on subjects of research, this may be the worst kind of stimulation for the work of a scholar and teacher. It very often results in his doing trivial work in ways which have little meaning to him as a person and less meaning to him as a teacher. If the system of university life has as a central component the demand that such publication be undertaken, then the pressures on the teacher and scholar are such that he is bound to consider time spent with students as wasted, or at the very least as a task made necessary by the terms of his employment. True scholarship is the result of a consuming interest in ideas directed by the disciplined intelligence of a person skilled in the field of ideas. It cannot be produced on demand nor induced by the wish to be promoted. Educational administration therefore has a serious responsibility to reward the development of the art of teaching, and to consider the publication of monographs, treatises, books, and research papers as increasing the value of the scholar only if his scholarship bears the marks of insight, importance, and intellectual usefulness.

I say therefore that the teacher at his best is a person who is enriched by the scholarship of his students, who gains nourishment and spiritual sustenance from the work with students. Creative teaching is an art, and it is an art which infuses one's own learning with the discoveries and contributions of the student. It is teaching which accepts the student as an intellectual colleague and which makes no separation between the intellectual problems of the young and the intellectual interests of the professional academic man. It is the teacher's responsibility to fuse the student's interests with his, and so to teach that the student will come to have the same vision of the possibilities and satisfactions of learning which the serious teacher and the serious thinker both have as their badge of office.

REFERENCE

1. James, William. *Pragmatism.* New York: Longmans, Green & Company, 1947.

Mr. Taylor is president of Sarah Lawrence College.

◄§ RALPH W. TYLER

The Evaluation of Teaching

In the American college community the evaluation of teaching is as common as the judgment of the quality of dormitory food — and often as subjective. "Professor Smith is a wonderful teacher!" "Course 101A is a terrible course, the teaching is awful!" "We are a select college, proud of our tradition of excellence in teaching." Comments like these are typical of college conversations. We know, though, they are not highly valid, objective, impartial appraisals. Sound and systematic evaluation of college teaching is exceedingly rare, and yet it is highly essential to the improvement of college instruction. This is true for several reasons, but three seem to me particularly important.

In the first place, as a teacher I can benefit from an appraisal of my efforts that indicates where I am relatively successful and where I am having difficulty, since this gives me a basis for concentrating my efforts to improve my teaching. Without such an evaluation I remain in the dark as to whether my teaching is relatively effective or ineffective and the respects in which it needs improvement.

In the second place, good teaching should be appropriately rewarded, but this is not possible without means for sound evaluation. Hence, rewards for research and publication are much more common than rewards for good teaching. This, in turn, directs the efforts of many instructors to activities other than teaching because such efforts are given recognition. Who has not heard faculty members comment on the fact that although the college talks about teaching's being important, what really counts in getting promotions and salary increases is the list of publications or other evidences of research productivity? Without well-grounded means for evaluating teaching we shall continue to base promotions and salary increases more largely upon other factors; faculty members, in turn, will be more likely to concentrate their efforts on the activities which will be rewarded rather than to seek to become more competent in teaching.

In the third place, to become good teachers ourselves and to help others to do so we need more than the results of our own trials, errors, and successes. We need to be guided by more fundamental concepts and principles of teaching which stand the test of practice. Hypotheses about effective or ineffective teaching become principles as they are tested out in practice and their effectiveness is carefully appraised. The development of a sound body of guiding concepts and principles in teaching is therefore mainly dependent upon means for evaluating teaching so that our principles have been tested rather than resting upon personal preference, or upon unsystematic impressions.

To sum up: evaluation is necessary to help the individual teacher improve his own teaching, to provide a valid basis for rewarding good teaching, and to develop a sound body of concepts and principles that will guide present and future college teachers.

What is involved in evaluating teaching? In essence, the task is similar to evaluating any other purposeful activity. It means finding out the extent to which the purposes of the activity are actually realized. This seems simple enough, but as we examine the purposes of teaching, we find certain complications. The purposes of teaching are to facilitate various kinds of desirable learning on the part of the students. Hence, the evaluation of teaching involves appraising students' learning. Learning is the acquisition by the student of ways of behaving — that is, ways of thinking, feeling, and acting — which he has not previously followed. Thus a college student may develop an understanding of the physical structure of the atom, an understanding he did not possess before; or he may acquire the ability to analyze a problem in plant ecology, an ability he did not have before; or he may develop greater skill in reading literary works than he had before; or he may acquire intellectual or aesthetic interests which he did not have previously. These are a few random illustrations of kinds of learning which college teachers may seek to bring about in their students.

Of course not all things students learn in college are desirable; for this reason, the evaluation of college teaching is not simply finding out whether students have learned, but whether they have learned the things the instructors were trying to teach. Students may learn bad habits as well as good ones, they may acquire misinformation as well as sound understanding, they may acquire a distaste for as well as an interest in various intellectual and aesthetic fields; these, too, are cases of learning, but not the learning that college teachers are trying to bring about. Furthermore, since the college years are relatively few — far too few to learn all that we wish could be learned — teachers must make a fairly rigorous selection of those kinds of behavior — thinking, feeling, and acting — that they consider most important for students to acquire. This, then, makes the evaluation of teaching a matter of finding out how far along the students are toward acquiring the important ways of thinking, feeling, and acting on which the teachers are focusing their attention.

The foregoing indicates the two essential tasks in evaluating teaching: first, to identify the behaviors, which are the teaching objectives; second, to make periodic checks of the extent to which students have acquired the desired behaviors. These tasks need badly to be done, they can be done; but one will encounter difficulties in carrying them out.

The first difficulty a college teacher, or a college faculty, faces is stating the teaching objectives clearly enough in terms of the behaviors that the students are being helped to learn so that one knows what to look for in trying to find out how far the students have acquired these behaviors. Many statements which appear in college syllabuses, course outlines, and catalogues are not statements of the things that students are expected to learn, but rather are listings of content to be covered or vague generalities, such as "to develop critical-mindedness." A list of the topics dealt with in a course does not indicate what the student is to learn to do with them, and yet it is the student's behavior which becomes part of him and is his learning. Several teachers may deal with the same topics; yet the students might learn quite different things. Some teachers might want the student to memorize certain facts or definitions under these topics; some might want the students to acquire an ability to use certain concepts in analyzing the problems and issues in the field; some might expect students to be able to explain various phenomena by the use of relevant principles; and some might want the students to develop an interest in this subject that would carry on long after the course was finished. The mere listing of topics does not indicate which of these or other kinds of behavior are being aimed at in the teaching.

The Evaluation of Teaching

Until we are clear about what we are trying to help students learn, we have no beginning point for evaluation. Each of us needs to answer such questions as What things am I really trying to get students to understand? What kinds of abilities and skills in thinking, analysis, problem-solving, and the like am I really trying to develop? What kinds of competence in reading, or writing, or mathematical operations am I actually seeking to help students to acquire? Am I trying to arouse certain intellectual and aesthetic interests, and if so, what are they? Am I trying to develop some study habits or practices that will aid the student in his continuing development, and, if so, what ones? Am I seeking to instill certain attitudes appropriate to understanding or appreciation of phenomena in this field, and if so, what are they? Until I can state quite clearly the different kinds of behavior I am seeking to develop in my teaching, I shall not be able to make a sound evaluation because I shall not know what to look for in the students.

Evaluation requires not only a list of student behaviors which teachers are seeking to develop but a clear definition of each kind of behavior, since the test of the clarity of the objective is whether one can recognize when students have acquired, or are acquiring, that behavior. One often hears teachers saying that they are not aiming at memorization of facts but are trying to develop understanding; however, when they are asked what they mean by understanding and how it differs from mere memorization, many are unable to define or explain it. Some teachers do have in mind a fairly definite meaning for the term understanding by which to distinguish it from rote memorization. They say that when students understand certain concepts and principles, they can explain them in their own words, they can point out illustrations of them, they can recognize illustrations when they are brought to their attention, they can compare and contrast related concepts or principles, and they can use them in explaining or analyzing phenomena. Each of us might have a somewhat different definition for understanding, but if we can define our objective in some such terms as these, we are able to use our definition as a basis for evaluation, since we know what we are looking for when we try to find out how far our teaching has been effective in developing understanding.

In similar fashion, we need to define every important objective toward which we direct our teaching. An excellent illustration of definitions of various commonly listed college objectives is found in a volume prepared by a group of college and university examiners and edited by Benjamin S. Bloom, called *Taxonomy of Educational Objectives*. The first of a series, this volume analyzes and defines objectives that involve primarily cognitive behavior. Later volumes will analyze other objectives, such as interests, attitudes, habits, and practices. These definitions are useful in suggesting possible form and content for clarifying the meaning of objectives we are seeking in our college teaching.

After the individual instructor has formulated and defined clearly his objectives, or after the department or college faculty has done the same thing for the objectives of the department or college as a whole, the next step is to decide on ways to get evidence of the extent to which the students are acquiring these kinds of behavior. For most fields, evidence of students' understanding can be obtained from paper-and-pencil tests. However, it is necessary to be sure that the tests actually require the students to do the things called understanding rather than simply asking for sheer memorization. There are a good many tests now on the market which include questions and exercises requiring students to recognize illustrations, to compare and contrast related matters, and to use concepts and principles in analysis and interpretation. Hence, it is not too difficult for a college teacher or the faculty as a whole to find tests for this objective, or to make up their own tests. To obtain evidence of the abilities of students to analyze and solve problems in particular fields, and to do other kinds of critical thinking appropriate to these fields, paper-and-pencil tests are also likely to be useful. A number have been prepared by testing agencies, by college examining groups, and by individual teachers. These developments make it possible to test for objectives of this sort with a fair degree of thoroughness. The same can be said for some of the intellectual skills like reading, writing, foreign-language skills, and mathematical skills.

When one comes to interests, attitudes, habits, and practices, however, paper-and-pencil tests will not prove satisfactory. To get at changes taking place in these kinds of behavior, one may use methods of observation, interviews, and questionnaires. There are a number of interest questionnaires on the market which deal with intellectual, aesthetic, social, and occupational interests, and many colleges will find them useful, either in their present form or with modifications. For attitudes that do not involve strong emotional reaction, straightforward opinionnaire items are reasonably satisfactory. For those involving more emotional content, either concealed-attitude items or informal interviews are likely to be more satisfactory. For study habits and practices, a combination of questionnaires and observation checklists are probably most useful.

Although this range of methods for appraising student attainments is necessary for comprehensive evaluation of teaching — since teaching objectives usually include the corresponding range of kinds of behavior we are trying to help students acquire — not all of the results should be used in grading the students. Interviews and questionnaires, if their results are valid, require free, honest reports from the students. Hence, these results should not be used as part of the student's grade because this would, in the end, affect the sincerity of students' responses. Information about interests, attitudes, habits, and practices can help us to learn how successful we are in teaching and to work more effectively with students even though we do not use the information in grading them.

The evaluation of the results of teaching requires more than one appraisal of the students' behavior. Learning is the acquisition of new ways of behaving. It involves changes in the students' reactions. This means that we shall need at least two appraisals, one toward the beginning of a course or the college experience and another toward the end, in order to see what changes have taken place and thus to estimate the effectiveness of the teaching in stimulating and developing learning. Furthermore, many of us are interested in the permanency of learning and we shall, therefore, want to make a further appraisal of the students' behavior some time after the course is completed, or after they have graduated from college, to find out the extent to which the learning which was noted while the students were taking the course or were in college is still evident some time later or whether a considerable amount has gone.

To recapitulate, to evaluate teaching most directly is to evaluate the extent to which students have learned what teachers are trying to teach. The same procedure is involved whether an individual instructor is seeking to evaluate his own teaching or whether a department or a college is seeking to evaluate its teaching. The first step is to state clearly each of the important educational objectives sought — to state these objectives in terms of the behaviors the students are expected to acquire. The second step is to devise the means for appraising the extent to which each of these kinds of behavior has been acquired by the students. Usually these means will include several methods of getting information, including tests, questionnaires, interviews, and observations. The third step is to use the means devised in actually appraising students' behavior. This appraisal will have to be done at least twice, once early in the course or college program, and once toward the end. In this way the instructor or the college gets direct evidence about the extent to which the teaching is effective — that is, evidence of the extent to which the students are learning.

Although the appraisal of students' learning is the most direct and the ultimate evaluation of teaching, there are other less direct methods which are useful. One of these is to examine the extent to which the conditions for effective learning are provided. Over the years psychologists, other social scientists, and educational practitioners have learned a great deal about the conditions necessary for effective learning. Since effective teaching consists largely of providing the conditions for effective learning, it is possible to make an indirect, but highly relevant, evaluation of teaching by noting the extent to which essential conditions for learning are actually present. In psychological literature one will find a number of lists of essential conditions, but most of the lists contain very similar elements.

One necessary condition is the student's motivation. The learner learns what he is thinking, feeling, or doing. Thus learning is not possible except as the learner himself is involved in it. This makes his motivation — that is, the impelling force for his own active involvement — a very important condition. In any college class, or in the college as a whole, it is possible to find out something about students' motivation. What proportion of them are interested in their studies? Are they deeply involved in the work of the class? Does the intellectual activity of the college represent a real concern on the part of the students, and for what fraction of the student body? These are typical questions that can be raised, and largely answered, by observation, interviewing, and the like.

A second condition for effective learning is that the learner finds his previous ways of reacting unsatisfactory so that he is stimulated to try new ways of reacting. As long as the learner does not recognize that earlier modes of behavior are inappropriate, he will keep on doing what he has been doing before and will not really learn anything new. It is necessary for him to discover the inadequacy of his previous behavior in order that he will not continue to repeat it. College students often carry over from their earlier school experiences the notion that study is memorization; called upon to study in college courses, they try to memorize textbook materials. The college teacher must help the student discover that memorization is not a satisfactory means to solve the kinds of problems or do the sorts of exercises which the college class requires. In seeking to evaluate teaching in a college one may ask, "What proportion of the students recognize the fact that they are facing new problems and require new understanding, new techniques, and new attitudes in order to deal with these problems effectively?"

A third condition is for the learner to have some guidance of the new behavior which he tries in seeking to overcome the inadequacy of previous reactions. If he simply tries new behavior by trial and error, learning is very slow and he is often discouraged and gives up. Some means of indicating to him more promising reactions will serve to guide him. Many ways are used to guide the learner in helping him to understand. Parts of syllabuses, textbooks, and manuals may be prepared or selected for this purpose. The instructor may ask questions which lead the student to look at various elements that he may have previously overlooked in his search for meaningful relations. He may be aided in learning a skill by direct demonstration. These are only a few illustrations. Every college teacher can check himself to see the extent to which he is providing some guidance of the student's efforts to acquire the new understanding or skills or attitudes or interests or other objectives sought. The extent to which the student gets needed guidance in carrying on the desired behavior is an index of the effectiveness of the teaching.

A fourth condition for learning is for the learner to have appropriate materials to work on. If he is to learn to solve problems, he has to have problems to attempt to solve; if he is to gain skills, he must have tasks which give him opportunity to practice these skills; if he is to gain appreciation, he must have materials that he can hear, see, or respond to in other appreciative ways. When students have only the textbook and the classroom lectures, they do not have enough of the stuff for study — that is, the problems, the exercises, and the other materials to think about, work on, and practice on to provide the necessary learning experiences. Hence, another index of effective teaching is the extent to which materials are provided students that give them the opportunity to practice the kind of behavior the teacher is seeking to help them acquire.

A fifth condition for effective learning is for the learner to have time to carry on the behavior, to keep practicing it. This is usually referred to as having study time. Often colleges assume that the student is spending time in study outside the classroom, when observation or an interview will indicate that the student thinks that if he comes to class and spends a half hour or so outside, that is all that is required. A more effective provision of study time is important for a high level of learning to be reached. Studies of college students show that time which is presumed to be available for study is often occupied in commuting, outside work, extracurricular activities, and social activities. Imaginative and realistic ways of providing study time can contribute to teaching's effectiveness.

A sixth essential condition for learning is for the learner to get satisfaction from the desired behavior. As the learner interacts in the various learning situations, the reactions which give him satisfaction are continued; those which do not are dropped. If the learner wants very much to acquire a certain kind of behavior, the actual satisfaction of getting it is sufficient. On the other hand, teachers are in a position to help learners derive satisfaction from desired behavior when this satisfaction does not automatically follow progress in learning. For example, to become competent in a foreign language so that one can read stories or articles in that language takes a long time. In the interim, the teacher may exercise a considerable influence by complimenting the student on his efforts, by helping to get the group's approval of reasonable progress, by providing tests or other means for him to perceive that he is progressing toward his goal. These are only a few of the ways in which the teacher may increase the effectiveness of learning by helping the students to get satisfaction as they make progress toward the desired goal. This too can become an index of the effectiveness of college teaching.

A seventh essential condition for learning is the opportunity for a good deal of sequential practice of the desired behavior. Sequential practice means that each subsequent practice goes more broadly or more deeply than the previous one. Sheer repetition quickly bores the learner and has little or no further effect. Only as each new practice requires his attention because of new elements in it does it serve adequately as a basis for effective learning. This is important for the student in gaining understanding: it means that concepts and principles are brought in again and again, but each time in new and more complex illustrations, so that the student continually has to think through the way in which these concepts or principles help to explain or to analyze the situation. It is important in the development of the skill for each new practice of the skill to provide opportunities for greater variety or complexity in its use. This is also true in the development of appreciation, for it means that each new work of art should demand something more of perception and provide opportunity for a greater variety and depth of emotional response. It is possible for the individual teacher, or the college as a whole, to examine the sequential nature of the learning experiences provided in various courses or throughout the college program to see the extent to which they capitalize on the opportunity for high-level learning through continuing sequential development.

An eighth condition is for the learner to set high standards of performance for himself. One of his common difficulties in college is that the student may become satisfied with mediocre performance and no longer put forth effort to learn. This is frequently a problem with the more able student. It is often necessary to help the student to acquire standards of performance that for him are high but attainable and to lead him on continually to seek greater excellence. One may ask of any teaching program about the kinds of standards that the students are expected to meet and how far they are relevant to the individual differences among the students in the class. By interviewing students one can find out what sort of standards each one has set for himself and how he knows that these are appropriate for him. One can make an independent estimate as to whether they are high but attainable, or for him relatively low and mediocre. This is one of the criteria of effective teaching.

The ninth condition is related to the eighth: to continue learning beyond the time when a teacher is available, the learner must have means for judging his performance, to be able to tell how well he is doing. Without them his standards are of no utility. Each teacher may ask himself, "Have I helped the students get some means by which they can judge the adequacy of their performance in this field? To what extent are they using this means?"

One purpose of outlining these conditions for effective learning is to suggest that their use as an indirect means of evaluating the effectiveness of teaching is less rigid, more flexible, and more relevant than the use of methods which set up an ideal description of good teaching against which teachers are checked or which arbitrarily define the proportion of lecture, discussion, laboratory demonstration, individual laboratory work, or other devices which should be used to do a good teaching job. It is possible for creative teachers to get effective results by a variety of procedures. But whatever methods they use or however they stimulate reactions, these methods of teaching do serve to provide the essential conditions for learning and may be judged fairly directly by examining the teaching in terms of the extent to which the conditions of learning are provided. Next to the direct appraisal of what students learn, this examination of the conditions of learning is most valid in evaluating teaching.

In checking the extent to which essential conditions of learning are being provided, two devices are frequently useful. If the individual teacher is doing his own check he will find the use of a tape recorder in his classroom helpful. After he becomes accustomed to recording class sessions, he and the students will not find recording inhibiting or artificial. Playing back the tapes in his own study gives him a better chance for checking on some of the conditions for learning than is possible by depending solely on his memory.

Where more than one faculty member is interested in evaluating teaching, a plan for visiting each other's classes is helpful. Using a list of conditions of learning as an observation checklist, the visiting instructor obtains information useful to talk over with the one being visited, and out of these observations and discussions often develop new and interesting ideas for trial.

A third procedure for the evaluation of teaching is the use of student opinion, which is, on some matters, very directly related to the effectiveness of teaching. Students can report on their interest in the course, on their understanding of what is expected of them, on their satisfaction with achievement in the field, on the amount and extent of their study, and the like. There are, of course, other important aspects of effective teaching which the students are not in a good position to judge, such as the soundness of the objectives, the validity of the reference material provided, the relevance of the approach. On the whole, however, it has been found that the summation of student judgments obtained from a questionnaire is positively correlated with other evidences of the effectiveness of teaching and is one of the devices which many teachers will find useful in their own efforts to improve their teaching.

A fourth procedure useful in evaluating teaching involves checking on the intelligent interest and effort which faculty members are putting into the planning and conducting of their instructional work. Effective teaching requires continuous attention. With objectives clearly in mind the teacher is reacting to clues provided by the students that indicate where his efforts are successful and where his difficulties are, and in the light of these clues the teacher modifies his own behavior so as to maximize the students' learning. This is a delicate and artistic application of all the understanding that the teacher has acquired.

One of the tragedies of colleges and universities, as with many other social institutions, is the fact that the central professional activities can become routinized and no longer occupy the focus of thought and interest of the professional staff. When this happens to faculty members, the effectiveness of their teaching drops and students do not learn nearly so much as they are capable of learning. Unfortunately, it is very common to find teachers who, after three to five years of interest and effort focused on doing a good teaching job, have shifted their concern to research, social life, campus politics, or some other sphere of activity, handling their classes in a pretty routine fashion and without the requisite continuing examination of objectives and of the learning process as it goes on in their classes. Because this is a frequent problem in colleges and universities, one of the positive evidences of effective teaching is the intelligent interest and effort put forth currently by the teacher in seeking to do the best job he can.

Such items as the following are useful indicators of this interest and effort: the development of new syllabuses, tests, reading lists, science demonstrations, films, laboratory equipment, and the like; concrete efforts to rethink and to clarify the major objectives of a course; plans

175

for new ways of teaching, for the use of new media like television, tape recorders, and the like; the development of programs for individual work, independent study, field laboratory experiences, work experiences. Evidences of interest and intelligent effort are also shown by the oral or written reports teachers make of their observations and interpretations of what students are doing in class, laboratory, or field. Faculty members may also show an active, intelligent interest in teaching by their concerned and thoughtful participation in faculty seminars on teaching. Conducting systematic studies of teaching — if they are fresh and not routine — may provide an additional indication of intelligent interest. These are matters on which the individual teacher may check himself; they may also be used by the college administration as an indication of the active intelligence of the faculty as a whole at work on the problems of teaching and learning.

These four major kinds of procedures seem to me the most promising, helpful, and practical means now available for the evaluation of college teaching. They can be used both by individual teachers and by departments or colleges as a whole. A comprehensive plan for evaluating teaching will involve all four: the development of a program of testing and other appraisals of the learning of college students; a systematic examination of the extent to which the essential conditions of learning are being provided; the use of student opinionnaires; and an inventory of evidences of continuous, intelligent interest and effort which faculty members are devoting to their teaching. To urge the use of all four procedures may seem to many to be a counsel of perfection. However, by careful planning, by distribution of responsibility among various persons and groups, and by working out a schedule which distributes the workload over the year, this comprehensive evaluation can be carried out without disrupting other important work. The need for evaluating teaching is very great. We must get to work seriously and systematically to meet this need.

Mr. Tyler is director of the Center for Advanced Study in the Behavioral Sciences at Stanford, California.

◄§ H. TAYLOR MORSE

Appraisal of the Educator: Proposals for Action

THE evaluation of teaching effectiveness is of crucial importance for two reasons. First, deans and department heads must have some assessment of teachers' competence to use when they are making recommendations for increases in salary and promotions in rank. This is an administrative reason — and external to the teacher. The second reason is internal: a teacher should have for his own use information about his teaching activities which will enable him to improve the effectiveness of his presentations.

Both of these reasons rest upon certain assumptions. The first is that the process of classroom instruction can be evaluated in a reasonably objective way by a person not immediately involved in a given teaching-learning activity — in this case the dean or department head. The second is that the individual classroom teacher can take a reasonably detached view of activities in which he is intimately engaged as party of the first part, and that he has a sincere desire to improve his performance in such activities.

Both aspects of evaluation are of intense personal concern to members of any college faculty. Both can and do provoke warm discussion in faculty circles whenever the topic is mentioned, and that is frequently. Much of this discussion is unstructured and discursive, so it should be of considerable interest to chronicle the reactions of faculty groups who address themselves systematically to the questions of the evaluation of college teaching for both administrative and personal uses.

Virginia Senders says that the most important product of the group discussions was not a collection of brand-new ideas, but the reaffirmation of the need for growth and for evaluating the ways in which growth might be achieved. Her statement would apply equally well to the discussions reported here.

The reactions of the groups to the statements of Harold Taylor and Ralph Tyler — especially to the latter — were strong but varied. Several groups believed that Tyler had so thoroughly and so satisfactorily answered the question of administrative or external evaluation of teaching that there was no point in discussing this aspect further; they went immediately to the discussion of the internal aspect: the teacher's evaluation of his activities.

Other groups were less satisfied with Tyler's proposals. It seemed fairly evident, both from the comments made in individual sections I visited, and in examining the statements of the recorders, that the idea of a systematic analysis and evaluation of teaching such as Tyler proposed was new to most of the conferees, and a number of them resisted it. One group, for example, recorded its opinion that English composition did not lend itself to the setting up of the kinds of objectives for "articulation and measurement" which Tyler proposed. They went on to say that "for an English teacher much of what he knows rates highest among his own achievements is necessarily not possible to measure." As examples of these they cited the development of students' insight into the real implications of literature, and their expanding awareness of these implications.

The fine and applied arts teachers were also uneasy about the criteria proposed by Tyler. They pointed out that the problems of evaluation in the specific fields of the arts are not uniform. "In evaluation," they specified, "no distinction should be made between teachers who do outstanding work in public performance (such as a concert pianist or organist) and those teachers who do an excellent job in the more obscure classroom teaching. In other words: the number of students a private studio teacher teaches and the number the classroom teacher has should not be a criterion for evaluating the effectiveness or value of an individual teacher." The group furthermore accepted a statement prepared by one of the members which read: "The responsibility of the art faculty at the college level is to create a foundation, not a finished product. Flexibility and the attitude of problem-solving is a more desirable end than a 'finished' painter." This is certainly not a contradiction of Tyler's proposals, and is a point of view which would doubtless have found acceptance among many representatives at the conference.

Another group, in debating Tyler's suggestions, felt that "very excellent teaching was self-evident and unusually poor teaching equally apparent. Many doubts were raised," their recorder noted, "about the possibility of establishing a set of criteria of effective teaching which could be administered, even by teachers, as a tool for appraising every teacher's effectiveness for either self-improvement or promotion." It was noted further, however, that most of the section members taught in colleges where there was in operation no systematic program of evaluation such as that proposed by Tyler. A number of them hoped that some such procedures might be introduced in their institutions, and several stated that they would attempt to review the literature in order to secure relevant materials so that these could be studied and considered by their colleagues with this end in view.

In considering some of the evidences of resistance to efforts to objectify as far as possible criteria for judging the effectiveness of teaching as a basis for promotion or increase in salary, one almost seems to find among some of the groups and individuals a contradiction, or at least an inconsistency. On the one hand some declared that teaching, especially a particular type of teaching or teaching in a particular area of instruction, did not lend itself to analysis and systematic evaluation. As one group put it rather flatly, "It was not felt that a truly analytical evaluation could be made of the artistic qualities characteristic of a good teacher."

But on the other hand, they accepted the fact that judgments and decisions had to be made. But many were reluctant to have college administrators make these decisions which have such an immediate and vital effect upon the professional career of the teacher. They felt that too often these judgments are too subjective, "based on hearsay, intuition, snap judgments, intangible impressions," and may frequently be affected by irrelevant factors. One group recorded its belief that one way to remedy this situation would be "through procuring less conservative deans. Since the good teacher [*as Taylor had pointed out*] is one who disturbs students, the really good teacher is often a radical. But deans are temperamentally unfitted for appreciating a radical." Therefore, they recommended, "Get radical deans."

Some felt that administrative evaluation of an individual teacher ought to be checked by a group of faculty colleagues, "in order that personality traits do not overweigh his value as a teacher." Others believed that promotions in rank and increases in salary should be recommended by a committee composed of administrators and elected faculty representatives. Another group, also affirming its belief in joint faculty-administration action, said further that "About one third of the group favored student participation in promotion and raising salaries of faculty members."

In still another group, which also favored joint faculty-administrative action in establishing standards and in evaluating teachers, one member was inclined to be openly skeptical about the real value of administrative judgments. This was reported by the recorder as follows:

"One teacher present assured us that he had received high praise from his superiors for one of the poorest jobs of teaching in his career. When he was writing his thesis, he set very limited objectives but concentrated his efforts on realizing them. One of them was to prepare his students to pass the examination given to all sections of introductory sociology students. His three sections had the highest average scores on the final examination. He had not even attempted to achieve many objectives that belong in such a course but their omission was not even noticed."

It is indeed unfortunate that so many classroom teachers seem to consider department heads and deans as unwilling or unable to make reasoned judgments about teaching competence as a basis for recommending promotion. Although some of the discussion groups went on record as being reasonably well satisfied with the procedures currently in use, a fairly large number expressed doubt and even opposition, as indicated above. Their belief that administrators should have their judgments supplemented or even checked by a committee of the teaching faculty is a further expression of this distrust.

As Tyler says so clearly and emphatically in his chapter, "Sound and systematic evaluation of college teaching is exceedingly rare, and yet it is highly essential to the improvement of college instruction." Teachers who are fearful lest administrative judgments be based on personal whims or irrelevancies should be heartened by reflecting upon the careful and thorough steps Tyler recommends. It could hardly be denied, moreover, that despite some instances of capriciousness, college administrators are well aware of the importance of the decisions they make, both in terms of individual careers and the professional well-being of their department or college. They are eager to make their judgments as objective, informed, and sound as possible, and surely most of them would welcome proposals for criteria which would enable them to do a more effective job in this respect.

Teachers at all levels, however, are highly sensitive about their individual teaching styles. It is almost no exaggeration to say that the great majority of college instructors consider themselves very good teachers, just as most people consider that *they* have good common sense, though admitting that this particular commodity is reasonably scarce among human beings in general. But teachers, especially at the college level, object, perhaps quite naturally, to any tendency toward the development of generally applicable norms for evaluating classroom instruction. One group summarized this feeling by stating: "There is a variety of types of good teachers. A department need not and should not be composed of all the same type."

The Need for Information and Communication

What conclusions may be drawn from the discussions of this topic by the various participants and from the reports of the recorders? It appears to me that two points emerge.

First, college teachers (if the sample attending the conference may be considered as representative) are in general not aware of the work which has been done — work involving research as well as careful analysis — to develop criteria for the evaluation of classroom teaching. Tyler's proposals should be heartening to these teachers, even though some of them felt that his points could not apply with equal validity to all subject-matter areas. It might be remarked in passing, furthermore, that presumably some of the delegates at the conference who now consider themselves "pure" classroom teachers will, in the normal course of events, assume administrative responsibilities. When this occurs they may have more occasion than they now do to refer to the proposals made in Tyler's chapter.

The second point that emerges is that there is not enough communication between administrative and teaching staffs concerning the criteria for recommending promotions and increases in salary. Studies such as that undertaken under the sponsorship of the Senate Committee on Education of the University of Minnesota (2) show that the three criteria most frequently mentioned by administrators as a basis for promotion are teaching ability, research ability, and extent and quality of publications, in that order. Administrators doubtless assume

181

that teaching faculty members are aware of these and other criteria, which may differ in relative emphasis from one department to another. Classroom teachers, however, may claim, often with considerable justification, that criteria for promotion are seldom made explicit, and that, even if items are mentioned — such as "teaching ability," which usually heads all such lists — the *means* by which such ability is evaluated are seldom if ever explained in detail.

It follows that it would be highly desirable, and would contribute both to better reciprocal understanding and to improvement of faculty morale, if the criteria for promotion and the means used in arriving at judgments concerning the facts could be discussed as dispassionately as possible by faculty and administration. This should be done at a time free from the tensions and pressures of budget-making.

Summary of Specific Proposals

The specific proposals made and recorded in the various discussion groups were fairly extensive, as might be supposed, and of course coincided with many of the suggestions made in the literature on this subject. It is perhaps sufficient for our purpose to catalogue the proposals here in summary fashion, without making any attempt to list them in any order of importance, or to elaborate them.

Among the criteria proposed were the following: research ability and scholarly productivity; results of student evaluation forms; reports based on visitation of classrooms; committee activity; extracurricular club advising; enthusiasm for subject; use made of time outside class; national recognition; students' achievement — preferably measured by pre-test and post-test; comments of colleagues; comments of students; classroom visitation by department head; systematic study of some outside field; production and revision of study guides, outline sheets, syllabuses, tests, and the like; change in teaching methods; membership in faculty research clubs for reporting current research; activity in professional associations and projects; community service; subsequent success of one's students; counseling activities; setting up of worthwhile objectives.

Because the first of these — research ability and scholarly productivity — was the subject of so much discussion, it may be desirable to comment upon it briefly. There were, of course, the usual debates about research versus teaching as the major factor in promotion. I will note two dominant aspects of this discussion — which can be triggered by merely mentioning the subject in almost any group of faculty members.

One of these was the opinion that research should not be defined too narrowly. Reference was occasionally made to what W. H. Cowley had said about *pandemic* teaching and *conceptual* research. Although it was evident that these concepts were fairly new to most conferees who discussed them, many were quite willing to accept this broadened definition of research.

The other aspect of this discussion was ably presented by one group, whose recorder wrote as follows:

"It was felt that teaching competence and research competence are both to be considered as bases for promotions; it was agreed that in the University situation, research competence is weighted more heavily, whereas in the small college teaching competence is in many cases the important consideration. Maybe then we should differentiate between criteria for promotion at the University and at the small college. We agree that research can be carried on in any situation, although, in general, research on a broad scale is handled by the University. We agree further that we should aim to produce at a high level whether we are engaged in either teaching or research."

Evaluation for Self-Improvement

The second subject for discussion, as noted at the beginning of this chapter, concerned the development of an analytical evaluation of teaching for the instructor's self-improvement. There was inevitably a considerable overlapping of the items proposed with those marshaled in answer to the first question — evaluation for promotion. The education and psychology group therefore decided that a definition of terms was in order. They pointed out the following interpretations of the word analytical: (a) implying more than mere helpful suggestions, (b) referring to a substantive evaluation, (c) diagnostic.

They recorded another qualification about the main question by distinguishing between *muchness* (quantitative and measurable aspects) and *goodness* (qualitative or nonmeasurable aspects) of teaching.

Among the numerous proposals made in answer to the major question there were two which were the object of considerable and extended (and often heated) discussion.

Tape Recordings

The first was the use of the tape recorder to preserve classroom lectures and discussions to be played back in the privacy of the instructor's office or study as a basis for his self-improvement. It appeared, significantly enough, that very few of the conferees had ever done this. Nevertheless many of them had decided opinions about it. One group which expanded its reactions came up with the following opinions about tape recordings. First, recordings require much time to listen to, let alone to analyze and evaluate. Second, there are no criteria by which to evaluate the results. Third, a criterion — some common denominator not yet pointed out — might be found to use in distinguishing between good and bad teaching. Finally, since at least one study has shown that when another class listens to a taped lecture, it gets different impressions than did the class originally lectured to, teachers might well give thought to clearer and better organization and presentation of their material.

In spite of the novelty of using tape recordings as a method for self-improvement, it appears reasonable to conclude that for a variety of reasons this technique will probably not be widely used among college classroom teachers. But those who are interested in discovering the uses which might be made of tape recordings to determine the relative effectiveness of the lecture and the discussion methods of presenting subject-matter content would do well to look up the fascinating experiments made by Benjamin Bloom and his associates at the University of Chicago (1, pp. 23–46).

The Use of Student Opinionnaires

The other matter on which considerable warmth and diversity of opinion was expressed was that of forms on which students rate the instructor. Practically all groups agreed that these had some value in self-improvement, but by no means were all of them ready to accept the ratings at face value.

One group stated that such student opinionnaire forms should be used only for the individual teacher's self-improvement, and not as an administrative device in determining promotions. With this position there was general agreement among the conferees, as there is in the literature on the subject. This same group felt that at times "students may have a myopic view which changes as years go by." Another group believed that students "tend to be too kind in filling out questionnaires."

In this respect it was possible to sample opinion directly from the consumers' point of view. There were fourteen students from Minnesota colleges, representing the National Student Association, who had been invited to the conference, and participated as regular delegates. With reference to rating forms one recorder stated: "The student representative from NSA expressed herself with considerable conviction stating no matter how 'threatless' the situation, students rate the professors higher than the students feel they deserve." The recorder went on to note that "Many members of the group agreed with the student but were inclined to believe that the criticism directed toward student reactions applied to the subjective type rather than the standardized form."

Another of the discussion sections had a good deal to say about student rating forms. Their comments are perhaps best presented in the words of their recorder.

Reaction was much more favorable to tests of student opinion. Most members present had had experience with student evaluation of teaching and courses. They seemed agreed that student questionnaires were useful tools for learning what students think of one's teaching, and that they provide valid results in this sense. It is common for student opinion reports tabulated by others than the teacher to contain only the class profile and to omit the differential reactions of individual class members. Some teachers please the top level, some the intermediate level, and some the lower level. Even colleagues rating their fellows may be pleased with teaching that is effective at a particular level and rate accordingly. In general students are found to be "moderate" in their evaluation of their teachers — as in everything else!

Several members related their violent negative reactions to professors during their first classes. Later they came to delight in classes with these same professors. Several copies of the student questionnaire used at the University of Minnesota were on hand. In checking over the items in the questionnaire, members challenged some items as irrelevant to the teaching-learning process. One item gave rise to considerable discussion. It concerned the methods of avoiding talking over the students' heads and the consequence of not avoiding it. It was felt that in ungraded classes a teacher had to make a judgment about the levels of student capacity present and make a decision about the level one would speak to. The result was likely to be that one talked over the heads of some students and provided tedium for others. It was suggested that a flexible method be used so that the levels of all students were met some of the time.

There is certainly no question but that college faculties are very much interested in student rating forms and in their potential usefulness for self-improvement in teaching. Many of them, it would appear, are nevertheless covertly or openly suspicious about their accuracy, reliability, and validity. They should be reassured to know that a very thorough study of this matter has been made by John Riley and his associates (3). Among other very interesting conclusions, these authors report that the ratings given college teachers by their students were consistent with those made by trained, experienced observers, and that the quality of work done by a student in the course did not significantly affect his rating of the instructor.

Conclusion

Many college teachers are skeptical about discussions or conferences concerned with pedagogy rather than with subject matter. It is conceivable that some of the delegates to this conference may have wondered, before they came, if any worthwhile results might be expected from attendance at a conference on college teaching. The great majority of them, however, were in an accepting mood, due, in part, to the careful briefing given the representatives before the opening of the conference. Once the discussion started, the delegates attacked the problems presented with vigor and spirit. That the conference will have a direct impact on the classroom teaching and other professional activities of a sizeable proportion of the teachers in the colleges of Minnesota for a long time to come cannot be better illustrated than by a conclusion drawn from the English literature group. "*A good teacher knows that there are specific behavior patterns for himself which he can acquire by effort and which will improve his teaching.* We must work out better evaluation methods for these, never losing sight of the more valuable immeasurables."

REFERENCES

1. Bloom, Benjamin S. "The Thought Process of Students in Discussion." Chapter I in Sidney J. French. *Accent on Teaching.* New York: Harper and Brothers, 1954.
2. Keller, Robert J., and John E. Dobbin. "Faculty Promotional Policies and Practices at the University of Minnesota Based on Letters of Administrative Officers." Bureau of Institutional Research, University of Minnesota, April 1948. Unpublished.

3. Riley, John W., Jr., Bruce F. Ryan, and Marcia Lifshitz. *The Student Looks at His Teacher*. New Brunswick: Rutgers University Press, 1950. o.p.

THIS chapter, prepared by Dean Morse of the General College of the University of Minnesota, sums up the Friday afternoon discussions of the nine groups mentioned in the footnote on page 148. Further details are given in Dean Morse's article, "The Minnesota Centennial Conference on College Teaching," in the June 1958 *Journal of Higher Education.*

ENDS AND MEANS

≈§ EDGAR DALE

New Techniques of Teaching

It would be remarkable and extraordinarily useful if any of us here at this centennial of a great state said something so significant about the improvement of college teaching that it would be a benchmark for another ten or twenty years, if we said or did something that would help our students get in charge of their own lives, their own minds. The chances are against it because some of the complex problems of teaching — or communication if you prefer a more inclusive term — are inherent in man and society. We show stubborn resistance to self-improvement and to seeing ourselves as others see us. Our capacity for self-deception is remarkable. We want to be comforted when we are troubled but not troubled when we are comfortable. Innovation is fun for some, enervating for many.

We do not readily admit that our educational system is shot through with a premature verbalism, an empty symbolism, an acceptance of signs or symbols of reality for the reality itself, a glut of second-hand experiences. The successful management and control of symbolic behavior is rough and tough to teach and to learn. Further, we are probably kidding ourselves if we think that some new scientific invention, some psychological discovery, is likely to give us an important educational breakthrough, lead us into the promised land. It would be folly indeed to predict that such a breakthrough was impossible, but I think we already know the major ingredients for a massive breakthrough in methods of improving collegiate teaching.

First, we shall have to know exactly what we want — to define our expectations in terms of actual behavior. We must know what outcomes to expect from our teaching, and aim directly at these learning targets. The work edited by Benjamin S. Bloom (2) at the University

191

of Chicago, which develops a rigorous classification of educational objectives, is helpful at this point.

Second, the teaching program must take into account the cultural characteristics of our democratic society. In short, our goals of teaching must get reinforcement, not antagonism, from the alumni, the parents of college students, and the influential public. Obviously this can be carried so far that a college follows but does not lead.

Third, there must be well-grounded, devoted, experimentally minded instructors who have spent their lifetimes working on improved methods for teaching their particular subject matters.

Fourth, these teachers must be highly rewarded through values held high in the society — in ours these would be money and prestige, sometimes synonymous terms.

Fifth, there must be especially skillful methods of determining the extent and nature of students' learning; samples of desired behavior must be recorded and then carefully analyzed and diagnosed by the instructors, with individual suggestions given the student for his improvement. The learner must have fairly immediate knowledge of where he is succeeding and failing and appropriate remedial practice should then be carried out.

Sixth, the teaching staff must have access to the latest equipment which might conceivably have a favorable effect on improved teaching. It must be the best that money can buy.

Is this visionary? Not at all. Indeed we have already achieved this kind of teaching effectiveness in one department of the Ohio State University. The chief instructor is W. Woodrow Hayes, affectionately known as Woody Hayes, the subject taught is football, the record of success is a series of Big Ten football championships.

This teaching excellence is nothing new. Around 530 B.C. Xenophanes, the Greek philosopher, was complaining that in the eyes of citizens the winner of a footrace or of the pentathlon, the wrestler, the boxer, the charioteer, would be resplendent with glory — that strength would be preferred to glorious wisdom. He went on to say that "the city is not on that account one whit better governed . . . does not enrich the innermost parts of the state." Obviously Xenophanes was a crank, an addled egghead.

Perhaps I was too sweeping in my remarks when I said we already know the ingredients of effective teaching. We know the ingredients of *training* but perhaps not of *education*. Let us define training as subjecting students (or should we call them pupils?) to an experience in which our aim is to have them reproduce that experience, master a very specific skill. To be perfect would be to imitate the model perfectly, to be a facile memorizer or imitator.

In education, however, our aim is to have a student learn more than the model exemplifies, to get something qualitatively different from what has been presented. In short, a creative element must be added.

Excellent educational materials are, in Whitehead's descriptive phrase, "suffused with suggestiveness." The instructor or writer or producer does not present a complete package for memorization or imitation. He presents a part of it and the student figures the rest of it out for himself. *Educational* material thrives on inference — on what is not there. With *training* materials inference is at a minimum, the experiences to be undergone are all preplanned. You do not need to think; you accept and imitate.

I do not say that there is no desirable element of training, of imitation, or repetitiveness in education. But the student imitates or reproduces a master (as have many artists), first to understand and then to transcend him.

The danger resulting from uncritical and unthinking imitation of what the professor, the textbook, or the film "says" is that our students become mere replicas or shadows of their instructors — unthinking conformers. We can be alike but we ought to be thoughtfully alike. We can be different, but we ought to be thoughtfully different. One hazard of mass education, of the use of larger and larger classes, is that the instructor must exactly define the right answers and give grades and marks on this basis. The student answers questions but he does not question answers. You may say that this is not a necessary concomitant of huge classes, but the mere fact of size makes it difficult to do anything else. We shall not get differentiated responses if differentiated responses are not rewarded by those who make up the tests.

As we turn to large classes as one way out of our present shortage of money and able instructors, we must face this question: Are we unthinkingly accepting a philosophy of training? Will our larger classes be instruments of training or instruments of education? If they are not to be instruments of training, what are we doing or what can we do in the larger class that requires and indeed ensures thinking?

As college instructors get shorter in supply are students going to be lectured to death, as President Charles W. Cole of Amherst has recently suggested? Will passivity rather than participation and interaction be a final result? What are we already doing? Paul L. Dressel and Lewis B. Mayhew say that "Observations of classes and interviews with students suggest that students in typical humanities courses read assignments from textbooks, and then come to class either to listen passively to a teacher tell them *about* some work of art or to listen to or see a work *about* which they have studied. In either event they are acquiring knowledge but have little experience related to other objectives." (5, p. 171.)

The other day on our campus an unusually frank student said to his instructor after class, "I can almost hear the wheels buzzing around in your head when you are teaching this class. But my wheels aren't buzzing. I'm just a spectator." Is there anything new that can be said about participation, about involvement, about interaction as we think about fresh approaches to college teaching? It is an old problem.

Plato discussed this and had Socrates say to Phaedrus:

You know, Phaedrus, that's the strange thing about writing, which makes it truly analogous to painting. The painter's products stand before us as though they were alive; but if you question them, they maintain a most majestic silence. It is the same with written words: they seem to talk to you as though they were intelligent, but if you ask them anything about what they say, from a desire to be instructed, they go on telling you just the same thing for ever. And once a thing is put in writing, the composition, whatever it may be, drifts all over the place, getting into the hands not only of those who understand it, but equally of those who have no business with it; it doesn't know how to address the right people, and not address the wrong. And when it is ill-treated and unfairly abused it always needs its parent to come to its help, being unable to defend or help itself. (8, p. 158.)

Plato was himself the author of the *Phaedo*, the *Symposium*, the *Republic*, and many other dialogues. Yet he remained highly sensitive to the influence of his mentor, Socrates, upon his own thinking and life. He was concerned about the possible dogmatism of the written word, and also about the inability of the reader to question the writer as he might question the speaker — the hazard of mastering words but not their meaning. Socrates says: "And it is no true wisdom that you offer your disciples, but only its semblance; for by telling them of many things without teaching them you will make them seem to know much, while for the most part they know nothing; and as men filled, not with wisdom, but with the conceit of wisdom, they will be a burden to their fellows" (8, p. 157).

Will our proposed use of television tell students of many things without really teaching them?

Jacques Barzun makes the point in *Teacher in America* that "every college should . . . be dedicated to intellect — not in the sense of pedantry, or verbalism, or highbrow superiority, but in the sense of mind, free and restless in its desire to experience, comprehend, and use reality" (1, p. 213).

Great teachers have always used this approach. I assume that when President Garfield talked about a college as Mark Hopkins on one end of a log with a student at the other, he meant that they were exchanging meaningful experiences that were rich with reality. But one hundred years ago Mark Hopkins was asking his students, "What do you think?" as contrasted with "What do you know?" Nor was he content to teach without the modern tools of that day. He used an anatomical model of a man which he had purchased from the Albany Medical College by pledging six hundred dollars of his salary. He was also one of the pioneers in the use of the blackboard. By the way, some of his colleagues didn't think he was much of a scholar. Hopkins made education personal. He made it real.

What new teaching methods will help us "experience, comprehend, and use reality?" Is there a danger as the mass media take more and more of our time that we shall have a glut of secondhand, shallow experiences? Will we in Macaulay's phrase "extinguish the feeble spark of intellect with huge amounts of fuel?"

John Herman Randall, Jr., in his presidential address before the American Philosophical Association in December 1956, quotes Herodotus as saying, "The eyes are better witnesses than the ears." Randall notes the occasion when it was said: the king, Kandaules, had been talking at great length about the beauty of his wife, Nyssia. A companion who could stand it no longer said, "Kandy, what you are saying is probably all true enough, but as Heraclitus says, 'the eyes are better witnesses than the ears.' " So, after arranging it with the king, he went to have a look at her — real, firsthand experience. Randall adds, "Now, for my money, that is a tough-minded, genuinely American philosophy. Looking is better than just talking. A good bull session is all right; but let's 'open our eyes, and go out looking — looking for what we can find in our world.' " (12, p. 18.)

How can college teachers make use of the real and — where this is impossible — the simulated reality? First of all, many of the great realities of life are going forward on our campuses. Could we perhaps think of our students as apprentice historians, scientists, teachers, musicians, mathematicians? Guy Stanton Ford in the *AAUP Bulletin* tells of the head of the history department in a small college who sent many excellent graduate students to the University of Minnesota. He was not a great historian, not a writer, not a great scholar, but he got results. Ford was puzzled by this and I can only guess at the nature of the apprenticeship. Perhaps the history professor had the spirit of a learner, perhaps his students learned how to shape their ambitions, use their talents wisely. Perhaps they witnessed the reality of an enthusiastic student of history. Perhaps they saw Emerson's "man thinking."

Our professional schools seem to have learned this lesson quite well. A professor of labor law who has an office next to mine is dealing in his classes with the complex cases of administration and arbitration with which he is personally concerned. The new medical curriculum at Western Reserve University introduces the student earlier to the realities of medicine by making him an "apprentice" doctor. The teacher in training spends time in the school long before she takes her practice teaching. In 1893 Woodrow Wilson wrote on the political student's need for firsthand experience.

He must cross-examine the experience of government officials; he must hear the din of conventions, and see their intrigue; he must witness the scenes of election day. He must know how men who are not students regard government and its affairs. He will get many valuable suggestions from such men on occasion; better than that, he will learn the available approaches to such men's thoughts.

This is not to commend the writer on politics to narrow "practical" views and petty comments; . . . it is only to keep his *generalizations firmly bottomed on fact and experience.* . . . You cannot lift truth so high that men cannot reach it; the only caution to be observed is, that you do not ask them to climb where they cannot go without leaving terra firma. (13, p. 36f.; italics mine.)

We are beginning to introduce more reality into our teaching of modern languages. Modern textbooks in foreign languages may be accompanied by recordings. Such new approaches aim to develop a command of the language for communication in speech, writing, and in reading; to help the student think automatically in the second language. George Borglum of Wayne State University, in describing the new teaching process (in an undated mimeographed report), says it bears "no resemblance to the decoding, word-learning, rule-remembering tyranny of the traditional language class." The course in French includes forty chapters, twelve hundred color slides, and forty tape recordings. There is a systematic program for class presentation of new lessons and this is coupled with a self-instruction laboratory.

This Modern Language Audio-Visual Project is an association of official representatives of several universities, national organizations, and public school systems interested in developing and testing audio-visual materials for use in language instruction. It includes the University of Michigan, Purdue University, the University of Tennessee, Wayne State University, and the University of Minnesota.

Middlebury College has long been experimenting with improved methods of teaching foreign languages. They think that language laboratories have in the past not adequately separated the spoken and written aspects of the language. Fernand L. Marty of Middlebury says that "too much attention is paid to pronunciation and that the main point in the audio language skills is to train the student so that he will be able to understand the spoken language and will be able to make himself understood without difficulty" (11, p. 177).

Simulating Reality

When we begin to analyze the reality principle in teaching we see that some realities are easily experienced, some are simple but rare (there are no live mongooses in the United States), and some realities are too costly or too complicated for classroom use. We must therefore simulate reality. *Fortune* for March 1958 describes a business game, run by the American Management Association at Saranac Lake, which costs each participant $500. Forty executives, divided into five competing teams, make decisions on price, production, marketing, research, and development, doing the equivalent of ten years' business in two weeks. The association says that the aim is to make generalists out of specialists.

ENDS AND MEANS

John Dennis McDonald and F. M. Ricciardi point out in the same *Fortune* article that "modern simulation . . . is a mathematical model expressed in formulas programed into a computer" (10, p. 140). They go on to say that the success of such simulation depends upon "the degree of participation of the players; how well the real world is represented by the model; and the application in real life of what is learned in the game. . . . the criteria of success are involvement, adequacy, and transfer."

The same kind of thinking is suggested in a speech by Dorothy Fosdick in 1955 at the Tenth Annual National Conference on Higher Education in Chicago.

> . . . the most useful training for all students would be one which gave them practical experience in putting themselves sympathetically into the situation of the responsible government official.
>
> For example, why could you not hold a series of required assemblies each year, or alternatively, give a special course, in which, on one issue after another, every student had to face the question, "Supposing you were Secretary of State: what would you do?" . . . What would you recommend to the President of the United States as a satisfactory disarmament program?
>
> . . . Why not hold model cabinet meetings, model national security council meetings, or even model planning staff meetings? To throw light on what senators and representatives are up against, why not set up model foreign relations and foreign affairs committee meetings, or a model meeting of the joint Congressional committee on atomic energy? Students intending to be specialists in foreign affairs could act as experts and prepare draft memoranda and position papers or present oral advice. Their job would be to analyze assumptions and estimates, evaluate alternative possible courses of action and their respective risks and costs, and make recommendations. (7, pp. 22, 23.)

Can we convey important direct or simulated realities by means of new teaching techniques? How effective, for example, is television teaching in the college? Will it help students experience, comprehend, and use reality? Or does it chiefly present shadows — not on the wall of a cave, but on a twenty-four-inch screen?

Hideya Kumata of Michigan State has prepared *An Inventory of Instructional Television Research.* Miami University has published its Report No. 2, "Miami University Experimental Study in Instructional Procedures." Charles R. Carpenter and others at Penn State have reported the results of extensive study of closed-circuit television in the fields of psychology, chemistry, economics, and music appreciation. Here are some tentative findings.

1. In courses whose aim is simply to convey information, television instruction does as well as but not any better than other methods of teaching. Its advantage, of course, is that it can teach large numbers of students at one time.

2. Costs of large groups taught on television by regular faculty members are roughly the same as the costs of small groups taught by graduate students. But careful accounting has not been done, and data on actual savings are lacking.

3. Sometimes when there is some initial advantage to the television teaching it seems to be counterbalanced by loss as determined by a retention test at a later date. We do not yet have any long-time retention data.

4. The benefits of interaction and feedback held as important in the small class do not seem to show up significantly when contrasted with a method of teaching with television by a superior instructor. This is not to say that feedback and interaction are not important parts of the teaching process. It is to say only that able instructors as lecturers can often anticipate, as a result of their previous experiences with smaller classes, just what kinds of reactions students develop and consider important. It may suggest, too, that the instructor of the small class teaches it in the same way he would teach a large class.

5. The tests used do not deal adequately with broad educational objectives such as motivation, problem-solving, tastes, and other general outcomes of education.

6. The Miami University Report No. 2 says that "students in television courses tend to become disenchanted with television as a means of instruction during the course of the year" (p. 56).

7. A policy report on college-credit courses taught over television at Michigan State University recommended that the university adopt a conservative policy with regard to giving credit until more evidence is in.

We should realize that television is a medium which conveys speech, pictures, demonstrations, charts, graphs, and the like. To ask if we can teach with television is almost like asking: Can we teach with books? with lectures? with demonstrations? We must not be led by the use of television for large classes and for individual viewing with the instructor absent into thinking that these are the only ways of using it. We might also pipe television into a classroom and the instructor could use it as a part of the class discussion just as he might use a film. Indeed if we think about television as a way of projecting an audio-visual-verbal message into the classroom or to a student's desk we are likely to be clearer about its function.

We should not assume, then, that the television medium will always be used only as a substitute for a large lecture room. Nor should we assume that what is taught is a kind of substitute for a textbook. What is broadcast may not be a typical lecture at all: it might be instructions on how to use the card catalogue and other facilities of the library, or safety precautions in the chemistry laboratory. The television camera can show the three thousand freshmen in a large university what they would see on a first visit to the college library — maybe they would see it even better through the camera's eye.

We should make use of what the camera can do — record or transmit a situation or experience which would otherwise not be brought to the class at all. This might be Harry Truman at Yale, Ezra Benson in our WOSU studio in Columbus, an interview with a United States senator, a briefing session of the United Nations delegation.

This is not fanciful. It is already being done by the Educational Television and Radio Center in cooperation with NBC in distributing "Briefing Session" and "Decisions for Research" live to about half of the thirty-one educational television stations and by film to the rest of them.

I'd like to put in here what I think may be an unlooked-for residue in the use of television for educational purposes. Perhaps there is a chance of using educational television for establishing better communication between town and gown. We have become so specialized in our universities that, as President Robert M. Hutchins once said, "even the anatomists at Chicago could not talk intelligently to each other unless they were both working on the same parts of the body." And a Columbus, Ohio, businessman, in chatting with a professor at Ohio State, said, "You know, you fellows don't make as much money as we do but you do have certain advantages. You have your quarter off each year and every seven years you have your bacchanalian year."

Through "Sunrise Semester" the people of New York are discovering what a professor of literature is like. Through the NBC program

"Decisions for Research" the viewers see what specialists in physiology and other fields actually do. Here is a way of relating ourselves to the public that will pay big dividends in making the university more personal, less anonymous.

In March 1958 there were thirty-one educational television stations operating. Of these nine were college- or university-owned — University of Illinois, Michigan State University, University of Nebraska, University of North Carolina, Ohio State University, University of Houston, University of Washington, University of Wisconsin, and the University of Utah. Five were campus-located with cooperative ownership — University of Alabama, Alabama Polytechnic Institute, Harvard University–M.I.T.–Lowell Institute–Boston Symphony, University of Minnesota, Oregon State College. And four of the stations were commercially operated by educational institutions — University of Notre Dame, Iowa State College, Loyola University, University of Missouri.

What about the Lecture?

First, there is a real place for an expert communicator to explain and demonstrate a field of subject matter. If the subject matter is a predictable one — does not vary sharply from year to year — if there really are standardized explanations, we had better *record* this material in a textbook, on a film, on a tape recording.

But where the quality of the students and the nature of the subject matter will vary significantly from time to time, then we may present it as a live lecture. The lecturer must, however, do more than demonstrate, more than explain, more than impart knowledge. He must demonstrate "man thinking," illuminating, qualifying, synthesizing, entertaining ideas, exploring, working on unfinished business. He ought also to be an exemplar of "man thinking" in the field of subject matter on which he is lecturing. Whether he gives this lecture to fifty or five hundred students does not matter much. Everyone must see and hear whether in the same room or another one.

Why not film what he says and use this instead of having him appear live the next time the course is offered? There are two defects. First, the recording, whether visual or aural, lacks some of the freshness and vitality of the original. Second, when you tape-record, or film, or kinescope a live event the student must use the whole thing in order to review it — he can't skim a recording or a film. We can read a lecture two or three times as fast as we can listen to it.

Today, however, the able lecturer can supplement his lecture with short bits of film, recordings, flip-over charts, 2″ x 2″ slides, or large cellophane slides shown with an overhead projector. If you read the report of the Miami University study on television you will find that this supplementation is now occurring. The staff developing audio-visual materials has increased at Miami from two to six. Just as we must have technical assistance in a chemistry or psychology labora-tory, so we need technical assistance in using the new tools of in-struction.

Improving Textbooks

Why have we said so little these past years about the improvement of college textbooks? I don't know of a single dime that foundations are giving for the improvement of the textbook, the most widely used teaching medium in the college. (Lee J. Cronbach (4) has discussed the problem of text materials.)

What are some of the things we need to know about textbooks? We need to know how wide and deep the conceptual range of a textbook can be. If you have one college group with a median at the twenty-fifth percentile of all college students and another at the ninetieth, something has to be shifted or changed in the instructional program to meet the needs of the groups. How do you do it? Obviously more concrete experience and more explanation by the instructor are re-quired for the less able class.

We need to know how textbooks are used by college instructors. Do they follow them closely? Adapt them wisely? To what extent is the text really the curriculum?

How can college textbooks have built-in flexibility, provide for local adaptations and changes? How can they be tied in with films and other educational media as McGraw-Hill has already done with some of its college texts?

I wonder if a series of systematic presentations might not be sound. Maybe at the outset of a course we could use film or television or drama (*Antigone*, for example) to sharply etch a key problem. Perhaps there are complicated explanations that could be visualized through-out the course. Must we write entirely new textbooks or guides to instruction to coordinate them with new audio-visual presentations? Sometimes we will.

Is there danger that highly systematized programs will over-plan for the instructor? Would we be better off to keep the systematic, organized, tightly integrated approach at a minimum and require greater resourcefulness from students and instructors? Certainly we need to discover which subjects can best be taught in this highly systematic way and which ones require much more adaptation to individual needs.

We need to have a better understanding of the grading of college textbooks. We need more artful exposition. A professor once told me of a student who complained about the difficulty of the textbook — one he had written. The professor replied, "Thank you. I certainly wouldn't be happy if you had found it easy to read." Textbooks should not aim to be either hard or easy; they should be clear. And if their prose is graceful, so much the better. Too many textbooks are juiceless, arid summaries of secondary sources.

Are we making adequate use of the paperbacks which enable the student to own, mark up, and re-read his own books? The paperbacks have changed markedly. Once they nearly always had a girl on the cover and no cover on the girl. College graduates — even from the best colleges — are reading too few excellent books. The college is a place to form the habits that will result in a lifetime of reading books. Here is where they get into the habit of using books either as stimulants for visionary thinking or as myopiates — tranquilizers for shortsighted people.

The Audio-Visual Center

If the college or university plans to make use of all the modern ways of communicating ideas, it will have to have some kind of audio-visual center. Large universities will be producing their own films as do Minnesota, Syracuse, Indiana, Iowa, Wisconsin, Southern California, and many others. Indeed there is a University Film Producers' Association with one hundred fifty members. Of these at least fifty are producing films as a part of a planned production program. Most of this production will be in subject-matter fields, some of it will be in the field of research.

Increasingly these departments are producing for combined campus and television use. Prints are sold to other universities and many programs are made available through the National Educational Television network.

Chart and graph service is a part of the work of the audio-visual center. Most of the departments of the Ohio State University have made use of this service — with most emphasis on agriculture, home economics, military science, business, accounting, bacteriology, psychology, music. Almost half of the work is in producing slides and filmstrips. Tape recording is a common activity of the audio-visual center. Some centers, especially those housed in libraries, will have extensive recordings, both tape and disk. Film projection service is usually a part of the work of the audio-visual center. On our campus such service is available merely through a telephone call. We also have professional assistance in film selection.

James Finn (6) has indicated that we shall not get far in our use of new kinds of materials until they are integrated into a system. We have done this pretty well with books through library service. Now we face the problem of efficient distribution of ideas through other media.

The NEA Department of Audio-Visual Education series of publications on planning schools for the use of audio-visual materials presents in pamphlet No. 4, *Audio-Visual Centers in Colleges and Universities*, illustrations and patterns of audio-visual centers in institutions of higher education; the price of the pamphlet is $1.50.

A New Concept of Librarianship

The body of knowledge has become so vast that not even the specialist can encompass his own field. Instead of trying to cover the ground, let us learn how to uncover it. The best we can do is to help the student to get his ignorance organized, to develop his desire to learn, and to master the methods of learning. In short, one of the major aims of a college education is to learn how to learn — how to read critically, how to frame answerable questions, how to find the answers to questions, how to develop and use bibliographies, how to learn to use the rich resources of the library.

The modern library is concerned with three problems: the storing, retrieving, and dissemination of ideas. The best ideas in the world are found in the college library. It does take a little too long, sometimes, to find them.

New Techniques of Teaching

Obviously we now have new methods of storing ideas which the library must use. These are tape recordings — some of them on continuous tape for language study, filmstrips, 2″ x 2″ slides, microfilms, 16mm films, microcards, transparencies for the use of overhead projectors, maps, models.

As we look to the future we shall have video tapes — the tapes that obviate the need for film. It may be that these will be in the form of a cartridge which can be easily loaded into a projector and viewed individually — returning to Edison's first idea of the motion picture projector. Already in Franklin County and elsewhere in Ohio, the public libraries are circulating huge amounts of excellent 16mm film to homes for individual and group viewing. Isn't it curious that the average professor has far more electronic equipment in his home than is easily available in his classroom? When will our classrooms catch up with our kitchens?

It is significant that the *Saturday Review of Literature* shortened its name to the *Saturday Review* when it became concerned with modern media such as films and recordings. If we really believe that students must become responsible for their own education we must give them guidance and materials in our modernized libraries.

As we begin to think hard about new techniques of teaching, especially those which emphasize the use of much larger classes, I suggest that we set up some standard questions to ask in this field.

1. Does the method make learning a joint enterprise of professor and student (Guy Stanton Ford's phrase). Does it in the long run give more time for a more personal approach to students, or does it depersonalize education — transform it into training, a strait-jacketing conformity?

2. Does it improve the self-esteem of the instructor, make him feel that he is doing a better job, enhance his respect for his own competence? Or does it make him feel that teachers are being robotized? A story is told about a psychiatrist who wanted to be more efficient. He decided that instead of taking time to sit and listen to his patients he would merely record what the patient said and listen to it later. It seemed to work well until one day when having a cup of coffee at the drugstore he saw his patient, who at that moment was supposed to be in his office. The psychiatrist asked how he happened to be there. The patient simply said: "Well, you found it very efficient to record my

thoughts so I did my own recording at home. Right now my recorder is speaking to your recorder."

3. Does it really economize the time of both student and professor, give them additional time to do those things they consider especially worthwhile? Let us also ask What are we going to do with the time we save? Further, it is not always appropriate to ask for efficiency. A straight line may be the shortest distance between two points, but is it art?

4. Does it give the student more time for intelligently practicing the reality of the sought-for skill, attitude, or understanding under the wise supervision of a professional? More time to think, to interact, to discuss? Is there an opportunity for maturely facing the realities of life or are there many rehearsals with no shows?

5. Does it put more and more responsibility on the student for taking charge of his own education or does it bind him more closely to routines set by others? Does it make the student a prisoner of a mechanized process or does he become increasingly able to learn without being taught?

6. Does the method provide for a variety of novel and useful experiences? Does it make use of all the modern tools for storing, retrieving, and disseminating ideas?

7. Where appropriate, does the method of teaching make use of the principle of graded experiences — taking into account the conceptual development within a field of subject matter?

8. Is shift or change within the subject so great that it is relatively pointless to make use of standardized, recorded experiences such as those of a textbook, a film or kinescope, or a tape-recorded lecture?

9. Is there a danger that we shall overemphasize the instrument of teaching and forget the student? A story from the January 1958 issue of *Supervision* (p. 33) tells of two zealous camera fans who met in New Orleans' French Quarter and immediately began gabbing about their experiences.

"This morning," said one, "I encountered a horrible-looking old hag in Jackson Square, huddled under a bundle of rags. She was homeless, penniless and hungry. But she told me that she was once a countess and lived in one of the Pontalba apartments. Nowadays she has no family or friends — just a wretched old woman living in filth and poverty."

"The poor thing," exclaimed the other photographer. "What did you give her?" "Well, it was sunny," the first replied, "so I gave her f:22 at 1/100th."

In Conclusion

For more than 2,500 years we have had sophisticated observations on the best ways of learning. Heraclitus told us that the eyes are better witnesses than the ears. Plato was worried about the use of manuscripts and wanted lively interaction with the author. The Duke of Urbino wanted only manuscripts in his big fifteenth-century Italian library — no printed books. Wordsworth, disturbed by wide use of woodcut illustrations in the newspapers of 1848, wrote a sonnet ending:

> Must eyes be all in all, the tongue and ear
> Nothing? Heaven keep us from a lower stage.

In the 1890's new methods of high-speed printing gave us ways of making pictures much more widely used in books and newspapers. Color processes are still so expensive that few college textbooks contain extensive color photographs.

In the 1900's we introduced motion pictures, added radio and sound films in 1930, and television and tape recordings about 1940. Our job now is to integrate these materials into a system of teaching, to get their costs down so that we can all afford them. Our problem is to get balanced communication — speaking *and* listening, writing *and* reading, viewing *and* overt doing, and a balance in the media themselves. The central aim always in colleges is to help students learn when they are away from their instructors — in short to learn how to learn and to love learning. I see no easy way of achieving that balance except through basic research plus sophisticated observation.

The word *new* in "new teaching techniques" has many nuances. It means fresh or unused, or recent origin, or occurring anew. Some of the techniques I have discussed are new in the sense of recent origin — television, for example; some are new in the sense of untried; and some are new in the sense of occurring afresh.

It is clear that we have many unsolved problems in this field. But we must use patience in trying to solve them. I think any new method of communication will aid us substantially, and small gains from a variety of sources will add up to an impressive total. I see no new magical methods of communication on the horizon. I see great possibilities for sharp improvement through little gains here and there.

ENDS AND MEANS

REFERENCES

1. Barzun, Jacques. *Teacher in America*. New York: Little Brown and Company, 1945.
2. Bloom, Benjamin S., and others. *Taxonomy of Educational Objectives*. New York: Longmans, Green & Company, 1956.
3. Carpenter, Charles R., L. P. Greenhill, C. J. McIntyre, H. D. Sherk, G. W. Smith, and R. W. Watkins. *An Investigation of Closed-Circuit Television for Teaching University Courses.*
4. Cronbach, Lee J. *Text Materials in Modern Education, A Comprehensive Theory and Platform for Research*. Urbana: University of Illinois Press, 1955.
5. Dressel, Paul L., and Lewis B. Mayhew. *General Education, Explorations in Evaluation*. Washington, D.C.: American Council on Education, 1954.
6. Finn, James. "AV Development and the Concept of Systems." *Teaching Tools*, 3:163–64, No. 4, Fall 1956.
7. Fosdick, Dorothy. "Higher Education and World Affairs." *Current Issues in Higher Education*, 1955.
8. Hackforth, Reginald, tr. *Phaedrus*. Cambridge: Cambridge University Press, 1952.
9. Kumata, Hideya. *An Inventory of Instructional Television Research*. Ann Arbor, Michigan: Educational Television and Radio Center, Michigan State University, December 1, 1956.
10. McDonald, John Dennis, and F. M. Ricciardi. "Business Decision Game." *Fortune*, 57:140–42, March 1958.
11. Marty, Fernand L. "Using the Language Laboratory." *Educational Screen*, April 1958.
12. Randall, John Herman, Jr. *Proceedings*, American Philosophical Association, December 1956.
13. Wilson, Woodrow. *Selected Literary and Political Papers and Addresses*, 3 vols. New York: Grosset & Dunlap, 1926–27.

MR. DALE is in the Bureau of Educational Research and Service at Ohio State.

◦§ C. R. CARPENTER

Teaching and Learning by Television

Amer ican higher education in broad perspective confronts two great problems.

First, how can it provide opportunities for advanced learning to increasing numbers of students, in expanding fields of knowledge, in spite of predictable proportionate decreases in the number of well-qualified faculty members? This is the problem of *quantity* — the problem I shall emphasize here. It seems to be the problem to which television is most relevant, appropriate, and applicable.

The second problem is, however, equally important, and to a certain extent it is the other side of the same coin: How can American higher education best encourage and facilitate the development of the full intellectual potentials of each individual student? This is the problem of *quality*.

We are deeply committed in this country to several propositions: first, that educational opportunities shall be provided to all in due measure relative to the person's needs and abilities; and second, that extensive and appropriate education is a necessary means and condition for the survival and development of a democratic national and world society. These commitments are increasingly justified, and their basic importance emphasized, by the essential requirements of our expanding and complex society. Conversely, we are committed to oppose the development of a thin stratum of a privileged intellectual elite, disassociated from the general population. These commitments, expressed in doctrine, formulated in law, and accepted in principle, are constantly to be implemented in fact.

Private and public educational institutions at all levels must accept the heavy central responsibilities for providing appropriate educational opportunities for millions of our exploding population. These same institutions are obligated, furthermore, to lead persons with superior abilities to the very borders of the advancing fronts of knowledge, and to encourage a few to penetrate the regions of the little known and unknown.

In general terms, therefore, our colleges and universities must accept responsibilities for solving both the *quantitative* and *qualitative* problems of education.

The Problem of Quantity

I submit that proposals to establish enrollment ceilings are hopeful dreams, but probably not very realistic confrontations of the situation that will exist in 1965. Let us look at the task a little more broadly. During the last six years the number of high school students has increased from 6,600,000 to 7,800,000 — or 1,200,000 additional individuals. During the same six years, college enrollments have increased from 2,500,000 to 3,200,000, and it should be observed that the groundswell of the college-age, college-potential population is *only beginning* to rise. The children now actually counted in schools, in increasing proportions, will soon be seeking admission to colleges and universities. The proportion of them who will do so may range as high as fifty per cent of all high school graduates. These estimates may not have taken into consideration sufficiently the numbers who *should* attend college because of their special potentials or capabilities, or because of society's critical needs for their full intellectual development, but who may not, under present conditions, go to college. Furthermore, in order to keep abreast of a changing and advancing culture and to meet the requirements of increasingly demanding professional training, larger numbers must spend more years of their lives in educational institutions. The numbers mount; the demands for adult education are also growing. In brief, vastly increased numbers of our people are requiring and demanding more education, of increasingly varied kinds, involving more years of formal study than in the past. How are provisions to be made for meeting these legitimate and justifiable requirements? What use can be made of television in accomplishing this task?

More specifically, it is estimated that by 1970, five hundred thousand teachers will be needed in colleges and universities. I sometimes see these referred to as *new* teachers. I don't think that is correct. It appears that proportionately five hundred thousand teachers including replacements will be needed in our institutions of higher education by 1970 if we continue to use the same conventional means of teaching, and operate under such assumptions as "the smaller the class the better the instruction."

As for the supply picture, we now graduate about nine thousand Ph.D.'s a year and only about half of these enter college or university teaching. Thus, it seems that we shall be compelled to find, develop, and invent new ways of solving new emergent problems and even some old ones. The vast dimensions of these are quite clear. The implications for the *quantity* problem in American education are also clear.

I should like incidentally to mention one other problem that fascinates and puzzles me: the national posture relative to educational problems. In the first place, it is puzzling to see our people — lovers of adventure, full of the pioneer spirit, and willing to spend almost any amount of money in peace and war to preserve our value systems or to achieve desired goals — so hesitant and confused in the face of the present educational crisis.

Viewing the situation in a new perspective, however, we find ourselves in a very favorable position. We have the means available for solving many of the problems, if we would only materialize them and apply them.

Television as a Means of Presenting Information

Turning to the quality side of the picture: if we assume that an important and major task of educating people (now note this, because I think it is of central importance) involves presenting to people for their reaction organized, intelligible information or instruction, we have the means developed and ready for use to accomplish this essential educational function on a vast scale. I should like to re-emphasize this and relate it to Keith Tyler's remarks. We must develop a taxonomy of the *varied functions of education,* and decide how each is to be performed. When we define specific functions of education we may find that television is a very important means for performing some of these functions, and not appropriate for serving other functions.

The means of presenting organized and intelligible information are available in radio, sound motion pictures, printing presses, and television. I should like to emphasize the fact that we have available these vast potentials for recording, extending, distributing, and presenting information. Why aren't we using these facilities? Why do we educators — good educators, concerned with the central questions and issues of education — still consider these means of communication as sideshows, gadgets, nonessential to the true and central functions of educating the vast numbers whom we must teach?

Evidence on Teaching by Television

Let us turn to the evidence on teaching by television, evidence for which special appreciation is due particularly to the Fund for the Advancement of Education. This fund has invested since 1954, principally since 1956, over $4,500,000 in nationwide experimentation and research, exploring the potentialities of teaching by television. This effort includes projects of closed- and open-circuit, and combinations of the two, operating at all levels from the elementary through the undergraduate levels of colleges and universities.

There are forty-eight projects, in as many schools, school systems, colleges, universities, and communities. There are seventy-five thousand students involved in the thirteen FAE projects in public school systems such as those in Cincinnati, Detroit, Miami, Norfolk, Greensboro, Oklahoma, and Milwaukee. I happen to have visited some of these schools. The vivid impression remains of 223 Negro children being taught the essentials of the Bill of Rights by a white teacher. It was a touching and memorable experience.

These seventy-five thousand students, plus twenty-five thousand in colleges, are being taught some fifty different courses. The operation is heavily oriented toward research and evaluation. Miami University in Ohio has led off at the college level with several excellent reports. New York University did a couple of years of exploratory experimental work. The Chicago City Junior College's junior college of the air is probably the project with the widest scope and the greatest momentum. The University of Houston, which had one of the first educational television stations, has emphasized research. A report is forthcoming from San Francisco State College. Penn State has done and is doing an extensive job. Rarely, if ever, in the history of education have such efforts been made to collect the evidence on an educational question.

Teaching and Learning by Television

Evidence from the Penn State Research

Against this background I shall report on the Penn State project merely as an example. I don't want to give the impression that we have done all of the research at Penn State, although we have in the past four years completed about sixty quantitative controlled projects. We have emphasized essentially two general phases of television activity: introducing closed-circuit television into a large and expanding university, and conducting research within the context of this ongoing activity and in a realistic setting. Balancing one phase against the other in due proportions is not always easy. For example: my impression at the moment is that our research is suffering because of the success and demands of the operational phase. We may also have somewhat exhausted our pool of good research ideas.

It might be interesting to suggest why Penn State is introducing closed-circuit television. To begin with, I'll say that we didn't have to use television. It is anticipatory behavior. We don't really need television to teach the students we have now. We have plenty of faculty members for them. However, we are anticipating that the situation will change very much by 1965, or even 1963; and that the same kinds of changes may occur at other universities. We have therefore undertaken not only to carry out extensive and continuing research programs in teaching by television, but also to create a model operation which may be adapted to other institutions. We are trying to define the problems and demonstrate how they can be solved. We are building *operational educational models* which can be copied by other institutions where their applications are appropriate. This is a promising and possibly an effective method for generalizing research results from one university to others.

The Strategy of Introducing Television into a University

I should like to comment briefly on the strategy of introducing television into a university. It is not easy. It is amazing that educational institutions which might be expected to spearhead social change frequently respond only to pressures and are among the most conservative of our social institutions. New techniques and new methods, new ways of doing things, new instrumentation, meet with considerable resistance in universities, even though the same methods and instruments may be recommended by universities for businesses, industries, and government.

We began at Penn State with certain basic assumptions or action hypotheses. One was that we were not going to impose television by the top-level administration. We planned to introduce television at a lower level, first at the department level. We think that imposing television from the office of the president, or worse still from the comptroller's, invites disaster in the semi-democratic educational institutions of this country. We also put television on a voluntary basis — voluntary with legitimate persuasion, and we can say, I think correctly, that no one is now teaching on television at Penn State who hasn't, within the limits (perhaps the narrow limits) of freedom of choice, elected to be there. This has slowed up research and especially retarded some of the aspects of sampling the various curriculums, but we think that it is a worthwhile approach because it is very necessary to have instructors who are enthusiastic for teaching over television.

Another important principle was making the instructor autonomous in the television situation. We have no directors, writer-directors, studio managers — in fact, we try to get away as much as possible from the professional television point of view, particularly when this tends to subordinate the instructor. The concept we are trying to establish at Penn State is that the instructor is in complete charge and everyone working with the television system is at his service.

Some of the strategy relative to other minor things will be described in a forthcoming report (1). The scope of the project at the present time, I think, attests its acceptance. We have now five thousand student course-units in some thirteen different courses being taught entirely or in part over television, and falling into the different categories which Keith Tyler will outline for you (pp. 222–25). A great many of them are total course presentations. Quite a few of them have supplementary exercise, as for instance problem-solving periods in accounting or in economics. We are operating two systems full time. We are teaching sociology over open-circuit, unmodified from the format of a good standard university course, and simultaneously to 560 students over closed-circuit. The intent is to show the public what goes on in a college or university classroom and at the same time do a good job of teaching resident students.

Four Main Research Areas

We are working in four research areas. The first of these is *comparative effectiveness,* where we compare the effectiveness of teaching over television with the effectiveness of the conventional method. Secondly, we compare different ways of presenting courses over television, concerning ourselves with the possibilities of television for the whole range of the university's curriculums, or the area of *appropriateness* — Is television appropriate for curriculums, or specific courses, or indeed for parts of courses? We are exploring the possibility of improving the quality of television, and in this connection we are studying the question of *acceptability* to the students, faculty members, and administrators. Finally, we are working in the area of *feasibility,* particularly on questions of practical and economic feasibility.

Methods of Research

Methods of investigation are critical and crucial to the interpretation of results. More rigorous controls and more carefully prepared experimental designs than now are used must be introduced into this field of educational research. We randomly assigned groups of students to the experimental and control groups. Unless we can randomly assign subjects into groups of sufficient number we do not count that activity as a quantitative experiment — it is just something else that we are doing because it is interesting or a necessary service operation or a qualitative demonstration.

The most critical part of this business of evaluating the effectiveness of television has to do with the testing and examination procedures. And here we are not satisfied with the kinds of tests and examinations that exist or that we have been able to develop. Nevertheless, we have had to use the best tests and measurements that we could secure or develop.

Comparative effectiveness. Using an auditorium, an instructor in general psychology taught as he would usually teach to this kind of class. We put a camera in the middle of the room, facing the teacher. The camera thus took the student's-eye view of the instructor and televised it to collateral television classrooms. The control consisted of the same teacher's teaching the same course in the same way at the same hour in other classrooms. We had two teachers — we alternated them and thereby canceled out the effects of differences between teachers. The following are the results on the final examination: For the standard lecture classroom (control group), with seventy-four students, which is a little larger than the average Penn State class, the final examination score was 85. For the television receiving rooms where we had proctors, the score was 82. For the television originating room the score was 83. No significant differences were found when we applied the F test of significance. I might say, however, that there were slight numerical differences which were not significant for the three examinations in this semester, all of them favoring slightly in raw scores the standard lecture-room presentation.

Three observations should be made: (a) We were using teachers who had never had any experience with television. (b) At least one of the teachers was not very sympathetic to the operation. He developed rather strong antagonism to teaching by television. Although he is one of the best teachers in the department, he is an informal person and likes small classes. (c) This was the first course students had taken over television, and I am pretty well convinced that there is an element of *learning to learn,* or at least being conditioned to learn over television.

This experiment was done in the spring semester of 1955; the next fall we got together all those students who returned to college and again gave them the final semester examination, to test for retention. In the second experiment we were interested in the question of differential *retention* of the control and experimental groups. This is a fundamental problem for television teaching, because someone is going to say someday, "It's all right at the end of the course, but those students who were taught in television classes are not as good in later courses as those who were taught in conventional classes." We must begin to work in the area of long-term retention of effects.

Now, essentially, the results of our study of retention after about four and a half months lined up with the scores of the different groups in the previous spring. There was no statistically significant difference among those students who had been taught conventionally in the class of seventy-four, those who were taught in the large originating room, and those who were taught exclusively over television.

Continuing the experiments in general psychology the next year, we set up a different experiment. We observed that some methods of presentation over television may be appropriate for television teaching, but exactly the same method, used in the interest of scientific control for a large group or a small group, may be putting television or the large group or the small group at a disadvantage. Therefore, we proposed to use appropriate methods for teaching over television, compared with appropriate methods for teaching a large class. We used the same instructor, the same course materials, and randomized the groups of students.

We did one other thing which we had previously hoped to do but thought impossible in a conventional university. We did not ask the students to buy textbooks. We were attempting to put a maximum amount of information through television channels, rather than have studying the textbook account for perhaps as much as ninety per cent of the variation in test results. We randomized our subjects and developed another interesting little technique: where it is impossible to randomize say three hundred subjects in one group and three hundred in another in large classes, we randomize *core groups* of subjects, about ninety in each category, and then let the rest of them come along for a free ride from the research point of view. We didn't count their scores in the experimental data. The mean total scores for the entire semester in what we called the adapted television-adapted large group comparison turned out to be 148.27 for the directly-taught large class and 148.13 for the television-taught classes. From these results we derived a generalization which we have been supporting with one experiment after another ever since: *the more strictly an experiment is controlled the greater the probabilities that there will be nonsignificant statistical differences between scores of students taught by television and those taught conventionally.*

What difference would methods make if we used radically different methods over television? We randomized about seventy students into one *core* control group (there were many more in the class in general psychology). These were our experimental subjects, and we did everything we could to improve the teaching materials and methods of presentation using television. We used films, live demonstrations and experiments, live interviews instead of talking about interviews, and the like. It was an enriched course. The other version of the course was taught by a straight lecture-blackboard method. The mean for three examinations on the adapted version televised and the lecture-blackboard types of methods is as follows:

Test	Television	Lecture-Blackboard
First	21.07	21.46
Second	25.59	25.62
Third	25.86	26.51

In two of the examinations the straight lecture-blackboard method was slightly but not significantly better. What do we conclude from this? That frequently students are confused by new methods, that there is a certain amount of learning to learn in different ways, particularly when students are accustomed to more or less straight lecture-blackboard presentations and suddenly are confronted with films or other complex methods that introduce a wide range of material. I am not so sure that most students today know how to abstract significance out of complex presentation — to get at the essential issues, particularly the issues thought to be worth testing by the instructors. Our examinations may not have adequately sampled the full range of information.

We go now to the chemistry experiments. We ran two full semesters of two sections of the lecture-demonstration parts of the general chemistry course. Note that this is not all of a chemistry course; it is the lecture-demonstration part only. For the standard lecture room, with about 220 students in a large lecture-demonstration room, the mean score on the final examination for 147 of the core group of students was 67.92. For almost the same number of students in the television receiving rooms the mean was 66.38. For the television originating room the mean was 66.49. That's for the first semester — the spring semester of 1955.

In the fall semester of 1955 we repeated the experiment in general chemistry; the adjusted mean for the directly-taught group was 83.49, for the students in the television rooms, 83.03. In another section of the same course, the scores were 83.49 and 83.60 respectively. We can observe as others have before, that with consistent monotony the non-significant results occur in these comparisons. What do we conclude? I think we can conclude conservatively under the *comparative effectiveness* category of research that college students are not placed at a disadvantage in their academic courses by having their main instruction presented entirely or in large part by television. And remember that this conclusion is drawn relative to the function that I talked about before: *presenting organized, intelligible information to individuals for learning.*

Teaching and Learning by Television

The challenge of the quality barrier. We are distressed by the fact that we have not been able to break through the quality barrier. This is the big challenge that lies ahead, not only for teaching over television, but also for any kind of methodological studies in relation to education. I am quite happy, incidentally, to see methodology subordinated in this conference. It would seem reasonable to conclude that students taught by television have as favorable an opportunity for learning as do students in conventional classes. But in addition, by means of television, a few superior teachers can be made available to very large numbers of students in college courses, either over closed-circuit or open-circuit television. Providing superior teachers alone might importantly affect the quality of instruction. That is the problem we are working on now. It is an extremely sensitive problem because teachers resist being compared on their effectiveness. (We do have some graduate-student volunteers who are daring to compare themselves with some outstanding teachers over television.) However, we can safely conclude that a significant contribution can be made by television to solving the *quantity* problem in American education. We have no evidence to support the fact that we can do a better job using television: the quality problem remains as a challenge.

Appropriateness. The main limitations of appropriateness as we see them in television have to do with some of the inherent limitations of the perception fields, and with the lack of color. We do not think that television teaching can stand alone in those courses that require extensive practice or performance, or long and intensive debate of issues. Otherwise we have not yet found a course which cannot be appropriately taught over television, and we have used it in about twenty-five courses.

Acceptability. I am happy to report that we are using the questionnaire less and less, and introducing instead what we call a behavioral choice method of testing the acceptability of television. The way it works is to provide students — say in general chemistry, where we had something like six hundred in the experiment a year ago last fall — equal opportunities to know what it is like to study over television and by the conventional lecture-demonstration method. After teaching them separately for four weeks and then reversing the groups for another four weeks, we brought the experimental and control general chemistry groups together in the lecture-demonstration hall and taught them there for another week. Then we said, "Ladies and gentlemen, you may have your choice — you can leave this hall and go back to the television rooms if you like, or you can stay here for the rest of the semester in seats to which you are assigned." It was an exciting experiment, because we didn't know what would happen. Thirty-three per cent left and went back to the television rooms.

In a similar experiment in political science, seventy-one per cent left the presence of the instructor and went to the television classrooms. In business law, forty-seven per cent chose television and the professor in the lecture classroom was one of our most dynamic and compelling lecturers. In an adapted course in psychology, sixty-two per cent voted for television.

In education the majority vote was used and there sixty-one per cent voted for television. The proposition was that if the majority voted for television it would be continued; if the majority voted against it, it would be discontinued.

These are all severe tests of television's acceptability to students. Of course you always have some students who are negative; I would say in general ten or fifteen per cent fall in this category. But the most distressing ones are those that just don't care: they don't care about television and they don't care about a great many things which are related to academic work.

We did a quick survey of thirty-five hundred students involved in television instruction the last fall semester on the following question: Would you like this course taught by television as was done this semester, or in a class of two hundred or more with a superior instructor — the best instructor available in the department, or in classes of forty-five with graduate assistants? The order, with low being highest on this scale, was 1.69 for television, 1.99 for forty-five in a course with a graduate assistant, and 2.8 for a class of two hundred or more with the best instructor. We might observe that in no course that we have taught over television has student opinion deteriorated over a full semester. Generally, pre-tests, intermediate tests, and final tests of their reactions have shown improvement in attitudes toward teaching by television, but this is directly related to the quality of instruction as perceived by students.

Feasibility. We think we have demonstrated that it is possible for a university like Penn State to accept the responsibilities of installing and operating not one system but several. We now have two such systems in operation for eight hours a week and three simpler systems which are used periodically for special purposes.

The television operations at Penn State have been staffed by people from the university. They have varied backgrounds, and have readily accepted the training necessary to operate the television systems. Only last year when we undertook regular broadcasting and the production of kinescopic recordings did we employ a television engineer. We have provided part-time work and practical training for many undergraduate students in electrical engineering.

The initial and research phases of the project were financed by the Fund for the Advancement of Education. However, now we are approaching the time, within a year, when all operation costs will be borne by the university. Teaching by television need not be more expensive than conventional methods. In fact, the present cost of teaching can be maintained or actually reduced. A cost analysis for four courses during 1956–57 showed a favorable balance over conventional (for Penn State) class management procedures of about $38,000. A similar analysis this year, 1957–58, for the same four courses with increased enrollments of students, showed a favorable balance of about $48,000. In the analyses the cost of vidicon equipment systems was amortized over a conservative five-year period.

Conclusions. We have the means in television for making a substantial contribution to the solution of the *quantity* problem in American education. It remains to be shown *how and to what extent* teaching by television can contribute to the related problem of improving the *quality* of college and university teaching.

REFERENCE

1. Carpenter, C. R., and others. *An Investigation of Closed Circuit for Teaching College and University Courses: Report Number Two.* University Park, Pennsylvania: Pennsylvania State University. (Copies of this report are available on request.)

Mr. Carpenter is head of the psychology department and director of the Division of Academic Research and Services at Penn State. The conference sessions having to do with teaching by television were presided over by Burton Paulu, director of radio and television broadcasting, University of Minnesota. In addition, Mr. Paulu served as analyst for a group discussion of television in college teaching; Norman DeWitt, College of Science, Literature, and the Arts, University of Minnesota, was chairman of that group and Robert A. Bauman of Macalester College was recorder.

~§ I. KEITH TYLER

Educational and Instructional Television: Some Definitions

MUCH is heard today about educational television and the phrase is used in varied and confusing ways. Recently, in higher education, there has been much discussion of instructional television, of closed-circuit operations, and of open-circuit or broadcast television. My task is to define these terms and indicate their relations.

Educational television. We can begin by suggesting some common misconceptions about educational television. Many people assume that this refers to some kind of quiz or panel program in which the moderator (who seems to fill the role of teacher) asks many questions, related or unrelated, of several persons (who resemble pupils in that they do or do not give back the right answers). When a research organization sends out its interviewers to ask people to identify an educational program, they often respond with "What's My Line?," "I've Got a Secret," or similar titles.

The Federal Communications Commission's definition is not accurate, either. The commission counts as an educational program only one that is broadcast by, or on behalf of, an educational institution. Now obviously an educational institution, such as the University of Minnesota, can broadcast a most educational program, but it can also broadcast football games, public relations programs, and swimming meets. Just the fact that the program is put on the air by the university does not make it educational.

I prefer a functional definition which enables one to distinguish educational from entertainment programs on the basis of intent. Thus, *an educational television program is one broadcast for the purpose of attaining one or more educational objectives.* More specifically, such a program is intended to inform, to develop concepts and understandings, to motivate interest and action, to develop skills and techniques, to heighten sensitivities and appreciations, to nurture convictions and values.

This is, of course, a very broad definition. It includes informative programs on weather, news, markets; skill programs about golf, gardening, sculpture, and painting; appreciation programs in music, ballet, art, and drama; background and thought-provoking programs of documentary interview, discussion, and lecture. It ranges from the casual, opportunistic, and occasional to the organized, orderly, and sequential. It runs the whole gamut of socially desirable behavior, because our educational objectives are similarly broad.

If we arrange these varied educational program types on a continuum from the casual and informal on the left to the formal, logically organized, and sequential programs on the right, it will be clear that (a) any one of these types may be found either on educational stations or on commercial stations, but (b) the commercial stations concentrate their educational endeavors on the informal left end of the continuum with fewer and fewer programs toward the formal, right end, while (c) the educational stations concentrate on the formal, right end of the continuum with fewer and fewer programs toward the informal, left end. The two services overlap but one assumes the burden of the informal while the other carries the burden of the formal.

I hope it is clear, also, that by this definition educational programs may be found not only on stations, that is to say, on open-circuit broadcasting, but also on closed-circuit broadcasting. A closed-circuit system may be defined as a system in which those putting on the program have control of the receiving situations — the programs are closed to the uninvited. When one broadcasts over a closed circuit, one knows where the program is received and by whom, whether the distribution is made by wire, by cable, or by ultra-high frequency relay. In open-circuit television there is not this control of reception.

Instructional television. This is the arbitrary selection of the right-hand end of the informal-to-formal continuum I have referred to. Instructional television is a part of educational television. It means formal, orderly, sequential programs usually organized in courses of instruction. Programs are done in series, broadcast with regularity, and there is progressive building from one program to the next. It may be found on commercial stations, on educational stations, or on a closed circuit.

Instructional television may be classified by types. I distinguish four, and for convenience I designate them by their initial letters.

The first type I call *total television teaching,* or TTT: the institution's entire activity, so far as a particular course is concerned, consists of the television presentation. Usually this is found only in adult education. A modern-language course is given over television by the institution, a syllabus is made available, and a text may be obtained, but the rest is up to the student. He must do his own reading, find his own opportunities for discussion, engage in his own drill. The institution does its part simply by providing the broadcast. This requires a great deal of maturity on the part of the student.

The second type I call *supplemented television teaching,* or STT. It is much more common at the college level. Here the main burden of instruction, usually a presentation by lecture-demonstration, is carried by television, but the institution supplements this with other learning opportunities — laboratory periods, quiz and discussion sections, field studies, and the like. Most of the current instructional television activity in higher education is of this type. Television is used for lecture-demonstrations in physics, three times a week; laboratory sections are given twice a week. English literature lectures are televised twice a week; discussion sections meet once a week. History is presented by television for thirty minutes with discussion in each receiving classroom for the remaining twenty minutes of each class hour. Supplemented television teaching assumes that the student is not yet completely self-directive and that other learning activities must be provided in addition to the television presentation.

With both of these types — the total and the supplemented — planning is done centrally. The classroom teacher, if there is one, either has the role of monitor or glorified clerk, on the one hand, or at most has the task of clarifying and enriching the presentations made by the television teacher, on the other.

With the third type of instructional television, the initiative passes to the classroom teacher. This type I call *television supplementing the classroom,* or TSC. Here the instructor develops and carries out his own teaching plans and uses a television program because it enriches, it supplements, the instruction. This use of a broadcast program is much more common at school levels and is currently to be found in such cities as St. Louis, Cincinnati, and Philadelphia.

Finally we have *television used as a teaching aid* or TTA. Here the electronic instrument is simply used as a means to make better observation possible on the part of learners. It may be a small closed-circuit system within a large science lecture room so that experiments may be observed on monitors rather than directly. Minute phenomena may be enlarged or picked out of a welter of confusing detail. Operations in medicine, veterinary science, or optometry may be seen close up, often in color. Children's behavior may be studied in more natural situations in child study courses by television than it can when observers are present; interview techniques may be observed intimately in guidance classes. Television is not used to present an organized lesson or even a case study; it simply transmits the raw data to be interpreted and explained.

While instructional television takes place on both open- and closed-circuit television, it is the spectacular growth of the latter which I shall briefly summarize. Preliminary results of a national survey by the Joint Council on Educational Television reveal that there are now two hundred closed-circuit educational installations operating in this country. These are on all levels, but the largest number appears to be at the college level with fewer at the high school level and still fewer at the elementary school level. They range from the very simple TTA, where the system merely enlarges a process going on in the same room, to the elaborate Hagerstown, Maryland, experiment with four channels connecting twenty-six schools and four programs on various grade levels being distributed simultaneously.

College subjects being taught over television include veterinary anatomy, military history, educational psychology, physiology, zoology, engineering, physics, chemistry, German, business organization, and speech.

Fortunately, research accompanies most of these uses of instructional television so that as new institutions undertake it they will know much more of values and limitations, of procedures, and of the human factors involved.

Mr. Tyler is director of radio and television education at Ohio State. (See note, p. 221.)

The Effective Use of Audio-Visual Materials

A<small>LTHOUGH</small> we commonly use the term audio-visual, it is merely a shorthand way of describing materials of instruction which are less abstract than words themselves. Even here we must exercise care because it would be more accurate to call them audio-visual-verbal materials because these relatively more concrete experiences are nearly always skillfully integrated with words themselves.

Television is audio-visual-verbal. A filmstrip has labels, titles, and is discussed while it is being shown. Some materials are chiefly verbal-aural, notably those used in tape or wax recordings.

I have found it fruitful to think of teaching materials as occupying sections of a cone of experience ranging from the most concrete, purposeful, firsthand experiences at the bottom of the cone, to highly abstract symbols at the top of the cone.

A weakness of all education is that the verbally stated concepts and principles are not firmly grounded in and based on the rich experience of the learners. Their concepts are not "suffused with suggestiveness" — a phrase used by Alfred North Whitehead. The student does not know and feel deeply what the instructor or the text is "talking" about. A visual symbol — a word or two written at this point — will help the student understand, and many instructors do use the chalkboard to help explain; but too often the small size of the statement on the board prevents its being viewed by the entire class. Here modern optics takes over to provide a picture big enough for everyone in the class to see.

The instructor might use simple handmade slides 3¼" x 4" with a lantern slide projector to help explain. He might have prepared his material and then photographed it on convenient 2" x 2" slides (35mm film). Full-color slides are easy to make. Modern automatic slide projectors ensure quick, accurate projection in the proper order; and with a long pushbutton control cord, the instructor can operate his own projector from the front of the classroom. If this material is used by many teachers, it is likely to be distributed in economical filmstrip form. There is much excellent filmstrip material available.

When a picture in a text or magazine will do the job the opaque projector steps in to do the projecting. Any opaque material may be quickly enlarged. These projectors do require almost complete darkening of the room.

To overcome the problem of inadequate darkening the instructor might use photographic slides made with the new Polaroid transparency film. With this film it is possible to project a picture with a slide projector only moments after the picture is snapped. The teacher can make use of newspaper headlines, weather maps, market quotations, and the like from the morning paper. Only partial light control is needed for these slide projectors. These instant slides are useful for any type of illustration, but the time feature is most important.

Still another projector which will enlarge the visual symbol is the overhead projector. Here the instructor writes or places transparencies on a level stage. A 45° mirror and lens put the picture on the screen over the head of the teacher who can keep his eyes on the class at all times. The large-diameter lens coupled with a 500-watt or larger lamp and efficient optics means the room does not require complete darkening. With prepared overlay transparencies the instructor may add superimposed portions of the illustration until the picture is complete. Then, with a marking pencil, further notes may be added as the class watches the picture on the screen. Still another technique would have the instructor write on a plastic roll the notes or symbols usually put on the chalkboard. The projector would enlarge these notes so that all could see; further, they could be saved for re-use again and again without further writing or drawing on the part of the user. The teacher would talk to the class and direct their attention to the screen. The visual-verbal technique helps the student get the picture that is necessary for comprehension.

In using audio-visual materials we often aim to help students move toward a greater degree of symbolization whether this be in mathematics, history, science, or a professional course. The student abstracts and generalizes from these experiences at varying levels of complexity.

He learns how to draw off and test inferences. Mere exposure to audio-visual experiences is not enough. Just showing a film or a filmstrip is not enough. The sensitively perceptive may learn by unguided experience, others will not.

But sometimes, it should be pointed out, we are not having an experience in order to compress, to abstract, or even to verbalize. Art experiences are an example. They are chiefly consummatory experiences, not aimed to be instrumental. Experiencing a painting, a play, music, statuary, or indeed an artful presentation or discussion is a good thing in itself. You've had it. The poet's "emotion recollected in tranquillity" is shared or it isn't. There are some experiences — and we hope that they will often occur in college — of which you do not ask: What is it for? If you do, you just didn't get it.

I object to the word *aids*. To some it carries the connotation of merely assisting, instead of being the experience itself. These audio-visual experiences are not always unique, *sui generis,* but we should try to select rich and unique experiences with this possibility in mind. At present we lack a wide range of excellent films at the college level. The market is, of course, more limited than that for elementary and high school films. However, the University Film Producers' Association, of which the University of Minnesota is a member, has produced more than two hundred fifty films during the year 1957–58.

May I offer a warning about the use of audio-visual materials? They are not for entertainment or amusement. They are to educate, to help students develop workable, useful generalizations in important fields of subject matter. If they can't help educate, they should not be used. While I would not go so far as to suggest as did Plato that learning is accompanied by pain, genuine learning is sometimes painful, sometimes frustrating, and often challenging.

Why is there sometimes a scornful reference to audio-visual materials as making education easy? Audio-visual materials are not to make education easy but to make it clear. When you give a person a map to find his way, you expect it to be clear to him. And you do not throw in any booby traps to make it hard, to test his character. There are plenty of hard things to learn in this world without adding to them needlessly.

Let us look now at some of the steps to be taken in the intelligent and effective use of audio-visual materials in the college.

Effective Use of Audio-Visual Materials

First, the instructor or group of instructors planning the work in a field of subject matter must know what they are trying to help students learn. Instructors at Miami University and Penn State who have been experimenting with larger classes and with television write down their objectives in enough detail so that they will have a guide for selecting and organizing the learning experiences necessary to achieve these objectives. And instructors have been faced with the need for evaluating the results of their teaching. This is the process through which every curriculum-maker must go no matter what the medium of teaching may be. The objectives may be skills, attitudes, information — none of them neat, independent categories.

After setting up objectives, the instructors must think clearly about the *kinds* of experiences to be selected and organized. Here we run into a problem that has not yet been adequately discussed and thought through: the great difference psychologically between the real thing, pictures of the real thing, and words (spoken and written) about the real thing. You can put words together to describe the real thing or to describe a photograph or painting but at best they are a substitute. Susanne Langer (1) says in *Philosophy in a New Key*: "Photography . . . has no vocabulary" (p. 77) and "In the non-discursive mode that speaks directly to sense, however, there is no intrinsic generality. It is first and foremost a direct presentation of an individual object." (p. 78.)

What I am raising here is the level of concreteness in collegiate education. William James once said: "You can't see any farther into a generalization than your knowledge of its details extends." What details, what concreteness do you plan to have your students experience? William James's great appeal as a teacher and writer is his wealth of pertinent illustration.

The problem of examples and illustrations was faced by a group of professors in our medical school who asked, "How shall we teach the heart to our students? By charts? Models? Tape recording? The living heart? A preserved heart? When is enough enough?" In our film "Accent on Learning" we can see faculty members studying visual materials for instruction as well as actual classroom use of some of the visual materials they chose.

My colleagues in anthropology do not think they understand other cultures until they go into the field — Japan, the Philippines, a city slum. But neither do they abandon statistical methods when they do so. How much can you generalize from one sharply-etched real case? The poet does this with a daffodil, a lark. The religious teacher does it with parables. But how many *com*parables do you need before you have made your point?

The historian is trying to reconstruct the past — help us see how people thought about slavery, or free silver, or World War I. The teacher of literature uses his subject to illuminate the past and the future. But too often the experience really does not move us — shake us loose, reconstruct us, change our perceptions, give us a fresh look at the world. Ludwig Lewisohn (2) says in *The Magic Word* (p. 149) that "He who grasps the particular in vivid fashion is given the general, whether he is aware of it or becomes aware only late." You can't summarize life for the other fellow. He must achieve an unsummarized reality of his own. You can't teach a century and a half in a page and a half.

You can also approach the problem in the more general way suggested by Henry James: "The power . . . to trace the implication of things, to judge the whole piece by the pattern, the condition of feeling life in general so completely that you are well on your way to knowing any particular corner of it — this cluster of gifts may almost be said to constitute experience, and they occur in country and in town, and in the most differing stages of education."

The power involved here is to see the new in the old and the old in the new, "to trace the implication of things."

Let's look for a moment at this question: What experiences shall be *systematically* presented by the instructor or through the textbook, what experiences shall the student undergo in class? On his own? How can we use audio-visual materials to help the student become an independent learner?

At Washington University in St. Louis, mathematics classes are being taught by means of television. There is a presentation or explanation or lecture — whatever you wish to call it — twice a day. The lecture is given in the morning and repeated again at night. There is a classroom where the student may go for help in working his assigned problems. And if the student wishes, he can hear the television lecture a second time.

Here we have a highly systematic use of audio-visual materials, with guided practice. The double lecture gives a chance for review or an opportunity to clear up a point missed from the first lecture. An able "explainer" does the job for a large number of students and if the explanation is not quite good enough for all students, there is an opportunity for further help. In this situation no large lecture hall is necessary to accommodate a large class. This system eliminates the assembling of all students in a room, maximizes practice, and gives the student individual help when he needs it.

Are there new ways of giving special practice in learning? B. F. Skinner of Harvard has a grant to do this with self-testing, self-correcting machines. I hope we don't reject such machines out-of-hand. We might make good use of devices for getting practice on important yet minor elements in learning. Maybe we can't, but we should experiment to find out.

Two of the necessary steps for curriculum-making have been noted. We have set up our objectives in detail so that we know the behavior, the learning we seek. Second, we have enabled students to undergo experiences necessary to achieve this learning. The experiences have been on varying levels of concreteness and abstraction — firsthand laboratory experiences, drama, mock-ups and models, field trips, role-playing, solving real problems through a case, writing and speaking about the problem or problems under study.

How do we know that we have helped students learn? Obviously we apply the tests appropriate to the objectives sought. We check the way the students feel about the materials, about whether they have learned something; we test information learned to see if it is appropriate. We sample students' skills: we may give them an unsolved problem in botany or zoology that does not yet appear in any textbook.

I hope that we shall also make wise use of the subjective judgment of the instructor regarding his own instruction. He should be an informed, dispassionate, sophisticated observer of his own teaching processes. And this means on a long-time basis as well as a short-time basis. I am concerned about the fact that our teaching in social science and literature does not make the able, interested, mature readers that this society demands. A recent study at Stanford noted that college students are not avid newspaper readers. They are too busy going to college to get an education.

I hope, too, that we shall have as one of our key objectives in all teaching: learning how to learn. You can learn how to look at a film, how to squeeze the juice out of a concrete experience, how to talk intelligently with someone who knows a lot more than you do, how to become a persistent interviewer of life. You can develop a persistent curiosity, keep in your mental file a reservoir of persistent questions. You can learn when to talk and when to listen.

To carry out the processes suggested above means that we must get organized to do it. We need audio-visual centers because we must select, make, or buy materials. They must be tied in with other library functions. Equipment must be kept in repair. Films must be produced, bought and rented. In short, we must build up a system. Questions of autonomy, of responsibility arise. But they also arise with our present libraries — getting the books and periodicals we want when we want them, how they shall be classified, how made available.

There are four stages in our efficiency with any new medium or technique: (1) Unconscious inefficiency — we teach badly but don't know it. (2) Conscious inefficiency — we know we could do better but don't know what to do to improve. (3) Conscious efficiency — we are applying new methods with painful proficiency. We are counting out the rhythm when we dance. (4) Unconscious efficiency — we have learned how and use the new method "without thinking."

REFERENCES

1. Langer, Susanne K. *Philosophy in a New Key: A Study in the Symbolism of Reason, Rite, and Art.* Cambridge: Harvard University Press, 1951.
2. Lewisohn, Ludwig. *The Magic Word.* New York: Farrar, Straus and Cudahy, Inc., 1950.

THIS chapter, prepared by Mr. Dale, who is in the Bureau of Educational Research and Service at Ohio State, reflects the discussion of a group of which Harry C. Webb, College of St. Thomas, was chairman, and Neville Pearson, College of Education, University of Minnesota, was recorder. Mr. Pearson supplied the material on visual presentations.

◄§ FREEMON G. MACOMBER

Panels and Reports in College Teaching

T_HE_ importance which one ascribes to student reporting — individual
or group, oral or written — is determined to a considerable extent by
the significance which he attaches to certain aims of higher education.
Doubtless reporting activities can and should contribute to several of
the major aims of college teaching. Indeed, it is difficult to see how
some of these aims can be achieved at all, except as the student finds
himself rather continuously in situations which call for investigation
and report. The following are objectives to which individual and group
reporting activities are closely related.

Most educators would agree that the ability to organize one's
thinking in regard to a problem or issue and to make a clear oral or
written presentation of this thinking to others is one of the earmarks
of an educated person. Psychologists are in general agreement that this
is an ability which can be learned, granting the potential for college-
level study, but that it must be learned primarily through experience
in such study, organization, and presentation. If this is an objective
with which we are seriously concerned, then reporting must be a major
learning activity of the college student.

The development of the capability of critical thinking is one of the
chief aims of a college education. There may be some disagreement
about what this constitutes, and certainly there is disagreement upon
how this capability may best be developed, but essentially all agree
upon its validity as a major aim of higher education. While not all reporting requires a high degree of critical thinking, a great deal of it
does. In fact, reporting should be required as a means of developing
this ability and of evaluating its growth. Critical thinking by the individual or group giving a report and by those receiving the report is
an essential of good reporting and listening. In general, reports should

require a great deal of library research (or investigation, if you prefer that term), a careful organization of the thoughts for presentation, and, where there is an audience, critical listening. These conditions must be met if the report is to contribute materially to the development of critical thinking.

There has been considerable argument as to whether or not high schools and colleges should be concerned with developing the ability of students to work and plan together. It is the old argument of co-operative versus competitive endeavor. From my point of view, this controversy makes about as much sense as the age-old argument over heredity and environment as determinants of behavior. Much of intellectual life is competitive, but so is it cooperative. We are in competition with Russia, for instance, in the exploration of space and in nuclear development, but it was largely cooperative scientific effort which produced the atom bomb of World War II, which launched our first satellite, and which has made possible much of the scientific and social progress of civilization.

Granted that experience in group study, organization, and presentation of a problem is desirable, the panel discussion is clearly a good way to get such experience. If desirable results are to be achieved, however, the panel discussion must be much more than the mere assembling of four or five persons, each of whom proceeds to expatiate upon his own ideas or prejudices. It must become a group experience in cooperative research, organization, and reporting.

So much for the educational aims to which reporting can make real contributions. There are certain basic principles — possibly I should say recommended procedures — which should make for better reporting.

1. The topic or problem must be of concern to the student. One of the great difficulties in English courses is finding topics for compositions which will meet this test. Entirely too much writing is done about subjects which are merely assignments rather than live issues, of real interest to students. I am not quarreling with the practice of assigning topics, but rather pointing out that the best opportunities for motivated reporting lie in those areas in which the student is keenly interested. Usually one would expect this to be in his major field of study. This, obviously, is not English, per se, for the majority of college students. The need for planned reporting in all academic areas should require little further elaboration.

2. Reporting activities, including the selection of topics for report, should be determined by recognized educational aims. For instance, if the ability to do library research and to organize the findings of such study for presentation to others are objectives of the particular reporting situation, then the topic must be one which requires research, and time and opportunity must be alloted for this research. It should be obvious that students normally cannot be assigned a report on Wednesday to be completed on Friday if this principle is to apply.

Likewise, materials must be available for successful research and report. All too often a librarian finds that with possibly two copies of a particular bulletin at hand he suddenly has some twenty-five or thirty students demanding it for a report due tomorrow or the next day. It is highly desirable to put students into situations in which they must exercise a good deal of ingenuity in finding materials, but the instructor must be certain that such materials are available in sufficient quantity, and that they can be found within the time limits of the study.

3. Reports must be evaluated if there is to be student progress in reporting. This does not mean a mere grading or marking of reports. It means constructive criticism by means of which the student may see the strong and weak points of his report and which may lead him to see ways to improve future reports. This is true not only of individual reports, whether written or oral, but of group reports such as panel discussions. The instructor of the class obviously is directly responsible for much of this evaluation. However, the ability to evaluate a report which one has prepared himself or to which one has listened is an important educational objective. Consequently, much of the desired evaluation should be self-evaluation and group-evaluation. Even here, however, the instructor must assume the role of guide; otherwise, there is no guarantee that students' evaluations will result in improved reporting. In saying this, I am quite aware of the difficulties involved, but I am quite certain that university-wide recognition of the problem can result in improved evaluative practices. In this connection I have some evidence for believing that a small number of reports per term, carefully prepared and evaluated, create a better learning situation than weekly reports and compositions hurriedly conceived and inadequately evaluated.

4. Topics or problems for panel-discussion type of reporting nor-

mally must contain issues or controversial elements. Anyone who has attempted to develop a lively discussion around a purely factual presentation will understand the significance of this recommendation. Of course one cannot stimulate discussion with nothing at issue except facts themselves. Factual presentations may make satisfactory symposia, but not panel discussions.

5. *Oral reports, whether individual or group, must be educational to the audience.* In other words, there is no point to having an audience unless the audience learns. It is the responsibility of the reporting individual or group to be both interesting and challenging to the audience. Again, there must be adequate guidance from the instructor during the preparation period to ensure a report that is worthwhile from the point of view of the audience. A poor report is a waste of time for all, including the reporting individual or group.

6. *Reports, to be really educative, require a high degree of study and organization, as well as effective presentation.* Regardless of whether the report is to come from a group or an individual, it has little if any educational value if it merely voices opinions and prejudices or pools ignorance — as so many panels do. Students must be led to understand the function of a panel discussion, which, primarily, is to provide intellectual stimulation for the audience — granted that the teacher's aim may be to provide a situation in which a group of students will gain speaking experience.

7. *There is a need for balance between oral and written reporting and between individual and group reporting.* I am not certain how this may be achieved in a college. I have been quite disturbed, however, by the apparent lack of any over-all faculty planning for reporting activities during the student's four years of college. I am of the opinion, which is not entirely unsupported by evidence, that many students complete a college program without making a single *major* written report. I am certain that guidance of the reporting activity must become a matter of concern for all departments of the university if this activity is to make the contribution to educational aims of which it is capable. More than this, there should be considerable interdepartmental planning so that there is some plan of over-all reporting which is neither feast nor famine.

8. *Students of high ability should have the opportunity and be faced with the requirement of high-quality reporting.* I am certain that we

could profitably devote a greater amount of the faculty's time and energy to making certain that all students of high ability were placed in situations where serious research and report were both necessary and required. An extension of the honors program or the senior thesis is at least a possible answer. I hope that we will not lose sight of this requirement of good education in the trying time ahead during which many institutions will be forced into a greater amount of mass instruction by the incoming flood of students, accompanied by staff and budget shortages.

THIS chapter, prepared by Mr. Macomber, who is director of the Experimental Study in Instructional Procedures at Miami University, reflects the discussion of a group of which G. T. Mitau of Macalester College was chairman and George H. McCune, General College, University of Minnesota, was recorder.

◦§ ARTHUR UPGREN

The Case Method of Teaching

THE case method is by no means new in higher education. Law schools for many years have built courses around concrete cases arising in the courts and illuminating the various points of law. Similarly, medical schools have long used hospitalized patients as cases for the medical student to examine and diagnose.

It is only recently, however, that the case method has come to have vogue among many other academic fields. A progenitor of the modern movement was the late Dean Wallace B. Donham of the Harvard School of Business Administration. Donham discovered that business-men frequently complained that the Harvard graduate was well versed in the theory and literature of business operation but frequently had great difficulty in solving practical business problems as they arose on the job. In a real situation, there frequently are four or five plausible solutions to a problem. The ability to weigh one factor against another, to gather relevant background information where needed, and to arrive at an independent decision, was an attribute that the Harvard busi-ness graduates often lacked. To meet this practical situation, the case method was instituted in the Harvard School of Business Administra-tion and gradually it came to be employed in certain liberal arts courses at Harvard as well as in other universities, such as Colgate, Ohio Uni-versity, and the University of Kansas. It is now so widely used by teachers in various fields throughout the country that it deserves analysis and assessment.

The case method is based not upon a systematic exposition of facts or theoretical material but rather upon concrete problems to be solved. Each professor naturally uses the method in his own distinctive way but there are some essential features always to be found. The prepara-tor of the case gathers all the relevant data concerning a concrete problem that has actually been faced in a subject field such as business, law, teaching, or human relations. He sets forth the problem as clearly as possible and describes the social setting in which it arose. The students are asked to examine the relevant data, search the literature for theoretical and factual insights that might be helpful, and eventually make a decision concerning the best solution. As the case is discussed in class, the students come to recognize more clearly the complexities of the situation and the human factors involved. It may be, indeed, that the student will identify himself with one of the characters in the case, developing thereby his capacity for thoughtful empathy with others.

The insight which a student gains from the case method is what William James referred to as the "knowledge of acquaintance" rather than mere "knowledge about phenomena." By forcing himself to think and feel into the very heart of an objective problem and to come up with a practical decision, the student derives a maturity and independence of mind that is not readily available in a typical lecture or discussion kind of course. It is what Dean Donham referred to as "education for responsible living," encouraging the student to make the kind of mature judgments that he could clearly espouse and responsibly defend.

Let us look at the educational assumptions underlying the case method. First there is a focus of attention upon student participation. In fact, most instructors who regularly use the case method require that the actual physical arrangement of the students in the class be such that they are really focused on each other instead of on the instructor. Thus, clearly a second assumption of the case method is the belief that students can learn from one another. To this can be added a third assumption: the belief in the student's taking responsibility for his own learning. Finally, the case method changes the role of the instructor from one who hands down doctrine from on high to one who leads and summarizes group discussion. Here the instructor no longer is the authoritative source of information, knowledge, and judgments.

In the case method, the student role involves extensive and thorough preparation. The "case" under analysis is not clean and crisp-cut as are our theoretical textbooks where doctrine has been distilled for as much as a century and a half.

In the case method of teaching, the student has a distinct role and responsibility for class participation. In fact, it is by this participation in the discussion that the learning process of the individual and of the group is advanced. Finally, the student is responsible for his own conclusions and cannot rest on the instructor's judgments.

In contrast to the role of the student is the professor's role. The instructor must establish a nonauthoritarian atmosphere in which the students are very free to speak in an uninhibited way — provided, of course, there is reasonable relevance in the students' discussion. The instructor should minimize his own contribution to the discussion. His primary function is to keep track of students' comments and be prepared at any time: (a) to summarize; (b) to point out dilemmas; and (c) to ask for relevancy or evidence.

The materials used in the case method of teaching are a common set available equally to all students. The materials are presented in depth so that hard thinking can be required and wishy-washy generalizations can be avoided. The usual focus is on either: (a) a problem to be analyzed and (perhaps) resolved; *or* (b) a procedure of evidence to be appraised.

Thus, the case system is one which emphasizes above all else student learning from materials which are more realistic to problems in life. These problems do not always have a single best solution, and in this respect the outcome of student work is different from the outcome of classroom presentation of principles or succinct statements of some distilled body of knowledge. The method aims at developing students in processes realistic to life.

The method does not result in elegance and neatness of digested principles and conclusions. Rather, the method aims at developing the student's ability to solve problems with all the resources he can bring to bear on them. The emphasis is upon maturity, not materials. Yet it is often found that the motivation derived from grappling with a tough case will lead to intensive reading and thoughtful reflection in an unusual degree.

It is difficult to evaluate the efficacy of the case method as compared with lecturing, Socratic discussion, and other classroom procedures. One can say, however, that where the method has been seriously tried, both professors and students have been enthusiastic at the results achieved. And there is no question but that many employers and others associating with persons schooled in case analysis have been impressed with the mature judgment that such persons can bring to new problems as they arise.

The method of course does not replace the other time-honored procedures of college teaching but it supplements them and makes a distinctive contribution to the student's development. It is a method well worthy of further experimentation in the many disciplines of the college curriculum.

REFERENCES

1. Andrews, Kenneth R. *The Case Method of Teaching Human Relations and Administration.* Cambridge: Harvard University Press, 1955.
2. Berrien, F. K. *Comments and Cases on Human Relations.* New York: Harper and Brothers, 1951.
3. Cabot, Hugh, and J. A. Kahl. *Human Relations: Cases and Concepts in Concrete Social Science.* Cambridge: Harvard University Press, 1953.
4. Donham, Wallace B. *Education for Responsible Living.* Cambridge: Harvard University Press, 1945.
5. Fraser, C. E., ed. *The Case Method of Instruction.* New York: McGraw-Hill Book Company, Inc., 1931.
6. McNair, Malcolm P. *The Case Method at the Harvard Business School.* McGraw-Hill Book Company, Inc.

THIS chapter, prepared by Mr. Upgren, who is at Macalester College, reflects the discussion of a group of which Charles McLaughlin, College of Science, Literature, and the Arts, University of Minnesota, was chairman, and Dorothy Dodge of Macalester College was recorder.

Role-Playing in the Classroom

For our purposes, the term role-playing will refer to a dramatic enactment of a social or interpersonal problem situation set up in the classroom. The students are the actors, and their preparation is largely a matter of getting them into role. This is a process of helping them reflect on their own relevant experiences, visualize the sorts of attitudes involved in the roles they are to play, and anticipate some of the attitudes they may expect to encounter. The action of the scene is simply the interactive working out of the interplay of attitudes and beliefs among the players — as expressed in a clearly defined problem situation. It is probably accurate to say that the student plays himself pretending to be someone else, and that that someone else is a projection of some facet of the student's own mixture of attitudes and orientations.

For classroom use, the major purpose of role-playing is simply to provide a slice of experience for the class to examine. This use is fairly similar to that of a laboratory experiment in physics. In both cases the experimenter devises the situation most appropriate to his inquiry. He makes adequate preparation, decides what to observe, and reflects upon his data. The two major differences are (a) the actors in role-playing can be interviewed to get their testimony, and this is another kind of evidence to weigh, whereas the weights and pulleys in an experiment in mechanics remain mute; and (b) the weights and pulleys interact in a physics experiment exactly as they would in a nonexperimental situation, whereas the role-players are influenced by the class and by the fact that the role-playing situation is partly imaginary. The dynamics of interaction are just as genuinely dynamics as they would be in any "real" situation, however, so that the scene is valid in its own terms; the fact that the actors are not playing for keeps makes it possible for them to follow their own impulses more directly than would be safe in a "real" situation.

'The acting out of impulses which are generally inhibited or expressed only indirectly leads, on reflection, to discovery of tendencies in themselves of which the participants had been only dimly aware. This is a major goal of role-playing when used for therapeutic purposes, where the emphasis is on the inner reactions of the participants (or patients). In classroom situations, however, the emphasis is more upon the analysis of the situation and its interpersonal dynamics than on the personality of the players. In fact, care is usually exercised to establish the notion that the players are not necessarily playing themselves; and that even if they were, they are being seen in only one specific and experimental situation, so that making any generalization about personality is going way beyond the data. In actual practice, the balance between the educational and therapeutic directions of emphasis is probably determined by the objectives of the lesson as understood by the class and teacher. But for out-and-out therapy, the kind of role-playing characterized in the first paragraph is far less effective than psychodrama, in which the situations are built upon diagnosis of personality and where the teacher is a competent psychiatrist.

Some Uses of Role-Playing

1. Marriage — anticipatory adjustment. Role-playing is used to explore the emotional dimensions of marriage relationships in the face of a variety of situational stresses. The class is small — about seven — and cohesive. The members tend to become quite involved with the players, and the exploration of the feelings of the players is probably to a large extent the vicarious exploration of the feelings of other students as well. The teacher is versed in the psychology of personality, and we may assume that he uses therapeutic skills to deal with self-revelations of emotional responses and to recognize and deal with personal anxieties.

2. Family living — development of objectivity. Role-playing is used to portray the range of relations among members of the family. The scenes show homely situations: father greeting teen-age daughter when she sneaks in at 2 A.M., after promising to be home at 12. The analysis deals with such tangled matters as relations between love and punishment, guilt and perceptual distortion, authority and autonomy. The students are helped to see these situations in terms of the frames of reference of the different participants, and thus to break away from their own anxious self-orientations.

3. Nursing — clarification and definition. As the student nurse moves from the role of student to that of nurse, she needs help to understand what is expected of nurses in different situations; what the roles of supervisors, aides, doctors, and others are in these situations. She needs aid to anticipate and structure her new professional role; she needs to know what to count on from other staff members and when to initiate action for them. These matters are communicated in scenes role-played by faculty members; the scenes help the student to formulate meaningful questions and to begin to rehearse herself for the actual situations she will encounter later.

4. Interviewing — role development and rehearsal. The students in the research class need to develop an interview schedule and to train themselves to collect and interpret interview data. They take turns interviewing each other, criticize and compare each other's techniques, and attempt to interpret the interview data. Through this experience they learn what sorts of questions give interpretable answers, and thus formulate their interview schedule. They also learn principles for guiding the conduct of interviews and, through practice, they overcome some of their anxieties and trepidations over this new role. Role-playing is quite regularly employed in many research projects.

5. Organizational problems — reality practice. In this use the participants test attitudes about their actual "real" situations. The scenes explore "what would happen if . . ." A suggested situation involved conflict between the faculty and the dean. It was proposed that a touchy problem (for example, leaves, salary, academic freedom) could be enacted before a departmental faculty — with one professor playing a professor and another the dean. In such a scene the "professor" would express many of the hostilities that the faculty felt but could not express to the real dean. The audience, witnessing such a frank portrayal, would realize that their hostility was shared by other members of the faculty, and this would reduce their anxieties about their hostilities to the point where they could be accepted. Presumably the faculty members would then be less awkward in dealing with the dean; they would have more energy available to apply to the problem and the dean because they would need less to deal with themselves.

This process of reducing anxiety through awareness of shared feelings is a result of most role-playing. The distinctive element in the present suggested use is the "real" situation with which the participants are currently living.

6. Community problems. In a course on community development, the whole class participates as citizens in a community they set up for the purpose. A survey committee gets the facts about the community; organizations are formed (usually with some conflicting purposes); and a problem is generated (for example, two delinquents burn down the high school). The citizens have meetings, devise organizational strategies, and attempt to influence each other. The action ends with the city council, school board, or other relevant authority listening to proposals, discussing them in open meeting, and arriving at a decision. This sort of project may go on for two weeks or more, with the students looking up data and arguments and principles between meetings, and with times during class when they step out of their roles long enough to analyze the situation and be helped to see the kinds of alternatives available for further steps. This has become a regular feature of several summer workshops in community relations.

7. Policy-making sciences. Role-playing could be used in a course on government — to personalize the rather abstract content of such a course: a group could portray a variety of incidents in the life of a congressman, for example. The first two scenes might show him talking with constituents who hold opposite views on an impending bill; then we might see him reacting to these conversations over a drink with a friend, or reporting them to his wife. Next we could see him discussing with his party leader how he will vote; and later he will offer his interpretation of the action of Congress to the same two constituents (or lobbyists) we saw in the first scenes. As in the community problems courses, these scenes would be spaced out over a period of time, with intervening activities such as looking up legislative procedure, talking with politicians, discussing the kinds of forces among which congressmen are trapped, and trying to understand the rationale of political action.

The same sort of sequences could be used to bring home economic realities (the travails of the manager of an automobile sales company, the vicissitudes of a labor leader on the eve of negotiations, for example). One can also go historical, and present such episodes as a sequence of critical and revealing incidents in the life of a hypothetical delegate from Virginia to the first Continental Congress.

Conditions for Effective Use of Role-Playing

There is probably a close relation between the kind of role-playing that will be effective and the degree of development of the class as a group. Thus, generally speaking, the closer to self the situation portrayed, the more cohesive the group needs to be. The use discussed above under *Community problems* can be effective at the beginning of the semester, because the problem lies in social conditions which are relatively non-threatening to any one person. On the other hand, one would hardly attempt role-playing of marriage or family matters until the class had developed enough security that the role-playing was seen merely as a way of making concrete feelings and attitudes that were already close to awareness.

Another way to put this is to say that a scene which is perceived to be the sort of thing that happens to other people but not to oneself — as in the theater — can be used early in the life of the class; but one which portrays problems in which students are actually involved — even though the particular situation may not be in their immediate experience — had better wait until the students have become better acquainted. In all of the uses, role-playing is emphatically not an end in itself. It is a device for getting involvement through identification and release of feeling; but its educational value depends on whether this involvement becomes motivation for study and analysis. It is a device for getting data in one instance of a more or less typical sort of situation; but the educational value depends on how rigorously and perceptively the data thus obtained are organized and reflected upon.

The most effective role-playing is likely to emerge naturally from the logic and purposes of prior discussion. Thus, for example, a class in management had been discussing the exercise of authority by bosses. Various students cited illustrations from their own experience. One of the students started on a further illustration, and the class was quite interested in it. At this point, the teacher said: "Why not show us how it was. You can be the worker, and I'll bet Joe could portray the boss. I suggest you take Joe out into the hall and give him the details of the situation, but don't tell him what to do. Then you two come in and act as boss and worker, and we'll all see what happens." While the students were getting ready in the hall, the teacher invited the class to predict what would happen in the scene, and had them discuss the kinds of behaviors to look for as evidence.

In this illustration, the briefing of the players had been developing through the previous discussions and lectures in the class. The students already had a frame of reference, knowledge of alternative courses of action, and general acquaintance with various types of boss-worker relations. The new element in the class was readiness to deal with problems in a personally meaningful — rather than merely academic — way; and this readiness was demonstrated in the engagement in swapping experiences and in the willingness to take the risks that go with expressing one's own feelings about specifically described events.

Preparation for role-playing involves two elements: defining the problem situation and briefing the players (that is, getting them into role). When the role-playing is for the purpose of comparing ideas about alternative ways of dealing with a situation, then the class may be asked to define the situation with an eye to building into it the problem factors they are concerned with. They can be expected further to give some characterization of the roles to be played, and to have suggestions about who might take these roles. The players themselves, however, probably should be free to fill in the details of situation and attitude, for role-playing is a spur-of-the-moment improvisation, and it cannot have the necessary spontaneity if the players are preoccupied with acting. Once the social status and duties of the players are decided, each player is expected to play his part in his own way. It is thus not expected that a player will accurately portray some particular person or some defined type, and discussion about whether the role was "typical" is fruitless. The simplest way to avoid such discussion is to have *two* scenes and to direct discussion to the differences or similarities between the scenes. Then the group deals with the evidence before it rather than evaluating the scene against some stereotypic but undefined expectancy.

The audience, too, can usually profit from some briefing as to what it will look for and who will look for it. Part of the group might be paying especial attention to one character, and another part to another. A third part might be looking not at the characters but at the development of the situation itself — the emergence of conflict, for example, or the techniques of critical thinking and persuasion employed by the players. Following the scene, the various groups of observers can meet, compare notes, and decide who will report their pooled perceptions to the class. This sort of meeting of subgroups is especially suitable when the role-playing situation is close to the experience of the class, for the observers have a chance to let off steam among themselves and gain a little more objectivity. Under these conditions, their comments to the class and to the role-players will be less likely to be threatening to the players and emotionally seductive of their classmates.

Probably the most important over-all requirement for effective role-playing is that it be dramatic (but not necessarily melodramatic). Just defining two roles and then setting them into interaction is not enough; the audience has no basis for interpretation and the players have no plausible reason for conversation. There must be a situation: a conflict in attitude, belief, or action *with respect to* a set of circumstances to be dealt with by the role-players. Probably most effective role-playing passes through the following phases: (a) initial communication through which are portrayed various aspects of the relations among the protagonists; (b) the development of a situation in which they are all involved and in which they disagree and, usually, covertly conflict; (c) the introduction of stress into the situation, either because of a demand made by one player on another or because of a demand made on their relationship by some element in the situation itself; (d) the emergence of conflict into the open, and the delineation of its dimensions; and (e) the effort at resolution — frequently through the need to reach some decision. Such a plot is probably in accord with the expectations of most people, and if these expectations are violated very seriously the audience is likely to feel that the scene is pointless and inconclusive.

Techniques and Educational Objectives

A role-played scene gives the class something to talk about; and, moreover, it ordinarily releases motivation to talk about it. But the educational value of the experience depends on the way the experience is structured and guided by the teacher. A number of techniques can be related to educational objectives.

1. Testing hypotheses. These may be hypotheses about policies dealing with objective, organizational, or interpersonal factors in situations. Thus, for example, in the study of leadership the question of the leader's style is likely to be of interest. Students think of leaders as democratic, autocratic, permissive, and the like. They seldom can define these terms very clearly, but they tend to believe that a democratic leader will get more creativity, growth, and motivation than an autocratic leader will. In such a case, the class has two educational problems on its hands: first, it needs to give terms like democratic and autocratic some operational definition so that it knows what it is talking about. Second, it needs to set up some way to compare or illustrate the important differences between the effects of the two styles. There are many ways in which these needs can be translated into role-playing techniques.

The same situation can be played twice, with all the characters the same except the leader. The leaders in the two scenes are briefed to try to act democratically and autocratically. The scenes are played, and the audience compares the responses of the leaders to criticisms, suggestions, bids for dependency, and other behaviors of the members; it also compares the behaviors of the members to similar demands, suggestions, and criticisms offered by the leaders within their respective frames of reference. The members themselves are usually interviewed to get their reaction to particular behaviors of the leaders.

Another technique involves playing the scene only once, but introducing the comparisons when the leader is making critical decisions. The leader is provided with two consultants who sit behind him. The scene runs along until something is said to which the leader's response will be crucial. The leader, instead of replying, stops the action, turns to his consultants, and asks for their advice. One consultant has been briefed to advise him from a democratic viewpoint, the other from an autocratic viewpoint. The audience and the leader hear the advice, but the other role-players, with the action frozen, are asked to hold their hands tightly over their ears. The leader, having heard the advice, may now look at the ceiling and introspect aloud as to how he will choose among the various suggestions made by the consultants; the leader may also decide to ignore their advice and do something else. He then turns to the group, the action is resumed, and continued to another critical point; then the consultation is repeated. Four or five such consultations are usually enough for the audience to deal with.

Another technique puts the audience in the role of consultants, living the experience with the leader. The scene is played once, with the leader dealing with the emerging problems in any way he wishes. The audience then divides into subgroups to discuss what advice they would like to give the leader (and why). The leader then interviews reporters from the subgroups, and decides (out loud) which of the various suggestions he will try to utilize. (The other role-players are sent out of the room during this phase.) Then the scene is replayed, with the leader trying to implement the suggestions he said he accepted. Members of the audience are usually filled with feelings of considerable suspense as they wait to see what happens to their suggestions. The follow-up brings out the perceptions of the role-players about differences they felt in the way the leader operated; the leader's perceptions of the suggestions he thinks he implemented well or badly; and the audience's perceptions of the extent to which the advice had any effect on the leader's behavior. This technique is especially suitable for raising questions about the problems of bringing about changes in behavior.

2. Developing sensitivity or analytical insight. It is one thing to know in an academic way that people have hidden as well as manifest motives for their conduct. It is quite another thing to detect and recognize which kinds of behavior are determined by motivations at which of these two levels. Of course, any situation can be discussed to bring out these differences, but there are real dangers here because the hidden level is arrived at through diagnosis, and the kinds of diagnostic comments the group makes may be as threatening as they are unsound. A technique is required to keep the analysis objective, focused, and within proper bounds of consideration for others.

One technique involves setting up a series of two-person situations. In each scene, one person is asking the other to contribute his time, his ideas, his money, his prestige; and the other person is resisting the request. The resistance is planned at the two levels of manifest and hidden reasons. Thus the resistant player gives the usual kind of evasions — lack of time, lack of sympathy with the campaign, and the like. But he tries to react at the deeper level with such responses as enmity toward the requester, feelings of injury at being presumed upon, adherence to some moral position which the requester or the requester's organization appears to violate. In the follow-up the audience tries first to identify the manifest resistances; then it tries to diagnose the hidden resistance which the player attempted to build into his act. The teacher keeps the discussion going until several alternative hypotheses have been offered. He then turns to the resistant role-player and asks him to comment on the shrewdness of the various hypotheses. Throughout the diagnostic discussion, the teacher insists upon specific evidence to support any hypothesis offered, so that the interpretative quality of diagnosis can be clearly seen. And the assumption, of course, is that there is no way to prove that any particular hypothesis is correct.

In addition to this diagnostic approach to sensitivity, in which the student operates primarily from the position of an observer, there is an approach to sensitivity through evocation within oneself of the other. That is, while one is actively interacting with another person, some part of oneself identifies with this other person — the interaction to some extent is internalized within oneself. As you and I chat together I am constantly anticipating the sort of tack you will take next, but this anticipation is not the result of intellectual diagnosis so much as the result of my feeling some of the things you are feeling. And between us we share enough of a common culture that I can expect you to react somewhat as I would when we both have the same feeling. This sort of identification is the essence of intelligent listening to another person. Two techniques may be suggested for helping students develop this kind of sensitivity. The value of both techniques accrues primarily to the participant rather than the audience, although readiness to profit from participation is undoubtedly developed in the audience.

The first technique uses alter egos. Each role to be played is assigned to two (or more) persons. One performs in the usual way — interacting with others, seeking to achieve his purposes, and so on. The second person, representing self-awareness, confines his attention to expressing the feelings that his other half in the role is suppressing or at best expressing only in a roundabout way. Thus the action-actor might say, "I would like very much to help you, but the fact is that dinner is waiting for me at home and my family is expecting me. Won't you call on me another time?" Whereupon the self-expressive-actor tries to express the "real" feelings of the action-actor, and says something like, "This pest! Can't he do anything for himself? Let me out." Such comments, made in the context of action, may tend to sensitize the action-actor to his possible reluctance to accepting another person's dependency; it suggests to the other actor that his request for help (whatever it was) has stirred up resentment; and it gives the audience an interpretative reaction against which to match its own reactions to the scene. In the scene itself, the expressions of the alter ego tend to increase the emotional involvement of the actors.

The second technique has been called role reversal; two variations have been used. The first calls for playing the scene twice; in the second scene, the actors exchange parts. Quite literally, the actors are forced to put themselves in the other fellow's place. Having felt what it's like on the other side one is frequently able to move a little closer next time to meeting the other fellow half way. One interesting result is that frequently the actors learn the extent to which their original positions are actually defensive façades. It is, for example, a rather chastening experience for the holier-than-thou type of liberal, who insists he is without racial prejudice, to play the role of a racially prejudiced person — and discover that he has rare talents in this direction. After such an experience he is more likely to be able to cooperate effectively to help prejudiced people. In the same vein, a troublesome student, given the role of a teacher and confronted by the teacher playing *him*, may develop greater sensitivity to the possible ways in which other people perceive his behavior.

Another type of role reversal has been suggested by several teachers who are interested in developing better communication. In a discussion, the rule is laid down that before anyone may express his own ideas he must first paraphrase the contribution of the last speaker well enough that the last speaker agrees that his point has been properly understood — only then may one go on to express his reactions.

These last several devices add depth to one's acting-out during role-playing. Teachers tend to feel that for maximum value these behaviors must be analyzed later to make explicit to the actors the various kinds of awareness toward which they are being pushed. Therapists, on the other hand, tend to argue that the acting-out under these conditions has values in its own right — quite apart from whether there is subsequent discussion or not. But even the therapeutically oriented teacher may feel that this sort of acting-out in front of the class is most useful as a stimulus; and that the most valuable experience takes place when the actor makes an appointment to come in and talk over his feelings privately with the teacher.

In Conclusion

First, role-playing can be used to make ideas concrete — so that people can observe and discuss behavior rather than characterizations of behavior. Second, role-playing when properly introduced tends to develop a good deal of interest, involvement, and motivation in the class. Third, this interest and motivation is likely to result in a good deal of student discussion outside of class; in fact one can point to a number of classes whose outside discussions seemed to have been considerably more worthwhile to many of the students than were the actual class discussions. Fourth, role-playing, if properly focused and structured, can be an educative experience of critical thinking. And, finally, some of the outcomes of enhanced meaning to the individual student are probably more likely to be realized through proper use of role-playing than through any other classroom technique so far available.

THIS chapter, prepared by Mr. Thelen, who is in the Department of Education at the University of Chicago, reflects the discussion of a group of which Ruth Weise, School of Nursing, University of Minnesota, was chairman, and Gerhard Neubeck, College of Science, Literature, and the Arts, University of Minnesota, was recorder.

Learning through Discussion

AT THE outset, let us be perfectly clear what it is we are examining. The dictionary is not too helpful, but it provides a starting point in suggesting that discussion is the "consideration of a question in open debate; argument for the sake of arriving at truth or clearing up difficulties." The important elements here are (a) that an issue, a controversy, an uncertainty is involved, as represented by "consideration of a question," "debate," "argument"; (b) that the process is "open" rather than restricted as in formal debate; and (c) that the object is clarification and "arriving at truth"—the latter a somewhat idealized concept of the learning process.

We might go further and indicate what discussion clearly is not, though each is often mistaken for it. It is not the posing of questions by the instructor to which students are expected to respond with answers gleaned from textbook or lecture. Neither is it the superficial exchange among students of opinions, without support of facts. Nor is discussion the overcoming of an opponent in debate, nor the random conversation in a group, nor the presentation of a series of student reports. Student participation per se is no guarantee of discussion. Rather discussion is a constructive process involving listening and thinking as well as speaking. It utilizes relevant facts and ideas to advance the group's understanding and action.

Discussion in the Teaching-Learning Process

It is important to recognize that discussion can be only a part of the total teaching-learning process. The complete act involves a series of steps. First, there is motivation—a desire or drive to acquire the learning, be it facts, skills, attitudes, appreciations, or understandings. Second, there is the presentation—the lecture, the demonstration, the text or reference reading, the film, the field trip. Third, there is clarification and practice — discussion, drill, laboratory exercise, shop and field work, home study. Fourth, testing for adequacy and proficiency — performing, writing, reporting, creating, constructing, taking tests. Fifth, the application and use of the information, insight, understanding, technique, or skill. Discussion can be of value in most, if not all, of these phases. However, it is only one among many instructional techniques and it cannot be expected to do the whole job. After all, students gain from reading, from observing demonstrations, from doing laboratory experiments, and even from listening to lectures!

Most instructors tend to think of the presentation phase of teaching-learning as being the primary, if not the entire, process. Thus History 106 is "taught" by the lecture method; Professor Horace Alback is offering Psychology 180 by television; the Marriage Course is "taught" by the discussion method. Actually, it must be understood that the institution provides facilities — laboratories, libraries, practice rooms, gymnasiums, lounges, common rooms, and study halls — for the other phases of the process and course effectiveness is dependent to a great degree upon the extent to which students engage in these other learning activities. This, in turn, is related to three factors: the student's maturity, particularly his self-directiveness; the motivation provided by the instructor, the environment, or the student himself; and the adequacy of the learning facilities which are available.

Discussion Little Used

Why is discussion so little used at the college level, as a teaching-learning technique? The lecture or lecture-demonstration method continues to be the prevailing mode of instruction not only in large classes but often in small ones as well. Perhaps it is because it has certain advantages from the instructor's point of view. Lecturing permits logical organization of a course, and it can be laid out in detail in advance. It is tidy, with everything important included and no loose ends of unfinished business. It is efficient and time-saving, for lecture notes can be assembled and kept up to date with a minimum of effort. The midterm and final examinations can be based solidly upon the material covered, and what could be fairer than that? Finally, there is the security of knowing exactly where one is and where one is headed.

There are, of course, other techniques used with considerable frequency at the college level. Many of these involve overt student participation without actually being discussion. There is the recitation or the quiz section which serves primarily to determine whether students have memorized "right" answers. There is the extensive blackboard work in mathematics and languages to test attainment of skills. Laboratory experiments are sometimes used to discover relations and principles but more often they are demonstrations of principles already presented. Finally there is the use of individual and group reports of surveys, projects, and investigations.

Basically, the dominance of these instructional methods may be traced to the assumption about the nature of higher education which is held by many college instructors, that it is a process of mastering predetermined content. If the student is to know the past — its events, its achievements, its culture, its great ideas, its techniques, the whole heritage of learning — then he must be exposed to it! What easier way is there than to tell it to him in lectures and have him read about it in books? And he must know it to the point of mastery so what is more logical than to question him orally and on paper and let him demonstrate at the blackboard and in the laboratory?

The difficulty about this oversimplification of higher education is that it fails to allow for other purposes to which we subscribe with equal fervor. Indeed, in a democracy, we usually give higher priority to such values as critical thinking, creativity, problem-solving, scientific method, independent judgment, refined tastes, humane values, and reasoned convictions. These represent goals not attained by the simple procedure of presentation and passive acceptance; they are developed through processes requiring initiative, independence, and creativity. Included are the practices associated with critical thinking and scientific inquiry: recognition of problems; formulation of hypotheses; gathering relevant data; weighing, comparing, and testing ideas and hypotheses; selecting and applying conclusions. Discussion, as an instructional technique, involves many of these very processes and contributes toward the students' attainment of these significant goals.

One must not conclude, of course, that discussion is not presently used in college teaching. Successful seminars and honors courses exist at undergraduate levels and the problem approach and the case method are certainly widely used in American colleges. Nevertheless many instructors who would like to employ discussion have not acquired the requisite skill. Others have tried from time to time to enliven classes with this form of student participation but do not feel as secure in the role of discussion leader as they do when they are in firm charge, ladling out wisdom and conducting recitations. And still others carry on what they assume to be discussion in an atmosphere so dictatorial that students respond only when specifically called upon and give back only what is obviously expected. Few college teachers have been trained in discussion leadership and few experienced it in their student days. In short, if discussion is to be more widely used on American campuses, opportunities must be given for instructors to become proficient in conducting it.

Purposes Served by Discussion

It is possible to become enamored of the process of discussion; indeed to become faddish about it. It is salutary to keep in mind that discussion is but a means to an end — not an end in itself. Some enthusiastic discussion leaders have seemingly become carried away by new vocabulary and tricks of the trade to the point where what is termed group process has become more important than the content of the discussion. Such extreme overemphasis can be avoided by being clear about the purposes for which discussion is employed:

Consensus. Sometimes, the evidence considered in discussing an issue becomes overwhelming in spite of initial prejudice and preconceptions, so that it is possible for the class to achieve consensus — to reach a group conclusion. Many issues in science, history, and the arts are of this type, though, even here, students learn that new evidence overturns accepted conclusions, thus illustrating freshly the tenuous nature of truth.

Group action. Discussion may be used as a means for determining group action. Thorough consideration ultimately ends in a choice among alternatives on the basis of a vote, the minority going along with the majority. The end product, however, hammered out in discussion, usually represents a compromise which comes closer to satisfying the divergent data and viewpoints than does any of the original proposals.

Individual conclusions. But most class discussion aims at the edification of the individual student who is not expected to accept a group conclusion. Rather he is exposed in the process to varied and conflicting data, points of view, and hypotheses, and must arrive at his own reasoned conclusions in terms of his own values and convictions. Much material in the social sciences and the humanities is discussed with such a purpose. Occasionally students may go beyond an intellectual conclusion to the logical action which it entails. Convinced, through discussion, of the importance of the United Nations, students may proceed to write letters to statesmen and politicians or to organize a student United Nations Assembly. Certainly action on the basis of reasoned conclusions is, in a sense, the ultimate goal of education; for if the student really reaches a conclusion, it becomes a part of him, thus influencing his behavior. Most of the time, however, the resultant action takes place outside the instructor's purview or at a deferred time so that he has little knowledge of the reality of the student's expressed conclusions. He must necessarily settle for what the student proclaims, orally or in writing, to be his individual conclusions.

Discussion can also be classified in terms of its functions in instruction. Merely to enumerate some of these is to suggest the usefulness of this process. Discussion can (a) stimulate interest in a new topic by exploring its relations to the students' concerns, needs, and preoccupations; (b) open up a new area of study by tracing relations to previously learned content, revealing issues involved, suggesting needed data to be gathered, and sketching possible ramifications; (c) clarify problems and suggest hypotheses; (d) be used to pool and evaluate data; (e) be employed to draw reasonable conclusions based on data including values at stake; (f) consider applications of principles and conclusions.

Value in Relation to Participation

The effectiveness of discussion is often assumed to be related to the proportion of the group engaged overtly in the process. Recent studies at the University of Chicago, as reported by Benjamin Bloom, indicate this is not valid. It was found that there was no correlation between overt participation in discussion and achievement in the course. Some students took part actively and made high marks, but others equally active made low marks. Similarly some who took no part outwardly in the discussion received high marks and others of similar overt passivity had low achievement. Retrospective analysis revealed that covert participation was the significant factor. It was the quality of this cerebral activity that was important. The task of the instructor, then, would appear to be to stimulate this active, though covert, process, whatever the instructional method employed.

It can be concluded that discussion can be effective in large groups as well as small ones and that it can be used on television with some success, as demonstrated at the State University of Iowa. The objective is not that all students shall speak up in class; rather it is that all shall be stimulated to active covert participation.

Suggestions for Discussion Leadership

It may be helpful to suggest some principles which appear to be essential in the leadership of discussion. This is not an exhaustive list of techniques. Rather they set the stage for lively and profitable give and take among class members.

Select issues. In preparing for discussion, the instructor must select those phases of his subject, or of a topic, which lend themselves to the process; he must look for issues, for controversies, for differences, which can be examined and evaluated. One cannot discuss a fact. In a sense this identification of issues is dependent upon the instructor's attitude toward his subject — whether he considers it relatively static and immutable or dynamic and ever-changing. My own belief is that there is no field of higher education which does not involve differences of opinion, require the weighing of evidence, and involve choices among alternative solutions.

Create a permissive atmosphere. To secure sincere and vital discussion, the instructor must create a classroom atmosphere which is permissive — which encourages original thinking, honest expression, and diversity in viewpoints and data. The leader must believe that young people can think, can express themselves fluently, and can contribute to the richness of group discussion. Students quickly sense a phony who lacks respect for their thinking and wants only to have his own ideas flung back to him.

Develop group tolerance. Beyond mere permissiveness there is needed a positive tolerance toward the expression of minority viewpoints — the outrageous alternatives, the rebellious utterances. Each sincere expression must be seriously entertained, rigorously examined, and severely tested. Youth needs the opportunity to express its rebellion against adult authority not in meaningless pranks, but in serious exploration of divergent views. The danger today is not that we shall encourage a host of radicals but rather that conformity will suppress all originality, independence, and creativity. The minority expression is a refreshing challenge to the majority, stimulating thinking, challenging stereotyped viewpoints, and suggesting new hypotheses.

Listen. Good discussion depends upon attentive listening on the part both of the leader and the class. This is what differentiates discussion from what Rebecca West called intersecting monologues. There is a progressive building of ideas, one upon another. The thinking of each is continuously modified by the others. A viewpoint shifts because of new data; a proposal is altered to take into account the reactions of an important minority; a concept must be broadened to avoid apparent inconsistency. These adjustments are possible only when group members seek to learn rather than to impose; when they listen as well as talk.

Choose appropriate type. There are several types of discussion commonly used today. Choice among them will depend upon the size of the group and the purpose of the discussion. The smaller the group the more general the overt participation. The larger the group the more reliance must be placed upon token or representative participation in the hope that most group members will take part covertly. Six types are described briefly below. They not only may be used singly, but in combination — as, for example, a symposium-forum in which a series of talks is followed by questions and statements from the audience. (a) *Small group discussion*: Discussion among a group of three to eight people with a nominal leader and great informality; often a working committee carrying out assignments for a larger group. (b) *Group discussion*: Discussion open to all members of a group from eight to fifty in number, though twenty to thirty is more usual; method informal with a discussion leader and frequently a recorder and resource people. (c) *Panel discussion*: A small group discussion carried on before a larger audience; panel members may be representative of the audience or consist of experts on the problem. (d) *Symposium*: A planned series of succinct presentations on a single subject given before an audience by representatives of divergent views, interests, or approaches. (e) *Forum*: A large group meeting offering opportunity for individual expression from the audience under formal rules. (f) *Buzz session*: The arbitrary breakdown of a large group into small groups for brief periods to secure individual expression on assigned questions, each group summarizing its replies for the larger audience.

Discussion must progress. The leader of a discussion must conduct it so that it progresses step by step toward the predetermined goal rather than bogging down in fruitless argument. (This goal, of course, is not a predetermined conclusion, but a decision to be made, an action to be taken, some alternatives to be formulated.) This is accomplished through frequent summaries of where the group stands; through calling attention to serious inconsistencies, significant omissions, and needed data; through clarifying emerging issues; through bringing the group back to the subject from which it has wandered; and by reminding the students of the tasks yet remaining.

Relate discussion to other learning activities. Discussion should be judiciously used only when it will best contribute to learning. It, in turn, will motivate a wide range of other learning activities. Discussion as the sole classroom activity soon loses its value; students become victims of what has been called progressive disenchantment. Discussion should grow out of, and feed into, reading, listening to lectures, research, writing, experimentation, drill, and creative activity.

Discussion about Discussion

Some possible issues which seem to be related to my analysis are as follows: Is the use of discussion in teaching compatible with scholarly standards? How important is discussion in the teaching-learning process? Is it practical to use discussion in combination with other instructional techniques? What factors determine whether a subject lends itself to discussion? Do large classes preclude effective use of discussion? How may college instructors acquire discussion leadership skills?

THIS chapter, prepared by Mr. Tyler, who is director of radio and television education at Ohio State, reflects the discussion of a conference group of which Ned Flanders, College of Education, University of Minnesota, was chairman, and Donald K. Smith, College of Science, Literature, and the Arts, was recorder.

◆§ LEWIS B. MAYHEW

Using Students as Teachers

Pᴇʀʜᴀᴘs the safest generalization one can make about the use of students in teaching capacities is that very little has been reported in the literature of collegiate education. Whether this paucity reflects the fact that little has been attempted or that people have just not written about their experience, of course, cannot be known. One suspects, however, that not much use has been made of students in the role of teacher. And this fact, if it is a fact, can be explained in several ways. There is some reason to believe that educational and psychological theory derives in part from the prevailing social and economic conditions. Thus, the 1930 theories that small classes were essential could be linked to the depression mentality which wanted to provide employment for larger numbers of teachers. In the 1950's one discovers that there are valid reasons for establishing large classes so that the supply of available teachers can be sufficient for the educational needs of society. Possibly an economic reason is responsible for the dearth of experimentation with undergraduates in teaching positions: the professoriate has not wanted the competition of nonsalaried workers. But in addition to the economic factor, students have not been used because of traditions of American education. Our university in part derives from the German university with its emphasis on research and the reporting of research to students. It also derives from the colonial college in which adults sought to impose a particular religious and moral ideology on students. In neither tradition was the student judged wise, mature, or knowing enough to fulfill even part of the role of teacher.

Some Examples of Teaching by Students

Evidence that these traditions are changing is the inclusion of a topic such as the one we are discussing and the few isolated examples of tentative experimentation with bringing students into a more central position in the teaching process. Sweetbriar, for example, uses its advanced students who have had a year of study abroad in teaching freshman language courses. Hastings College habitually uses its foreign students as coaches in its language courses.

Stephens College has a course required of all students which is taught over closed-circuit television. Twice a week a twenty-minute lecture over television by an expert is followed by discussion of the points raised in each of fifty-two small classes. These discussions are usually led by faculty members, but in each of a few of the larger sections one girl who has taken the course the previous year assumes the responsibility of leading the discussion for half the girls in the section — the other half being led by a faculty member. This student-led discussion goes on in the same classroom as the one led by the faculty member, so the girl is really under the supervision of an adult.

At Taylor University a senior course in leadership is organized along practicum lines, with each senior being responsible for the orientation of freshmen and for working with a limited number of new students throughout the first semester. Seniors attend classes on leadership and then put their new knowledge into practice by teaching freshmen how to adjust to the college community. A number of schools have used advanced undergraduates as lab assistants in science courses and a few have used them as quiz section leaders following a lecture. A few other colleges have made undergraduates responsible for laboratory equipment and the preparation of demonstrations.

Another use of students is represented by several attempts to ask students to grade written work. At Chatham College a few years ago students were asked to write themes. One example was shown on a screen by means of an opaque projector and analyzed in detail by the entire class. Themes were then exchanged and each student graded another's paper using the criteria established by the entire class. Those who have worked with this speculate that it is possible to double the amount of written work required in rhetoric or communication classes without increasing the theme-reading burden of teachers. Further, they hold that the experience students gain in criticizing and judging written work improves their own facility with language. I have used the same device in courses in social science and find that in general student judgments of papers agree with mine at about the same level as the judgments of faculty colleagues agree with mine about students' performance.

At St. John's University students construct test questions and then grade other students' papers written in response to them. In various remedial courses at the college level this same rationale has been applied. At Michigan State the speech and listening services have extended the effectiveness of the professional staff by using a coach-and-pupil method. For example, the teacher will present some ideas on clarity of diction. Then the class practices in pairs. Students may sit back to back with one student speaking and the other recording what is being said. Apparently such activities result in improved speech patterns for both students and improved listening and writing habits as well. At Howard University courses in remedial English and social science are being taught experimentally by lectures given by experienced teachers, followed by discussions led by advanced undergraduate students. These students are given special instruction to enable them to cope with each week's work.

A by no means new idea is the long-established practice of the United States military and naval academies of using upper-class students as company officers for the entire student body. To these young men is assigned much of the responsibility for inducting new students into the military way of life and for developing the high *esprit de corps* which is said to characterize those institutions.

Of a similar order is the use of undergraduate students as assistants to faculty resident advisers in dormitories in civilian institutions. At Michigan State, men are housed in large four-hundred- to six-hundred-man buildings, each under the guidance of a faculty member and his wife. The dormitory is divided into sections, each of which is assigned to a student. In the past these students were selected and appointed by administrative decision of the faculty member. It was found, however, that use of sociometric devices with all students to identify a group of natural leaders from which appointments could be made resulted in better student leadership. Students looked to their natural leaders for instruction in the ways of the university, for help with their academic problems, and for many other reasons. Dormitories using this selection technique had fewer disciplinary problems and more cases of recognition for academic and extracurricular achievement than did dormitories selecting assistants by traditional means.

Using Students as Teachers

While not particularly saving of the total time teachers spend on each class, increased educational values have been claimed for course organization stressing student leadership. At Ball State, classes in freshman English are organized into committees of five students each. One student is chosen chairman to assist the teacher and to help stimulate other students. At Capital University, five or six capable students are placed in each section of English to assist the less able members. One man at Michigan State has organized his sections of Communication Skills so that students work on their own or under student leadership in class. The teacher himself remains in his office and encourages students to come to him only when other sources of help or knowledge prove inadequate. He sees important counseling outcomes for classes so organized, and has been influenced by some of the theory and practice of group psychotherapy.

Since some of my work takes me away from the campus a good bit, I have been forced to make use of students enrolled in the course in social science to act in leadership capacities. Typically, I schedule an examination for the first day of my absence. The papers are picked up in my office by a member of the class, who administers the test, takes it himself, and returns the papers for machine scoring. The next day the class (forty to fifty members) is divided into groups of ten to twelve and each group keys the entire examination. If I am absent a third day, the entire class reconciles differences among the keys worked out by each smaller group, and this becomes the key which determines grades on the examination. All of this is done without adults present.

With unselected groups one encounters some student resistance, but with students selected on the basis of their flexible, adaptable personality structures, this procedure seems to work and to give students values they otherwise would miss. One student, for example, reported to his counselor that he had been caught cheating on an examination in one course. That same week he had taken the examination in which students were on their own; he remarked that he wouldn't dream of cheating in such a situation. This does not minimize the very real morale problem in asking students to apply sanctions to each other. It simply says that the morale problem can be alleviated by careful selection of student groups.

Many of the projects suggested for the education in citizenship of college students are also of this general order. These courses are most often organized around projects. The instructor helps committees of the class prepare their undertakings, suggests materials they might read, and, of course, is available to help them overcome difficulties. The bulk of the time, which in orthodox social science courses is spent in classrooms with a teacher, is spent outside the classroom under the leadership of a student. Poll-watching at election time, working in a local party headquarters, making surveys for proposed annexation of territory, or surveying local housing needs are some of the activities which have been attempted. A particularly interesting project was the effort of one class to introduce an honor system to its college. Committees checked local practices and the experiences of other schools with honor systems, and then undertook the social action necessary to get a plan adopted by the faculty and student body.

Such a few examples are certainly inadequate as a basis for any sort of generalization. However, certain principles do seem to be implicit in most of them. If students have special skills, as had the students who studied abroad, these can be utilized with some confidence in teaching other students.

Secondly, a number of the examples assume that students gain from being required to assume responsibility for others. Most teachers could probably testify that they never really understood parts of their subject until they tried to make them clear to others. Apparently students find the same thing to be true. The nuances of language, for example, are difficult for students to assimilate until they are forced to judge someone else's paper and then justify their appraisal. And students apparently welcome the opportunity to tell someone else about a subject.

Thirdly, there appear to be some values, legitimately part of the objectives of a collegiate institution, which are more effectively handled by students than by faculty. Such things as discipline, procedures for group living, and orientation to the campus culture are made more intelligible and are more quickly accepted when students themselves assume responsibility for them. Courses such as those designed to orient students or to develop facility in interpersonal relations would seem to be adaptable to students' assuming a greater role in teaching. If dormitories and the extracurriculum were brought into closer harmony with the curriculum, these would also provide opportunity to use students as an important educational resource. For example, one of the dormitories at Stephens College became the focal point for Sunday afternoon dramatic performances. Students staged plays which were viewed by other girls and their dates and which were tied into the regular curricular work in dramatics.

Lastly, there seems to be an assumption in the examples given that students can be used to save teachers' time and that the educational gains for students thus employed make their working without pay defensible. The time teachers save from such tasks as reading themes, listening to group discussions, reviewing examination questions, and routine drill on skills and procedures could be used for more individual guidance of students, deeper professional preparation, and handling more students in the same amount of time.

The Development of Principles

While these assumptions seem valid and capable of considerable extension into classes now using students in teaching capacities, a broader theory is necessary if the use of students is to become anything more than a collection of interesting episodes. If a series of principles could be advanced which would support broad experimentation with students as teachers, ways could then be found to have students carry an important share of the tasks of education. Whether or not principles, once developed, can be validated, of course, will require considerable research. Perhaps all that can be accomplished now is the presentation of some principles and suggestions of how they might be applied.

The most important theoretical premise involves the nature of teaching and the role of the teacher. If teaching consists chiefly of one who knows much telling someone else or showing someone else what he knows, there can be little justification for even considering the use of students in teaching capacities. Obviously, a seventeen-year-old freshman is not going to know as much as a forty- or fifty-year-old professor. He is not going to possess the skills of thought which have come from years of research. If deep knowledge about a subject is necessary before one can teach, then only mature men and women should be allowed an opportunity to modify the minds of students. It is only if one assumes that the transmission of specialized knowledge is but one of the tasks of a teacher — and possibly not even the most important one — that the subject of this discussion makes any sense. It is only when the teacher is supposed to provide some focus for the attention of students' study, to stimulate students to want to learn on their own, to serve as one means by which students test their own perceptions of reality, and when he is as much responsible for students' opinions, attitudes, and values as for students' knowledge, that undergraduates can appropriately be expected to help.

If the task of teaching implies a variety of separate responsibilities, then several principles may be suggested which allow for student assistance. Despite the best of intentions, it is virtually impossible for members of one generation to comprehend what really interests the members of another. Many of us have possibly had the experience of wondering what young people could possibly see in Elvis Presley. Yet teen-age young people do see something and react to whatever it is that they perceive. To this observation we must add the note that learning takes place most effectively when the learner is sincerely interested in the materials. The value of interest can most plainly be seen in the success which athletic coaches and band and orchestra directors have had in getting students to give virtually professional performances. Now, if students are the ones who can most accurately detect the interests of other students, use of this phenomenon in education might be a possibility.

A second principle, allied with the first, implies that all learning is in reality the solving of problems. The human organism grows, matures, and becomes richer as it encounters obstacles, overcomes them, and incorporates each new synthesis into the total pattern of personality. Much of what any teacher does is to present problems to students in the hope that they will come to grips with them, solve them, and thereby grow. Not infrequently, however, students don't see as real problems the carefully contrived situations presented them by their teachers. The social scientist, for example, presents his class with a situation involving the analysis of a particular culture — only to have students see as the essential task the simple memorization of a few terms. Yet students in their friendship groups become concerned about highly abstract matters and will debate such things as the good life, the nature of God, or the psychological bases of marriage with a spirit any teacher would welcome in the classroom. The use of students in helping to set problems that other students may regard as real and significant and which at the same time will deepen their knowledge of an academic discipline may be the way of using students as an aid to learning.

A third principle involves the matter of communication. A person who knows a great deal about a subject is quite likely to assume a greater degree of sophistication on the part of his hearers than is actually warranted. We have found, for example, some slight evidence that students in the Basic College at Michigan State University learn more in the portions of the broad interdisciplinary courses which are not the specialty of the teacher than in those portions which are. Thus, a historian may frequently do the best job with the social and psychological portions of a course and the poorest with essentially historical materials. If this is so, perhaps a judicious blending of the mature scholar's knowledge of his subject and the ability of one undergraduate to communicate with other undergraduates might be a partial answer to a continuing problem of education. One does, however, need to be careful that undergraduates do not try to become so like their professors that they too shoot over the heads of other students.

A fourth principle also involves the relationship between generations. The nature of the growth pattern of the human being makes considerable tension the rule in relations of young people with adults. From infancy on, the adult, capable as he is of granting or withholding from a child affection, love, or even life itself, places the child in a potentially threatening situation. As the child moves from home to school, the teacher takes on many parental attributes. In the presence of a possibly threatening adult, the child or youth inhibits much of his natural curiosity for fear of alienating his powerful adversary. It may well be that much of the arid, moribund classroom work one sees in American colleges has its roots in the students' fear and resentment of the adult teacher. When almost all classroom work is conducted in such situations, important aspects of the students' willingness and ability to learn may atrophy. Again, perhaps a wise and prudent blending of situations in which adults are present with situations where they are not present may maximize the learning possibilities in collegiate education. Adults cannot abdicate from the classroom. There are times when students want and need their presence. On the other hand, there are important times when adults are really in the way.

A last principle implies that the teaching-learning process has many aspects. Some of these seem to require the concentrated efforts of a well-trained adult, while others require the efforts of the peers of students and a laissez-faire policy from teachers. Perhaps an analogy from childrearing practices may make the point clearer. Parents, as informed adults, have a responsibility to show children how to dress, how to express themselves, and how to react to certain kinds of emotion. The age group of the child, when he reaches adolescence, inducts him into the actual ways of expressing sexual urges. One could not claim that adequate heterosexual adjustment was an unimportant part of the individual's life history. Yet it is a part of life the training in which we adults leave chiefly to young people. Those of us who are parents of boys consciously leave to the girls of the same age group certain teachings about the regulation of one's personal behavior. The point of this principle is that colleges and universities attempt to do many things to and for students. Some analysis of these purposes can suggest that some are clearly best dealt with by other students, while some require the attention of adult teachers. And these principles probably have relevancy in the strictly academic side of education as well as in those parts emphasizing socialization and recreation.

Some Possible Practices Based on These Principles

There is a variety of practices that could be attempted which would be consistent with these principles and which would place considerable educational responsibility on students. Some of these have actually been tried, while others are sheer speculation at this time.

Students could be brought into the planning of all courses and programs. Antioch College has done this for years, with a student serving as a member of every standing committee and every department in the institution. As new courses are planned, as old ones are reviewed, and as teaching techniques are discussed, these students have ample opportunity to make their ideas effective in educational development. At Stephens College the Research Service has begun interviewing groups of students to get their ideas for curriculum revision. At Sarah Lawrence a committee composed of faculty members and students worked with a planning committee of the governing board in charting the future of the institution. In any attempt to bring students into the planning, care should be taken to ensure that they feel free to express opinions and that they believe that what they say will really be taken seriously.

Using Students as Teachers

A second use of students is in residence halls. At the present time there is a scarcity of trained people willing to live in student residence halls for more than a few years. Yet colleges could use the experience of these personnel workers for longer periods of time. Possibly using adults in guidance roles during the day, while making students solely responsible for the dormitory at night, might alleviate a serious staffing problem and at the same time gain significant educational results. For example, the values of the student subculture could probably best be transmitted to new generations of students in a dormitory situation, without the interference of adults. Further, the experience of assuming full responsibility for an entire dormitory might help students mature faster and hence stand to profit more from the rest of the collegiate program.

The third use of students is in connection with closed-circuit television. The substance of a variety of courses might be presented over closed-circuit television to several sections. After each day's presentation, a student might assume leadership in the discussion, lab work, or group project suggested by the lecturer's remarks. The pattern of the Stephens College Ideas and Living course of a twenty-minute presentation followed by thirty minutes of discussion seems feasible in other kinds of courses. The particular pattern, however, might vary. In some courses the first hour each week might be a lecture, with discussion sessions on subsequent days. While there should be some adult supervision of these student teachers, faculty members should not try to make them into younger models of themselves. The students' conduct in class should be free enough to preserve the advantage of the fact that they *are* undergraduate students.

A fourth use of students has but scant relevance to the subject of this discussion but seems significant enough to warrant some comment. Students in America probably have been trained to rely on teachers too much. Quite possibly breaking the pattern of classes meeting three or four times a week and replacing it with a system of classes meeting perhaps one hour each week might improve education and free some faculty members' time as well. Such a system would place great responsibility on each student for his own education and in this sense would be using student assistance. A scheme like this could, of course, be modified so that a class might meet with a teacher once a week and as committees chaired by students once a week; the remainder of the available class time could be devoted to independent study. In this connection, there does not seem to be evidence to warrant colleges' maintaining heavy class-hour requirements. In an experiment at Michigan State, a four-hour course was offered in three hours with the result that students taking the accelerated course performed better on a common final examination than did students who had attended the full four hours of class.

A last suggestion involves further experimentation with the residence hall as the real center of the total educational enterprise. Instead of students' leaving the halls to attend classes, the reverse might be done. Professors could go to the dormitories to deliver their lectures to students who lived there. These lectures might be followed by scheduled discussions conducted by the natural leaders of the residence hall. This might lead to informal discussions in which the full force of student interest, and the impact of the peer culture, might serve to enhance learning. Some will say that such a scheme could not work in large multi-purpose institutions, where the odds are several million to one against any two students' taking exactly the same pattern of courses. One can admit that the plan would present many difficulties and might have to be modified in important respects. However, the example of the oldest British university, which is broken into small, self-contained colleges and makes maximum use of students and of tutors to turn out educated men, leads one to believe the problems are not insuperable. Possibly the time has come for us to restore students to a position as fully recognized members of the university as a community of scholars in which they will fill teaching as well as learning functions.

THIS chapter, prepared by Mr. Mayhew, who is a professor of social science at Michigan State University, reflects the discussion of a group of which Thomas W. Chamberlin, Duluth Branch, University of Minnesota, was chairman, and Emil A. Erickson, Virginia Junior College, was recorder.

⊷§ C. GILBERT WRENN

Student Personnel Services and Teaching

STUDENT personnel work has developed rapidly on American college and university campuses during the past thirty to thirty-five years. It has expanded so rapidly, indeed, that many faculties have little intimate knowledge of these services — too little at least to make use of them. Such a lack of understanding is frequently tinged with distrust, and attention will be given in this chapter both to seeing student personnel services as a function of the instructional program of the institution and to an examination of faculty skepticism about personnel work and personnel workers.

We speak of rapid development, but it should be made clear that many of these services have existed on American campuses, often under different labels, for a century or two past. Attention to admissions and record-keeping is not new, nor is a lively concern for students' welfare outside of the classroom. What is new, however, are the following: (a) attention to a wider variety of needs, (b) the utilization of new psychological and administrative procedures to meet these needs, (c) recognition of the total constellation of student personnel services as a major function of the institution's educational program, (d) the staffing of these services with professionally qualified people.

An American Development

Student personnel work in college and university is a distinctively American development. Very little in the way of organized student personnel services exists elsewhere, although there is a stirring of interest in Europe and Australia. Japan is taking decided steps in this direction as a result of its experience during occupation by United States troops. My textbook, *Student Personnel Work in College* (9), has recently been translated into the Japanese language and at least three waves of student personnel specialists have been invited to visit that country.

The growth of student personnel work on American campuses has several causes, some psychological and some philosophical and social. Some of the influential features of our American educational culture are (a) the sheer size of student bodies: on any one campus there exist a relatively wide range of student abilities and a number of cultural and vocational curriculums. This condition will of course become accentuated in the future (1957 fall enrollments in the United States up to 3,068,000 students — an increase of 4.1 per cent over 1956, of 25 per cent above the peak enrollment of 1949, to become 150 per cent above 1949 in another decade); (b) a widespread acceptance of the psychological realities of individual differences and of the emotional in behavior as a determinant in all intellectual experience; (c) the development of a wide variety of usable psychological tools and procedures; (d) the impact upon higher education of a distinctively American educational philosophy involving a concern for the development of the social and aesthetic factors in personality as well as the intellectual; (e) the relative closeness of the college to parents and the community.

Faculty Use of Personnel Services

Three centrally useful student personnel services. There are at least three personnel services which the faculty could well use or, better still, could amalgamate with the instructional function. (Instruction is here broadly conceived as any planned function which contributes to learning, whatever the nature of the learning. Student personnel work is therefore seen as an integral part of the total educational program, not as a function separate from the total instructional activity.)

The first area is *counseling,* which is performed by a staff specially selected and prepared for a task of considerable complexity. Almost all faculty members counsel students, some of them infrequently, often superficially, but nevertheless they do counsel (4, 8). Faculty members need professional consultation on this, or the student needs more help than a teacher can give, in situations that arise almost daily.

The second area includes *student organizations* of a social, intellectual, literary, political, and religious nature. What students learn in these organizations may bear a close relation to classroom learning and should be understood and used by the faculty. The tendency to think

274

of activities as merely time-filling and of little basic significance for learning shows an appalling ignorance of them (7, 9).

The third area covers *student personnel records,* whether these exist in a departmental, registrar's, or admissions director's office, or in a counseling center (2, 9). The information in them may be invaluable to a teacher, both for understanding his students and for making possible a richer and more effective relation with a given student.

Meeting the reasons for faculty members' reluctance. Why don't faculty members *use* counselors as specialists in counseling, a function for which each teacher is responsible, not *use* student organizations as field situations and reality-testing laboratories for the very concepts and values stressed in the classroom, not *use* records as rich sources of understanding of the very students the teacher is pledged to serve? *Why* indeed is a puzzling question. Let me suggest three reasons.

1. Faculty members do not *know* the range of personnel services available on their campus. They act as if they did not care, but their attitude is more often to be explained as the result of ignorance. They may pretend that personnel services are no concern of theirs and refuse to listen to any evaluation of them. (Sometimes there is a question as to whether this is real disdain or a reaction to what they consider a threat to their status as teachers.) The teacher should know of the many other resources available to his students in addition to counseling, student organizations, and records. He should also know about such resources as loans and scholarships; part-time employment; dormitory counseling and social life; health services; job placement; special facilities for foreign students, married students, and commuters. He has a responsibility to seek out and to know, but what a man is ignorant of he often distrusts. Sometimes he not only does not use personnel services, but he condemns them. This is worse than ignorance; this is professional malpractice.

2. Faculty members do not *ask* personnel workers to help with the very problems of student need and development of which the faculty may be most aware. No one, unless it is a dormitory counselor, is more at a front-line observation post than is a teacher. And although he may be distressed by what he sees, he often does nothing. He may see gifted students and not know that a counselor is even more interested in such students than in the academically troubled or crippled. He

may be fearful of betraying his ignorance by asking for help or by referring a student. He appears not to know that the personnel worker *wants* to be asked, exists for the purpose of complementing the faculty's skills. The personnel worker will not consider an inquiry or a request for help as an imposition but as an opportunity to do what he is qualified to do.

What the personnel worker cannot do is to suggest that the teacher *needs* help! He has regard for faculty members' self-respect as well as concern for any resentment that might be aroused if he took the initiative. No, he must depend rather heavily upon the assumption that a faculty member will indicate any need for his services. We may wonder why this is not more frequently done, since both teacher and personnel worker are dedicated to the service of the student and the advancement of knowledge.

3. The teacher may not *use* available records about students because he thinks he does not have time to go to the appropriate office or is puzzled about what he sees on the records. On the other hand, consulting one student's record may prevent a real academic blunder, or may save a student from disaster. This failure to use records is often a fault of both personnel worker and teacher. The records *should* be accessible, *should* be in a translated form for easy use by the staff, *should* be seen against a prepared set of local norms.

That improved use is possible was demonstrated by a study conducted under my direction of English classes in the College of Science, Literature, and the Arts at the University of Minnesota (6). Biographical, academic, and test data for each class were presented in interpreted, profile form to the instructors of the classes. Three instructors had asked for this kind of aid, three had said they were not interested. Follow-up at the end of the quarter revealed substantial use by the instructors of the psychological descriptions of the classes, increased referrals of students to the Counseling Center, requests for and use of information on individual students, and approval of the project by all six instructors.

A personnel worker makes a clear distinction between confidential and nonconfidential information about a student. He will not release information that is given to him in confidence, nor should the teacher expect this. But there is much that is not confidential, much that could be learned that would aid the teacher in relating himself and his teaching most effectively to a single student or to a group. Neither he nor the personnel worker wants to use information to manipulate a student — both are committed to the principles of autonomy and self-determined growth for students. Both should also be committed to the principle of acting in ignorance as infrequently as possible.

Faculty Relations with the Student Personnel Worker

The dilemma of specialization. It has been appropriate and essential that personnel workers become professionally self-conscious, that they strive for professional standing so that they might secure the respect and collaboration of other educational and noneducational professions. It is important that they develop specialized tools and skills, that they promote consideration of students' characteristics and the needs they deem significant, and the like. Such activities are appropriate to any professional group, particularly one that is as yet incompletely developed. After all, college faculties are still striving to secure recognition by their administrations of *their* profession as a distinct and essential influence in determining policy.

What has happened to student personnel workers is that they have sometimes alienated their teaching colleagues in their attempt to secure professional recognition. They may have become so professionally self-conscious that they have isolated themselves from the faculty; they may have developed a jargon and a set of I-know-something-about-students-that-you-don't-know attitudes that are injurious to faculty–personnel worker relations.

Most student personnel workers recognize the danger of their isolation, but the development of a healthier relation is not a unilateral affair. They need help from the teaching faculty to enable them to stay in the main stream of educational activity, that of instruction and research. Their special knowledge should be used by the faculty, to be sure — that is the main emphasis of this chapter — but also they need to be recognized by the faculty as blood brothers. They should be invited to faculty meetings, included on department or college committees. The personnel worker cannot of himself be successful in effecting this rapprochement. One reason is that he may not recognize his alienation from the faculty as clearly as does the faculty. At any rate, the latter, in the interests of student welfare and institutional cohesiveness, could well become interested in effectively relating the personnel worker to the central stream of the academic institution (2).

The philosophy of the student personnel worker. It has recently been my task to relate the basic concepts in student personnel work to their philosophic foundations (1). There seems little doubt but that many of the purposes and goals of student personnel work have their basis in the philosophic approach known as *experimentalism* or *instrumentalism.* The ontology and epistemology of this school of thought focus upon the continuity of knower and to-be-known — the concept that knowing is operational, not simply a beholding. The problem-solver and the problem both change in the process of knowing. This is a naturalistic and relativistic theory of knowledge in which truth is forever emerging. Reality does not consist of universal truths but resides in particular experience in the present and the emerging future. Truth is dynamic in a world which is constantly changing.

For the experimentalist, values are not universal nor can they be separated from the observer and a particular experience. Values are the results of human choices involving a person and his environment, and their character must be found within that context.

It would be manifestly unfair to assert that this is *the* philosophy of student personnel work. Rather, I believe that it bears the closest relation to student personnel work of any systematic philosophy. On the other hand, most college faculty members are probably *rationalists* (holding the belief that knowledge, truth, and values pre-exist in the abstract, to be discovered and rediscovered by man) or *realists* (conceiving of reality as existing in the world of physical and biological fact, truth to be discovered within the physical world and apart from the knower). But personnel workers are also academicians in education and in environment — if their background and interests have been in the humanities they are likely to be rationalists in philosophy, if in science to be realists; if they have been operating within a religious frame of reference they are likely to be idealists.

So the personnel worker is thoughtful — his task appears to depend upon experimentalist assumptions, but he as a person has been nurtured upon realism or rationalism. With all of his belief in individual integrity and uniqueness, with all that he knows of values as operational and relative, deep within himself he may well be an *idealist* in value concepts. He believes in great immutable values, timeless and, perhaps, having their origin in the nature of God. A student personnel worker is the child of two worlds, the world of science and the world of humanism. His philosophic conflict is therefore understandable and very real.

All this is to suggest that the personnel workers are plagued by the same philosophic problems as are many of the teaching staff. For the faculty also may struggle between experimentalism, realism, or rationalism on the one hand, and the idealist's belief in basic values on the other. There should be much profit in the faculty's thinking through its philosophic bases in conjunction with the personnel worker's consideration of his philosophy. The personnel worker may well not be a rationalist, yet he was brought up in that atmosphere and understands the reasons why it is a satisfying philosophy for some faculty members. Since he is likely to be research-oriented, he will probably have a healthy respect for those in the sciences who are realists or positivists. Yet the nature of his relations with students and their complex needs and growth situations may well require him to stress process and not product, to see reality more in terms of "does it work?" than "is it true?" Because of the personnel worker's dedication to working with the student as a total, functioning personality, it is not too remote to suggest that the faculty rationalist or realist may learn something about *people* from the personnel worker.

Although the philosophy of a college teacher may have a different core than that of a student personnel worker, their educational nurture is similar and some aspects of their philosophic beliefs are likely to be the same. After all, both are educators with many assumptions and beliefs in common.

Although other goals, such as the application of college facilities to the solution of urgent social problems, are emerging, the two traditional and almost incontestable roles of higher education in America are (a) to operate as a socializing agent both in transmitting the culture and in preparing young people to assume their individual responsibilities in American society (transmission) and (b) to contribute to the advancement of that culture through new knowledge, skills, and values (innovation). To these two ends student personnel work may contribute richly in the development, on the one hand, of greater interpersonal effectiveness, more mature and realistic personal goals, greater tolerance of personal differences, and the like, and on the other to the advancement of knowledge of human behavior through research and procedural tryout (5).

The personnel worker as a person. In the two foregoing sections I have suggested that the faculty can use personnel services more effectively by developing a more satisfying personal relation with the personnel worker. He needs to be seen as a person who in some situations has perhaps unwittingly and unwillingly developed his task tangentially to the instructional task. *Of course* he stresses different student needs and different procedures than those seen and used by many faculty members. If he did not, he would be of little complementary value to the faculty. But he is quite definitely as much an educator as is a faculty man and their common elements of interest and purpose need to be seen more clearly by both. He needs help in remaining close to instruction. Can the faculty help him? His philosophy may be less fixed than that of some teachers but some of his assumptions exactly parallel those held by his teaching colleagues. If one can see the *reason* for a disagreement in aim or procedure and the *reasonableness* of it to the differently oriented person, it is easier to accept the other person as possessing integrity and as deserving of respect.

Often a teacher fails to use a personnel service because he does not understand the personnel man back of the service, has made little attempt to understand him — and assumes the worst! Lack of meaningful communication between the persons involved in an academic transaction is as common as lack of understanding or distrust of the services themselves.

Summary

Developing the relation suggested in the title of this chapter will be furthered by

1. Faculty *understanding* of the personnel worker as a person, as a member of a related profession, as a fellow educator.

2. Faculty *acceptance* of the student personnel worker as an educational colleague who desires to contribute to the effectiveness of the teaching function.

3. Faculty *knowledge* of the services available and of the kinds of students for which such services exist.

4. Faculty *use* of professional counselors, student activities, and stu-

dent personnel records in the furthering of their own instructional aims and the more complete development of their students.

Can the student personnel services be used by faculty members to save time in the crowded days ahead? The answer I am sure is yes. In the coming years when every teacher will have more students for whom he is responsible, can the student personnel worker help the teacher become more intelligently aware of the human learner in the class and thus contribute to the effectiveness of the teaching-learning process? The answer seems undeniably in the affirmative — but the outcome is in the hands of the faculty.

REFERENCES

1. Hardee, Melvene, ed. *Personnel Services in Education.* Chicago: University of Chicago Press, 1959. 58th Yearbook, National Society for the Study of Education (Chapter 2, by C. Gilbert Wrenn, "Philosophical and Psychological Bases of Student Personnel Work").
2. Lloyd-Jones, Esther, and Margaret Smith. *A Program for Student Personnel Work in Higher Education.* New York: McGraw-Hill Company, 1938 (Chapter 16, "Student Personnel Records").
3. ———. *Student Personnel Work as Deeper Teaching.* New York: Harper and Brothers, 1954.
4. Shank, Donald J., and others. *The Teacher as Counsellor.* Washington, D.C.: American Council on Education, 1948, Series VI. Personnel Work in Colleges and Universities, No. 10.
5. Shoben, Edward Joseph, Jr. "A Rationale for Modern Student Personnel Work." *Personnel-O-Gram,* 12:9–11, No. 3, March 1958.
6. Smith, Robert E. "Presenting the Psychological Dimensions of Classes to Instructors." *Journal of Educational Research,* 47:149–51, 1954.
7. Sutherland, Robert, and others. *Students and Staff in a Social Context.* Washington, D.C.: American Council on Education, 1953. Series VI. Personnel Work in Colleges and Universities, No. 18.
8. Williamson, E. G., ed. *Trends in Student Personnel Work.* Minneapolis: University of Minnesota Press, 1949 (especially chapters by Daniel D. Feder, William M. Gilbert, Donald J. Shank, and John L. Bergstresser).
9. Wrenn, C. Gilbert. *Student Personnel Work in College.* New York: Ronald Press Company, 1951 (especially chapters by Ruth Strang, "Education through Guided Group Experiences," and "Administrative Policies Regarding Admissions and Student Records").

THIS chapter, prepared by Mr. Wrenn, who is professor of educational psychology at the University of Minnesota, reflects the discussion of a group of which Donald Swanson, Hamline University, was chairman, and Theta Wolf, also of Hamline, was recorder.

The Community in College Teaching

COLLEGE education has three operational poles or centers: the student, the teacher, the community. The interaction of these with one another may be called the educational process. Of the three the function of the community is the least clearly understood and the community itself the least well defined.

The community usually is taken to be the total social environment of the college — not only the people and institutions among which the college operates, but the cultural environment, the intellectual heritage, the financial and economic backgrounds, the tax and administrative areas and instruments. The community in this general sense is big and heterogeneous. It may include all of Minneapolis, the state of Minnesota, the Scandinavian migrations, the Mayo Clinic, the Farmers Union, the Kensington Stone controversy, and so on indefinitely. Almost everything is there, laid out in showcases for the college teacher to select as educational material for a thousand uses.

This social environment, called the community, has increased vastly in complexity, availability, and range. Its resources and illustrative materials are bewilderingly rich and diverse. In certain limited ways it serves as a laboratory where educational and social hypotheses may be tested; a technique of tax collection, a theory of control of business recessions and inflations, a new style of football offense, an interpretation of modern poetry may move from the campus to the experimental laboratory of social life and be tested under actual conditions. Though the modern environment may not exert any greater pressure on the college than in an earlier day, it is unquestionably more diversified and fragmental in its impact. It requires a multiplicity of adjustments as compared with the situation a century ago.

The community, thus regarded as the total social environment, is not organized as an educational function or instrument. Its impact is fragmental. It is a wilderness around the frontiers of the college where educators may hunt for game or gather berries useful in their work. Usually it is set off sharply from the campus.

This vast miscellany outside the campus stockade is impressive and important, but as a party in the basic interaction among the three poles of the educational process it is not adequate. An organic relation between the college and the community is something different from the discovery and mining out of items of educational use in the environment. It implies a conception of the community different from this environmental one. It requires a greater degree of organization and reciprocity.

I shall describe this different and more limited conception of the community very briefly. The community, as I see it, is necessarily small. It is a familiar, face-to-face group, such as the family or village. It is cooperative in many or most of the main functions of living. It is a group whose members are associated with each other as whole persons, not as fragments. These primary groups are probably essential in human society, basic both in educational and in moral development. I doubt that any other type of social organization, such as the state or the corporation, no matter how large and powerful, no matter how socialized and detailed in control, can adequately replace them. The larger groups may, and indeed must, supplement the small community. If they replace it, however, social breakdown is probably inevitable.

I realize that the community in this sense is not easily available to many colleges. The trends of our time are in many ways unfavorable to it. Though the small college in the little place, or in close contact with it, has many advantages in establishing an organic relation between the campus and this fundamental community, those advantages may be unrecognized in the little school. On the other hand, a larger school with vision may go far toward the integration of community and college life. But the educational advantage — probably a critical advantage in educational and social development — still lies with the smaller types of organization.

The Student and the Community

At this conference one great area of students' motivation seems to have been neglected: the motivations that arise when a person finds himself in functional and operational relation to significant events. This area is neglected because the student in his campus habitat is usually segregated in a play-world that is withdrawn from the decisions, the actions, and the intellectual conflicts and controls of the world outside. The protected world of the student — and of the professor too — has some advantages. Sometimes it provides serenity and distance; presumably it gives teachers the opportunity for contemplation and research and allows students to dream their dreams and flower eventually into the life of intellect and the arts. But the campus culture is hardly this. The student's outlook is more likely to be play-centered and juvenile, his motives frivolous and immature.

There is little doubt about this, if the entire campus life is considered. Frank statements such as those of Nevitt Sanford (see pp. 11–14) bear out the experience of many college teachers. But this play-centered world is not necessary. The overgrown juvenility of the campus is largely the result of a system of education that is no longer in touch with the needs and realities of the times. If ways can be found whereby the student can have a significant part in events he will respond maturely in most cases. The evidence is all around us. When military, social, or intellectual emergencies arise we often draw upon these college-age people with magnificent results. But in less disturbing times we thrust them back into juvenility. The college is less alma mater than mom and momism at their worst.

In the development of functional relations between the college and the community the student can have a mature part. This development can be and indeed has been of importance educationally to the college and socially and culturally to the community. It can also be a motivating influence on the student. Critics who say at this point that the college should try only to do better its present job without resort to such diversions and frills probably do not recognize the ineffective results of our system of liberal education or the structural failure of the so-called present job. More than classroom techniques and special stimulants of student motivation are required.

Some assumptions that seem to underlie a functional relation between the college and the community are as follows: (a) The college and the community have certain values and objectives in common and can be supplemental to each other in action. (b) The traditional segregation of the college from the community is not necessary. (c) Young people of college age have profound resources of energy, imagination, responsibility, and social concern that modern society greatly needs. (d) Only in operational situations can education have a really significant impact. This is true in the arts, the intellect, the sciences, as well as in technology and the professions.

There is little doubt that such assumptions, if carried into action, would be revolutionary in higher education. Here I shall attempt only to sketch some of the work that has been undertaken. I shall also describe a limited, matter-of-fact project based on these assumptions. Projects of this sort are perhaps having more effect on higher education than is generally realized.

The Community's Contribution to the College

How can the community contribute to the college in an organic and significant way? The college town now serves as a reservoir from which day students and some financial help are drawn. The familiar marginal services by churches, elementary schools, doctors, dentists, rooming houses, eating places, clothing stores, smoke shops and night spots, movie theaters, real estate and rental agencies, and the like also are drawn from it. These are important services, to be sure, but haphazard. Their educational value to the college is accidental. As laboratories for higher educational projects they are at best casual. They have no part in college policy. Nor has the college much part in the functional structure of the community except as a consumer and tax resource. An organic relation between the community as such and the educational process of the college is rare.

How may this organic relation be established? In a few cases it already is present in the tradition and development of the college. At Antioch, for example, this came about years ago through the enlightened policies of Arthur E. Morgan and was firmly established by their vigorous and flexible continuation. The initiation of this kind of relation between the college and the community is today more difficult, perhaps, but not impossible. Illinois College at Jacksonville little by little entered cooperative projects not only with state and county agencies but also with villages in the vicinity. Joint study groups and planning sessions composed of members of the respective communities, the faculty, and the student body were held — always with action in mind but also with a three-way educative purpose. The work, begun by former president C. Gary Hudson and Professors Malcolm Stewart, Phillips Ruopp, and others of the philosophy, psychology, and sociology departments, undertook problems such as health, recreation, juvenile motivation, and tried to make them joint problems for students and adults. Because it requires mature, functional action the work has great educational value.

Colleges find, indeed, that the contributions of the community may have significant educational impact. Goddard College in Vermont and, in certain ways, Bennington have oriented themselves successfully toward the integration of educational values with community life. This involves an ideology rather different from the individualistic career dynamics that mark, or are supposed to mark, most programs of college work. Goddard under the leadership of President Royce Pitkin gives evidence that the career motive is not solely necessary to engage the aspirations and responsibilities of young college people.

Another example is Parsons College in Iowa. Several years ago, under President Tom Shearer, a community program was begun there by combining general coaching of the faculty in the concept of college-community cooperation with an opportunity for doctoral training in the field for a selected student at a nearby university. This man later became executive head of the program. Thus Parsons was able to bypass the indifferent or rejective attitude toward the community idea that often is characteristic of graduate schools. It secured in Professor L. R. Davison a trained leader whose approach to the problem is sympathetic and informed.

Marietta College in Ohio, Chico State College in California, Berea College in Kentucky, and others have recognized the contribution of the community and made a place in their educational program for it. This is carried on through key men in appropriate departments or through extension work. The University of Kentucky through the leadership of sociologist Irwin Sanders, and the University of Virginia through Jean and Jess Ogden, have carried out extensive programs of community analysis and development. In Kentucky the Louisville businessman Harry Schacter, working through the Committee for Kentucky, brought about a major improvement in community life in the region. This in turn served as a demonstration to educational institutions of the unlimited possibilities in this field. At the University of Utah Dean

Hal Bentley introduced community studies and with the cooperation
of the Mormon church gave wide prestige to the functional association
of education and community life. Mississippi State College, within its
racial ideology, is also undertaking a program, while far to the north
of it the province of Saskatchewan put into operation a full-scale,
many-sided community program under David Smith that is bound to
be educationally influential.

The Catholic church and some of its colleges, such as Saint Francis
Xavier University through the work of Father J. J. Tompkins and
Father M. M. Coady at Antigonish, are pioneers in bringing the values
and ideology of the small community into higher education. The so-
called peace colleges of the Quakers, the Brethren, and the Mennonites
also are firm in their insistence that higher education shall remain within
the cultural pattern of the small organic group, such as the family and
village. At Earlham College Professor W. W. Biddle organized a program of community dynamics which has considerable educational influence. His studies and experiments in the training of community
leaders and in the special problems of the community educator are of
importance in the further development in this line.

Only in the laboratories of community life itself can these leaders
be trained. The lack of such leaders slows down the work. The public
junior colleges, for example, could well be of great importance in the
orientation of education on the community. Sometimes they do accomplish this purpose, but not too often. They could become people's
colleges here as they are in Sweden, Denmark, and to some extent in
England. They could stabilize and enrich the community and give it
cultural integrity. Many of them fail to do this adequately because
they imitate the university or serve only as feeders to it. Their faculties are likely to have the current academic ideology and outlook because they are trained that way. They may fail to see a difference
between local college objectives and those of the larger institution.
Arthur Morgan, former president of Antioch, has said ironically that
one of the surest ways to ruin a little town is to put a college into it.
Because the college does not value the community, it is likely to serve
only as a drainage ditch for able students away from the hometown
where they are needed to the great centers where they are needed far
less.

ENDS AND MEANS
The College's Contribution to the Community

How can the college contribute to the community? The usual answer is that the development of the individual student will in turn bring about the development of the community. This of course is true. But it is not the whole truth. Nor is it always true when the community is defined as the organic, familiar group in contrast to the aggregative, fractionated life of the big city. Integrative education requires more. The individual career is not enough. The answer must include taking thought of the community and of its values in the higher educational process.

In recent years efforts have been made to find out how this can be done. In 1944 a program of community development under my direction was initiated at the University of Montana by Chancellor Ernest Melby with the help of a three-year grant from the Rockefeller Foundation. The purpose of this program, called the Montana Study, was to bring the resources of the University to the aid of the small communities of the state. It was a self-help program and in spite of its name was geared to community rather than statewide action. It was set up in the belief that each small town or rural neighborhood has its percentage of thoughtful persons concerned about the welfare of their community. The director assumed, further, that the main decisions, the local research, and the financing of the operations could best be made by the community itself. Even the initial invitation was left to the local group. The program was not introduced into a community except at the firm request of a representative group of residents.

This program in the community may be outlined as follows:

1. A community study group is organized with meetings at least once a week for ten or more weeks. These meetings are open to those who wish to come. They are planned in such a way, however, that persons from the major cliques and factions of the area, the different economic, racial, and religious groups, are all represented around the big table. The group is not organized around official representatives of the various community organizations, although it includes persons from those groups through a reasonably definite advance commitment.

Thus in Stevensville, Montana, where members of the Farmers Union were at swords' points with the businessmen, the program was undertaken by the university on condition that a number of representative members of both groups would attend regularly. So too housewives, young people, the Catholic and Protestant clergy, professional men and women, employers and members of labor unions, members of the D.A.R., Indians, Negroes, Mexicans, or other racial, national, or ethnic groups represented in the community are invited to sit around the tables of the study group and deal with the common problems of their community. They do just that to a remarkable degree.

2. A temporary chairman and steering committee are secured and later a permanent chairman is elected by the group. Here again the preliminary canvassing is very important. The chairman should be a man of prestige in the community, a man of energy and ideas, and above all a man who is not too closely identified with any one faction. Through him the work of the entire program is focused.

3. The chairman appoints the key committees or at least their chairmen. On these committees rests the burden of most of the research and the operations of the project. These committees may vary according to the situation. Usually there are committees on boundaries and population, agriculture, industry and business, education, recreation, religion, beautification, new industries, jobs, youth, art, local history. They report to the general study group, and the order of these reports is really the order of operation of the entire project.

4. The committees report the relevant facts about the problem in the local situation. The facts are subject to criticism and correction by the study group. This factual picture of the local situation is exceedingly important. Assembling it often requires painstaking research by the committee. Experts and resource men are made available to the committee by the university so far as that is possible. Often much material is reported that neither the members of the community nor the resource men previously knew. These reports are mimeographed; if the community is very small, this may be done at university expense. On the basis of factual reports the committee recommends a course of action which is later approved, modified, or rejected by the study group as a whole.

5. These courses of action are the second major function of the committees. Usually an action group is set up separately from the fact-finding and advisory committee. It may even extend beyond the membership of the study group. But the work of the study group and its committees always is geared to action.

The committee on recreation, for example, may study the local situation for several weeks or months, interview informed persons both young and old, consult specialists or bring them in to survey the field. Eventually it reports to the study group. In addition to the factual report, it usually will discuss the community's recreational needs, if any, and make practical recommendations for action. On the basis of these reports the study group will make the decisions that seem best.

The chairman of the study group then may appoint an action committee to put the plan into operation. This action group may well include interested persons not only in the study group but persons outside, such as the city manager, a county commissioner, the superintendent of schools, the basketball coach. Much, if not most, of the action will be carried out by members of the community itself. They are assembled and briefed by the committee. Special days may be set aside for group work.

6. What place does the working staff from the university have in all this? The members of the staff, if wise, try to keep in the background, but their service as sparkplugs, discussion leaders, advisers, coaches, procurement men, and intermediaries between the community on the one hand and the resources of the university and of national, state, county, and city service bureaus on the other, is of critical importance to the success of the work. Students and faculty members as well as entire classes may be associated with appropriate projects in the community. Some may be part-time members of the staff. Other may volunteer for work requiring their special skills and interests. Almost every community has able men and women willing to help in the stabilization and enrichment of their community life. But the contribution of the university in original initiative, know-how, organization, and quiet leadership is very important.

University Programs of Community Development

Procedures such as these have been highly successful not only in a number of Montana communities but in other states. They have of course a profound educative value to all who participate in them. Those who benefit include not only the residents of the communities where such work is undertaken but many faculty members and students in the cooperating university. Entire departments are likely to be drawn into the work.

At the University of Washington work based on the Montana program was undertaken by President Raymond B. Allen and Richard W. Poston with great success. Poston's work was carried out on a much larger scale than was the Montana Study and was somewhat modified to suit different conditions. As a result of this program dozens of small, failing communities in the state were regenerated by their own energies. New industries, new schools, new recreational facilities, new programs of art and beautification have transformed these little places. When the community thus makes plans and takes action concerning the whole pattern of its life the benefit is almost incalculable.

At Southern Illinois University a program, again similar to the Montana Study, was undertaken by President D. W. Morris in 1953. This work was laid out by me in a six-year plan, covering thirty-one counties of southern Illinois. To execute the program Richard W. Poston was brought in as chairman of the newly organized Department of Community Development. His success has been amazing. Here as in Montana and Washington the demand by communities far exceeds the present supply of services. Although the department has expanded rapidly at Southern Illinois, with a staff at present of twenty or more persons, a long waiting list of communities remains to be served. Dozens of communities in southern Illinois — including Cairo, Eldorado, Du Quoin, Chester, Golconda, East Saint Louis, Edwardsville, Carbondale, Rosiclare, Pope county, Hardin county, Cave in Rock, Carlyle, West Frankfort, and Cobden — have requested services and have gone to work on the program. In some cases the community's survival itself depends on the service.

In summary I suggest that the community as a laboratory for the college will serve best when the relations between the college and the community are mutually significant, responsible, and functional. Some churchmen and moralists as well as some sociologists have begun to see that the small community is fundamental to human welfare. Perhaps more educators will begin to realize that the welfare of the college and that of the community are interdependent. Those responsible for the one are also responsible for the other.

REFERENCES

1. Biddle, William W. *The Cultivation of Community Leaders; Up from the Grass Roots.* New York: Harper and Brothers, 1953.
2. ———. "People Grow in Communities." *Earlham College Bulletin,* Fall 1956.
3. Bishop, Claire Huchet. *All Things Common.* New York: Harper and Brothers, 1950.

4. Brownell, Baker. *The College and the Community; A Critical Study of Higher Education.* New York: Harper and Brothers, 1952.
5. ———. *The Human Community; Its Philosophy and Practice for a Time of Crisis.* New York: Harper and Brothers, 1952.
6. ———. "The Montana Study." *School and Society,* December 16, 1944.
7. ———. *The Other Illinois.* New York: Duell, Sloan and Pearce, 1958.
8. Campbell, Olive A. *The Danish Folk School.* New York: The Macmillan Company, 1928.
9. Coady, Moses M. *Masters of Their Own Destiny, The Story of the Antigonish Movement of Adult Education through Economic Cooperation.* New York: Harper and Brothers, 1939.
10. Dahir, James. *Communities for Better Living; Citizen Achievement in Organization, Design and Development.* New York: Harper and Brothers, 1950.
11. Hart, Joseph K. *Education in the Humane Community.* New York: Harper and Brothers, 1951.
12. Hayes, Wayland J. *The Small Community Looks Ahead.* New York: Harcourt, Brace & Company, Inc., 1947.
13. Henry, Nelson, ed. *The Public Junior College,* I. 55th Yearbook, National Society for the Study of Education. Chicago: University of Chicago Press, 1956.
14. Hitch, Earle Vann. *Rebuilding Rural America, New Designs for Community Life.* New York: Harper and Brothers, 1950.
15. Hoiberg, Otto G. *Exploring the Small Community.* Lincoln: University of Nebraska Press, 1955.
16. Holm-Jensen, Paul Henry. *The People's College.* Blair, Nebraska: Danish Lutheran Publishing House, 1939.
17. Ligutti, L. G., and J. C. Rowe. *Rural Roads to Security.* Milwaukee: The Bruce Publishing Company, 1940.
18. Manniche, Peter. *Denmark, A Social Laboratory.* Copenhagen: G. E. C. Gad, 1939.
19. Melby, Ernest O. *Administering Community Education.* Englewood Cliffs, New Jersey: Prentice-Hall, Inc., 1955.
20. Morgan, Arthur E. *The Community of the Future.* Yellow Springs, Ohio: Community Service, Inc., 1957.
21. ———. *The Small Community.* New York: Harper and Brothers, 1942.
22. Nisbet, Robert A. *The Quest for Community; A Study in the Ethics of Order and Freedom.* New York: Oxford University Press, 1953.
23. Ogden, Jean, and Jess Ogden. *Small Communities in Action; Stories of Citizen Programs at Work.* New York: Harper and Brothers, 1946.
24. Poston, Richard W. *Democracy Is You.* New York: Harper and Brothers, 1952 (a manual for community development programs).
25. ———. *Small Town Renaissance, A Story of the Montana Study.* New York: Harper and Brothers, 1950.
26. Redfield, Robert. *The Little Community.* Chicago: University of Chicago Press, 1955.
27. Ruopp, Phillips. *Approaches to Community Development; A Symposium Introductory to Problems and Methods of Village Welfare in Underdeveloped Areas.* The Hague: W. van Hoeve Ltd., 1953.
28. Sanders, Irwin T. *Making Good Communities Better.* Lexington: University of Kentucky Press, 1950.
29. Schacter, Harry W. *Kentucky on the March.* New York: Harper and Brothers, 1949.

THIS chapter by Mr. Brownell was discussed in a group of which Arthur Naftalin, Commissioner of Administration, State of Minnesota, was chairman, and Walter H. Uphoff, Industrial Relations Center, University of Minnesota, was recorder.

⋖§ THEODORE C. BLEGEN

Trustees of the Centennial Heritage

Some lines from a sonnet, "Perspective," by that genial philosopher Irwin Edman seem particularly apropos for this occasion.

> Remember, there were ages before this,
> Nor do we breathe an epilogue to time.
>
> . . . .
>
> Today is yesterday, it is tomorrow;
> It is a dusk, a dawn, a death, a birth.

Today is the sum of all our yesterdays, the past projected into the living hour. The idea of a centennial heritage invites one to look back to the hopes and achievements of the pioneers of a century ago, but for this North Star state, as for all our states, the roots of our heritage spread out far beyond a hundred years or a single state or this country. By the same token the heritage embraces the whole of our past up to the fleeting instant we call the present. For yesterday is as definitely a part of the past as May 11, 1858, when Minnesota was admitted as the thirty-second state of the Union. To many people history seems far away, but it can be near at hand in time and it is always near at hand in impact when we think about institutions and ideas and practices that have blossomed across the decades or ages and are a part of the current scene.

Though my thought here will center on our heritage and trusteeship in the realm of education, I should like to point to a few lines of general interpretation which, with differences as to places and names, can perhaps be applied to most of our states — lines not entirely remote from the educational world.

One is so simple that we sometimes fail to see it. It is that our past is a story of curiosity, of a stubborn and courageous will to find answers to problems — to open new paths or widen old paths to trade, agriculture, industry, education, and human welfare. This is a key to the achievement of a long line of explorers, from Radisson, Hennepin, and Carver to Schoolcraft and Nicollet.

Pierre Radisson, a Frenchman, came into this region, a tangle of lands and streams and lakes in the seventeenth century, with no map to guide him, and he wanted to know. And he dreamed of what these lands, "so pleasant, so beautiful and fruitful," might mean to millions of people in the Old World. How map a country nobody had mapped? What were those great fresh-water lakes of America? Where did the great river start its journey to the sea? How get to the Pacific and the dominions of the Khan of Cathay? So Radisson and many others asked questions, and their answers lifted the age-old curtain of mystery that had hidden, not Cathay, but mid-America from the world.

Sometimes these inquisitive explorers broke into almost lyrical prophecies. Thus Jonathan Carver, a colonial traveler of the eighteenth century, who was almost at the spot where we meet today, wrote, "There is no doubt that at some future period mighty kingdoms will emerge from these wildernesses, and stately and solemn temples, with gilded spires reaching to the skies, supplant the Indian huts, whose only decorations are the barbarous trophies of their vanquished enemies."

Another tradition so simple that it is not often noted is the vital tradition of work and enterprise. This state was not built by lazy people. Nor was it built in a day. We are part of the American tradition of the strenuous life. Here as in every state people responded to an immediate challenge, telescoping into a few decades a job of building that countries of the Old World spent centuries doing. And frontier people had to be not only strenuous but also versatile. For their age was an unspecialized age when rewards went to vigor and a handy ability to do many things. Much of our social, professional, and educational history is related to the shift during the intervening years from a general to a specialized society.

Work was a means, not an end for the pioneers, and here we come upon the American tradition of hope, allied with the belief in progress. Imbedded in it was an optimism that could explode into wild exaggeration and booming, but which, as we review the frontier era, could also stand up in the face of cruel disappointment and ordeal. This optimism was extravagant, but so also was the growth. In a decade, from 1850 to 1860, the Minnesota population jumped nearly three thousand per cent as Yankees, Germans, Scandinavians, and others came up river or over rough trails to this region, landseekers eager to translate dreams into reality for themselves and their children. There was clearly a pioneer exuberance, a basic faith in progress, which has exhibited itself through all American history until our own time — when some historians and philosophers have raised critical questions as to the validity of the very concept of progress.

Loneliness, Indian wars, and the burden of ordeals did not, for most of the pioneers, shake their fundamental belief in progress; but in our day two devastating world wars, a long-continuing depression, the anxieties of a sharply divided world, and other considerations have made thinkers about American life skeptical. Underlying the optimism of the pioneer era was an unshakable conviction that people were building, in initial stages, a great society, a great state. Doorways to the future were land, work, and vigor, opportunity, freedom, and education. In no small measure people still regard these as doorways to progress. The belief that they existed and were open is a clue to the democratic concept of Western and American life, a concept so fervently held that even in our own time few will accept the notion that progress is a myth or a shibboleth. "America," as Clarke A. Chambers remarks in a recent essay, "was not yet prepared [*in the middle of the twentieth century*] to reject as no longer relevant or viable the belief in progress, rooted as that faith was in the experience of generations. Continuity of thought and hope survived the discontinuities posed in an age of anxiety."

Another point is that we have been a moving people, a restless people through much of our past. We have moved from frontier to frontier, from country to town, from crop to crop, from job to job, from level to level, from house to house. We have moved economically, socially, politically — and in this state our political moves have been spurred in part by critical, protesting third parties through much of our history. The tradition of migration merges with that of immigration and with the larger tradition of opportunity and freedom of choice. There has been much jostling, and in the process the reflective life may have suffered, but it may be doubted that mobility tended to make people complacent.

Through our history, from the time when the flags of France, England, and Spain flew over our lands, we have perforce been a part of major currents of national and world history. People have talked about isolation, and we have had our isolationists, but Minnesota has never been an island, cut off from the world mainland. The trade and ambitions and hopes, the wars and ideas and aims of nation and world have left their marks, through three centuries, upon this region. Frenchmen sang ballads on our rivers. Scotsmen ran our furtrading posts. Our furs went out to Montreal and London and Leipzig and Russia, even to Canton, China, in early days. Our northern boundary was set by international treaties. We have been caught up in national and international wars; and our people, only a generation after the state was founded, were two thirds of European blood in the first and second generations. The languages and customs, faiths and traditions, ideas and institutions of more than a score of peoples and cultures of the world have been and are a part of the merging people of Minnesota. We have bridges reaching back to New England, New York, the lower Middle West, the South, the Scandinavian countries, Germany, and all the other countries in which so many of our people have ancestral, linguistic, religious, educational, and cultural roots.

So this people has had some schooling in tolerance; the amenities of intercultural living are part of its breeding. The record is not without blemishes, but the kind of schooling we have had has helped us to weather with some balance and sense a good many national storms of intolerance, hate, and the fears that feed upon ignorance.

The battle against ignorance has been fought on many fronts, and here it is interesting to note that our pioneer founders had a genuine sense of history. They looked to yesterdays and tomorrows, and it is almost startling, in this centennial year, to realize that nine years before statehood, in the very year when Minnesota became a territory of the United States, it created a historical society. Through all the hundred years of statehood and more this society has collected contemporaneously the records of the people who have built the state; and this was foreseen by one of the founders of that society, the first territorial governor, Alexander Ramsey, who incidentally had studied at Lafayette College. "Let us save that which is interesting in the fleeting registers of the day," he said, "and which in the years to come will be esteemed rich mines for the historian."

The sense of history merged with opportunity, with hopes that could blossom for coming generations, and with a conviction that humble beginnings were leagued with a great future. And these ideas are in-terrelated with the driving eagerness of the pioneers to build a system of education that would open doors of opportunity for their children.

The faith of the Minnesota people in education, in schooling from the earliest years to the top levels of college and university education, is rooted in the pioneer past and is a vital part of the centennial heri-tage — a heritage passed on through periods of rapid change, difficul-ties, criticism, and attack, with a high measure of support and confi-dence. For this heritage we of today are indeed trustees — trustees in a time of fear and reappraisal.

Nearly every educational level and interest represented in this con-ference makes a junction with events and movements in Minnesota in its frontier era — the 1850's and 1860's. Our very first territorial legis-lature, in 1849, passed an act to establish and maintain common schools; it set up a fund "for the education of all the children and youth" of the territory; it made provision for state and local taxation in support of the schools; and it declared that the common schools were to be opened "to all persons between the ages of four and twenty-one years, *free.*" The originators of this measure looked to both grade schools and high schools; and this was the initial move in this region toward uni-versal education, toward what Oliver Carmichael has called "one of the boldest social experiments ever undertaken by any people."

Only two years later, in 1851, a territorial legislative committee — re-member, we were then only a straggling little frontier community — declared that the "cause of education in the Territory demands the early establishment of an institution of learning which shall afford to the youth of the Territory an opportunity of obtaining a liberal, scien-tific and classical education." Men, said the committee, do not "gather grapes of thorns, or figs of thistles. Neither does society grow virtuous citizens from the haunts of vice, or exalted minds from the abodes of ignorance and stupidity." And so the children of that day, said the committee, were the "citizens and rulers of the future" upon whose education depended the character and destiny of the commonwealth. In advocating a charter for the university, the committee looked east-ward and recalled the establishment of both Harvard and Yale in early New England. The legislature acted. The basic document of the uni-versity dates from 1851 and was given constitutional validity in the state's constitution. The charter plus the land-grant act of 1862, under which the University of Minnesota became a land-grant college, has been fundamental to the later course of the university.

The creative 1850's also saw the emergence of private colleges in Minnesota, led by Hamline University, Methodist in church relationship, which opened its doors in 1854. It symbolized a movement that in the next few decades brought onto the Minnesota scene, alongside public education, close to a score of excellent private colleges, church-related in their origins and most of them still thus related. Dedicated to liberal education and the Christian religion, they have made invaluable contributions to Minnesota and American higher education through all the period of our statehood, and they are sturdy and thriving to-day. Viewing these colleges — Methodist, Presbyterian, Lutheran, Congregational, Baptist, Catholic, and the rest — one is forcibly reminded of the migration of dynamic ideas and faith from the lands of our European ancestors, and of lines of religious and educational influence that reach back to Luther, Wesley, Calvin, St. Benedict, and yet others, as well as those reaching Oxford and Cambridge, in part by way of Harvard, Yale, and other colleges of the East. So, as I have suggested, the heritage of which we speak is bounded neither by a state nor by a century of time, but in fact encompasses ideas and forces in our Western world from ancient to modern times. Trusteeship has resided in every generation for the precious institutions and values that we cherish and support.

Yet another landmark of the 1850's calls for mention in this review. As the common schools multiplied and high schools began to appear, as acceptance of the philosophy of universal education deepened and widened, it became apparent that the education of qualified teachers was crucial and that the established schools could not produce the needed supply. Here undoubtedly we come into the orbit of influence of the apostle of public education, Horace Mann, crusader for training schools for teachers. In any event, it is highly interesting to learn that in 1858, the very year of statehood, the frontier legislature of Minnesota passed a law establishing this state's normal-school system — the foundation of the state teachers colleges that now play so large and important a role in the preparation of teachers. Only two years later we had our first normal school, that at Winona, which also takes rank as the first normal school in America west of the Mississippi River.

Even this sketch must make it clear that the heritage of which we are trustees includes a very comprehensive system of education founded in our frontier years — and founded with a view to permanence. This long view is nowhere better expressed than in the inaugural address of President William Watts Folwell of the University of Minnesota in 1869 — one of the major educational state papers of America — the address in which he declared that the university was "not merely from the people, but for the people." "We thank God," he said, "for foundations now laid here which may endure to the end of the world, to the blessing and upbuilding of all the generations which shall follow ours."

Underlying the founding of a system of education was not only a faith in education as an avenue to social progress, but more: a belief in *universal* education as a means of meeting the needs of our democratic society. The very variety of schools, colleges, and universities suggests a further item in the heritage — namely, diversity in educational ways and functions. Foundational also is the liberal arts tradition rooted in England, transmitted by way of our eastern universities, and strongly marked in all our colleges.

The belief in education was held, not just by the intellectually elite, but by citizens of every rank, and it has been translated into support and sacrifice through decades of growth and adaptation to changes, many of which were not clearly foreseen in the days of institutional pioneering.

And the growth and transition with the passing years constitute also a part of the educational heritage. Our educational system has never stood still. It has not been static. There has been much appraisal and reappraisal, and that, too, is linked with the heritage. Education has moved forward, as I believe, in response to needs, to leadership, to criticism, and to the will of our supporting public. Thus establishment of the land-grant college system, a profoundly significant development in higher education, with its emphasis upon agriculture and mechanic arts, was a reflection of a national purpose; and as we view it in perspective we must see it as a sidepiece to an educational interest that embraced all segments of our society and also to the compulsive advancing specialization of function that has marked the hundred years we now celebrate. In my view the land-grant idea, coupled with certain other forces, was crucial to the development of the modern American university with its sweep of graduate work, its far-flung researches, and its championship of professional education.

Often when we speak of heritage we think less of institutions than we do of people, of human character, of integrity and devotion, and this chapter would quite miss its mark if it did not make place for this aspect of our heritage. Every college and school in the state has welded into its life and traditions the minds and characters and service of men and women — teachers, scholars, leaders — who, in ways humble and distinguished, have turned the idea of school and college into the reality that has meant education for thousands of young people and made immeasurable contributions to state and nation and world.

Trusteeship is responsibility. The Old Norse derivative is *traust,* which means confidence—security. Our trusteeship does not mean merely guarding what is. It means looking forward, improving, and strengthening. And so this centennial conference on college teaching, with its forward-looking inquiry into vital questions of student learning and faculty teaching, is attuned to the spirit of responsible trusteeship. The program is one of appraisal and scrutiny of ideas and practices with the purpose of helping us all to meet, with increasing effectiveness, the challenge of high quality in the work we are trying to do.

This head-on grappling by college teachers with the problems of learning and teaching in college is in pleasant contrast with the practice, all too common, especially in times of apprehension, of shifting responsibility to other levels, lower or higher, and placing the blame for what seems wrong on everybody except ourselves. I have no magic prescription for our school ills, but I think it wise for every level in our school system to be looking critically at itself, to be engaging in self-study, and to be seeking ways of improving the quality of its work. I have been urging the graduate schools of the country to find ways of improving the education of college teachers and to adopt many other reforms, and I have done so in conformance with my belief in appraisal and self-study. As I said a few years ago to my fellow graduate-school deans at a conference in Washington, "Time, numbers of students, and the pressure of unmet or ill-met needs now confront graduate education with problems that cannot and should not be shunted along that familiar buck-passing line that leads ultimately to the kindergarten, pre-school, and home."

It must be obvious to every mature person that our school and college problems are not simple, coping as we are with varied objectives and constantly increasing numbers, including the gifted and highly gifted along with all the others. The problems are complex and difficult. They are not to be solved by jeering and emotion-stirring slogans which at best represent only partial truth and often are grave distortions. It has seemed to me that especially in the realm of professional education and the so-called subject-matter fields we have need of cool and objective thinking. As I said in 1952 at the Duke University Centennial Conference, we need efforts by professional education and by subject-matter specialists to find a common front against the chief enemy of those who teach — namely ignorance and unenlightenment. The answer is not to sweep away achieved gains in a policy of topsy-turvy, but to seek a common front. Probably many measures can be found to aid us in that search. At Duke University I urged, as I do now, increased devotion on the one side to careful and critical educational research plus pilot-plant demonstrations, and on the other side removal of patent distortions, sincere efforts to understand the complexities of universal education, and a willingness to look fairly at the fruits of scholarship applied to the learning process itself.

I believe that many of our schools are making notable progress in their efforts to solve the problems they face, just as I believe in the integrity and good purpose of our teachers all along the line. It would be absurd to pretend that there are not shortcomings at every level, as indeed there have been at every stage of our history. We know well that objective and critical studies leading to action are needed, and we know equally well that at many stages in our long past they have been both needed and supplied.

It is in the setting of such thoughts that I welcome conferences, study projects, committee investigations, all efforts locally and nationally to deal responsibly with our school and college problems. In this spirit I look with interest to the studies now being carried forward by Dr. Conant, not only because he understands the imperatives of universal education and the need of identifying and encouraging high talent for tomorrow's leadership, but also because he is visiting the schools to see for himself what is going on.

From his studies and from concerted efforts throughout the country to find out, to make known, to improve, to strengthen, to face honestly the problems of American education, we shall move toward greater and better-informed public interest, more vigorous support of education, and more encouragement and recognition to those who devote their lives and talents to serving our schools and colleges.

Just after World War II, John Masefield spoke at the University of Sheffield. He spoke of a university, but I think we may add *college* to his lines.

There are few earthly things more splendid than a university.
. . . In these days of broken frontiers and collapsing values
. . . when the dams are down and the floods are making misery
. . . when every future looks somewhat grim
. . . and every ancient foothold has become something of a quagmire
. . . wherever a university stands, it stands and shines
. . . wherever it exists, the free minds of men, urged on to full and fair inquiry, may still bring wisdom into human affairs.

So, as I, today, think of our university and of all these colleges and schools which in their ongoing represent the centennial heritage, I echo the poet's words and say — they stand and shine. It is our task as trustees to see to it that they continue to stand and shine.

MR. BLEGEN is Dean of the Graduate School of the University of Minnesota.

THE CONTRIBUTORS
BIBLIOGRAPHY AND INDEX

The Contributors

HARALD C. BAKKEN was graduated from the University of Minnesota in 1956. He was president of the All-University Congress while at Minnesota, was elected president of the United States National Student Association for 1956–57, and is now director of the Foreign Student Leadership Project of the United States National Student Association.

THEODORE C. BLEGEN is dean of the graduate school of the University of Minnesota. In 1949 he was chairman of the national Conference on the Preparation of College Teachers and he later served as chairman of the American Council Committee on Preparation for College Teaching. He has been president of the Mississippi Valley Historical Association and superintendent of the Minnesota Historical Society, and is the author or editor of many volumes of history.

BAKER BROWNELL is professor emeritus of philosophy at Northwestern and Southern Illinois Universities. For twenty years he has been concerned with community development, particularly as related to education. He was director of the Montana Study, which served as a model for several other community-university programs, and at Southern Illinois he organized the Area Services Division and set up the Department of Community Development. Among his publications are *The Human Community, The College and the Community*, and *The Other Illinois*.

C. R. CARPENTER has, since 1940, been at Pennsylvania State University where he is director of the Division of Academic Research and Services. He is a graduate of Duke and Stanford Universities, has served on the faculty of the Columbia University College of Physicians and Surgeons, and was a pioneer in the development of teaching by television.

MARJORIE CARPENTER is chairman of the Division of the Humanities at Stephens College. She has been vice-president of the national Educational Association for Higher Education, has served as chairman of the Committee on Evaluation of Courses in the Cultural Area for the United States Armed Forces Institutes, was sent in 1951 and 1952 to serve as humanities consultant to German universities, and is particularly concerned with the development of values in the student.

W. H. Cowley has been David Jacks Professor of Higher Education at Stanford University since 1944. He has also served as president of Hamilton College, professor of psychology and member of the Bureau of Educational Research at Ohio State University, and member of the administrative staff at the University of Chicago; in addition, he has been associated with the Bell Telephone Laboratories and other businesses.

Edgar Dale is professor of education in the Bureau of Educational Research at Ohio State. His work with audio-visual aids to education has been done as head of the Coordination Division of the Bureau of Motion Pictures of the Office of War Information, as a member of the advisory board of the Institute of Propaganda Analysis, as president of the NEA Department of Visual Instruction, as chairman of the Motion Pictures Committee on Visual Education for the National Congress of Parents and Teachers, and as member of the United States National Commission for UNESCO. He is the author of *Audio Visual Methods in Teaching* and co-author of *Motion Pictures in Education*.

Elizabeth Drews teaches in the College of Education at Michigan State University and also does research, particularly in the field of critical thinking. She has been a member of the staff of the University of Michigan Psychological Clinic, director of psychological services in the Lansing public schools, and is now president-elect of the Michigan Reading Association.

Robert L. Ebel is vice-president for testing programs and services at the Educational Testing Service, Princeton, New Jersey. He is a graduate of the University of Iowa, and served as professor of education, director of the Examinations Service, and director of the Bureau of Educational Research and Service at the University of Iowa.

Reuben G. Gustavson is president and executive director of Resources for the Future, Inc. He served as professor and chairman of the department of chemistry, dean of the graduate school, and president of the University of Colorado; as vice-president and dean of the faculties of the University of Chicago; and as chancellor of the University of Nebraska. He has also been a member of the board of governors of the Argonne National Laboratory.

The Contributors

WILBERT J. MCKEACHIE is in the department of psychology at the University of Michigan. He is the author of *Teaching Tips: A Guide Book for Beginning College Teachers* and other works on psychology, college teaching, and general education.

FREEMON G. MACOMBER is director of the Experimental Study in Instructional Procedures at Miami University. He has also served as professor of education at the University of Oregon and dean of the College of Education at Miami University. He is the author of *Psychological Factors in Education* and *Teaching in the Modern Secondary School*.

LEWIS B. MAYHEW is professor of social science and member of the Office of Evaluation Services at Michigan State University and Director of Research at Stephens College. He is chairman of the National Committee on General Education, was executive director of the North Central Association's Study of Liberal Arts Education, and was associate director of the American Council on Education Evaluation of General Education.

HORACE TAYLOR MORSE is dean of the General College at the University of Minnesota. He has written numerous articles on general education, college teaching, and evaluation, and served as editor of the volume *General Education in Transition*. During the fall and winter of 1957, he served as a consultant to the University of Delhi and the Ministry of Education of India.

NEVITT SANFORD is in the department of psychology at the University of California at Berkeley and director of the Mary Conover Mellon Foundation study of Vassar College. He has served as research psychologist at Harvard, research associate of the Institute of Child Welfare, associate director of the Institute of Personality Assessment and Research, and co-director of the Berkeley Public Opinion Study, as well as practicing psychoanalysis. He is co-author of *The Authoritarian Personality*.

VIRGINIA L. SENDERS is lecturer in psychology at the University of Minnesota, and author of *Measurement and Statistics*. She has taught at Wellesley and was a member of the department of psychology and director of the Laboratory for Research in Aviation Psychology at Antioch.

MORRIS I. STEIN is in the department of psychology and director of the Center for the Study of Creativity and Mental Health at the University of Chicago. He has been a research associate at Harvard, a clinical psychologist in the mental hygiene clinics of the New York and Boston Veterans' Administration, and a fellow at the Center for Advanced Study in the Behavioral Sciences, Stanford, California.

HAROLD TAYLOR, a graduate of the Universities of Toronto and London, is president of Sarah Lawrence College and was formerly a professor of philosophy at the University of Wisconsin. He is the author of *Education and Freedom* and editor of *Essays in Teaching*.

HERBERT A. THELEN is professor of educational psychology and director of the Laboratory for Study of Teaching-Learning in the Department of Education at the University of Chicago. He served on the planning and policy committee of the National Training Laboratories and was a trainer in human relations for the European Productivity Agency. He is the author of *Dynamics of Groups at Work* and *Methods for the Study of Emotionality and Work in Group Interaction*, and co-author of *Emotional Dynamics and Group Culture*.

I. KEITH TYLER is director of radio-television education, director of the Institute for Education by Radio-Television, and professor of education at Ohio State University. He has been president of the Junior Town Meeting League and editor of *Radio and the School*. In October 1957 he was given the annual Award of Merit by the National Association of Educational Broadcasters.

RALPH W. TYLER is director of the Center for Advanced Study in the Behavioral Sciences, Stanford, California. He has served as professor of education at Ohio State and was associated with the Bureau of Educational Research. He was chairman of the department of education, university examiner, and dean of the division of social science at the University of Chicago. He was also director of evaluation in the Eight-Year Study of the Progressive Education Association and director of the Cooperative Study in General Education of the American Council on Education. He is the author of *Service Studies in Higher Education, Construction of Achievement Tests, Appraising and Recording Student Progress, Cooperation in General Education*, and *Basic Principles of Curriculum and Instruction*.

ARTHUR UPGREN is a professor of economics at Macalester College. He earlier served as dean of the Amos Tuck School of Business Administration at Dartmouth and at the University of Minnesota. He has acted as economic analyst and consultant for the United States government, and was secretary to the congressional commission that set up the International Bank for Reconstruction and Development. He was for many years vice-chairman of the National District Committee for Economic Development.

The Contributors

GEORGE R. WAGGONER has been dean, since 1954, of the College of Liberal Arts and Sciences at the University of Kansas. He was formerly associate dean at the University of Indiana. He is a member of the executive board of the Inter-University Committee on the Superior Student and director of the Experiment for Gifted Students at the University of Kansas.

C. GILBERT WRENN is professor of educational psychology at the University of Minnesota. He is a past president of the American College Personnel Association, the National Vocational Guidance Association, and the Division of Counseling Psychology of the American Psychological Association. He is on the Council of Representatives of the latter association, has served on the American Board of Examiners in Professional Psychology, and on the national advisory board of the Air Training Command of the USAF. He is author or co-author of *Studying Effectively, Building Self-Confidence, Guidance Procedures in High School, Student Personnel Problems,* and *Student Personnel Work in College.*

Bibliography

Function and Status of College Teaching

Berkson, Isaac B. *The Ideal and the Community*. New York: Harper and Brothers, 1958.

Biddle, William W. *Growth toward Freedom*. New York: Harper and Brothers, 1957.

Bloom, Benjamin S., and others. *Taxonomy of Educational Objectives*. New York: Longmans, Green & Company, 1956.

Brameld, Theodore. *Cultural Foundations of Education*. New York: Harper and Brothers, 1957.

Brownell, Baker. *The College and the Community*. New York: Harper and Brothers, 1952.

———. *The Other Illinois*. New York: Duell, Sloan and Pearce, Inc., 1958.

Brubacker, John S., and Willis Rudy. *Higher Education in Transition*. New York: Harper and Brothers, 1958.

Conant, James B. *The Citadel of Learning*. New Haven: Yale University Press, 1956.

Earnest, Ernest. *Academic Procession*. The Bobbs-Merrill Company, 1953.

Eddy, Edward D. *Colleges for Our Land and Time*. New York: Harper and Brothers, 1957.

Greene, Theodore. *Liberal Education Reconsidered*. Cambridge: Harvard University Press, 1953.

Hofstadter, Richard, and DeWitt C. Hardy. *The Development and Scope of Higher Education in the United States*. New York: Columbia University Press, 1952.

Hutchins, Robert M. *University of Utopia*. Chicago: University of Chicago Press, 1953.

MacLean, Malcolm S., and Edwin A. Lee. *Change and Process in Education*. New York: The Dryden Press, Inc., 1956.

President's Committee on Education beyond the High School. *Second Report to the President*. Washington, D.C.: U.S. Government Printing Office, 1957.

Schmidt, George P. *The Liberal Arts College*. New Brunswick: Rutgers University Press, 1957.

Smith, Huston. *Purposes of Higher Education*. New York: Harper and Brothers, 1955.

Instructional Procedures

Andrews, Kenneth R. *The Case Method of Teaching Human Relations and Administration*. Cambridge: Harvard University Press, 1955.

Association for Higher Education. *Current Issues in Higher Education*. National Education Association annual.

Axelrod, Joseph, and others. *Teaching by Discussion in the College Program*. Chicago: University of Chicago Press, 1949.

Blauch, Lloyd E. *Teaching in Colleges and Universities, With Special Reference to Dentistry*. American Association of Dental Schools, 1946.

Bibliography

Bonthius, Robert H., and others. *The Independent Study Program in the United States.* New York: Columbia University Press, 1958.

Buxton, Claude E. *A Guide to College Teaching.* New York: Harcourt, Brace & Company, Inc., 1956.

Cantor, Nathaniel. *The Dynamics of Learning.* Buffalo: Foster and Stewart Publishing Company, 1946.

———. *The Teaching-Learning Process.* New York: The Dryden Press, Inc., 1953.

Cole, Luella. *Background for College Teaching.* New York: Farrar & Rinehart, Inc., 1940.

Committee of Fifteen. *The Graduate School Today and Tomorrow.* Fund for the Advancement of Education, 1955.

Committee on Utilization . . . *Better Utilization of College Teaching Resources.* Fund for the Advancement of Education, 1956, 1957.

Cooper, Russell M., and others. *Portfolio of College Teaching Techniques.* Washington, D.C.: Educators' Washington Dispatch, 1951.

Cronkhite, Bernice Brown. *A Handbook for College Teachers.* Cambridge: Harvard University Press, 1950.

Dale, Edgar. *Audio-Visual Methods in Teaching.* New York: The Dryden Press, Inc., 1954.

Dobbins, Charles G., ed. *Expanding Resources for College Teaching.* Washington, D.C., American Council on Education, 1956.

Drummond, Donald F., and Charles Hudson, eds. *The Teaching of the Humanities.* Columbia: University of Missouri, 1954.

Educational Policies Commission. *Mass Communication and Education.* National Education Association, 1958.

Eells, Walter Crosby. *College Teachers and College Teaching.* Southern Regional Education Board, 1957 (annotated bibliography).

Ellis, Elmer, ed. *Toward Better Teaching in College.* Columbia: University of Missouri, 1954.

French, Sidney, ed. *Accent on Teaching.* New York: Harper and Brothers, 1954 (o.p.)

Goode, Delmer M. *Improving College and University Teaching.* Quarterly since 1953, published by Oregon State College.

Highet, Gilbert. *The Art of Teaching.* New York: Alfred A. Knopf, Inc., 1950.

Justman, Joseph, and Walter H. Mais. *College Teaching, Its Practice and Its Potential.* New York: Harper and Brothers, 1956.

Kelley, Earl C. *Workshop Way of Learning.* New York: Harper and Brothers, 1951.

Kelly, Fred J., ed. *Improving College Instruction.* Washington, D.C.: American Council on Education, 1951.

McKeachie, Wilbert, and Gregory Kimble. *Teaching Tips: A Guidebook for Beginning College Teachers.* Ann Arbor: George Wahr Publishing Co., 1953.

Macomber, F. G. *Experimental Study in Instructional Procedures.* Miami, Ohio: Miami University, 1957.

National Society for the Study of Education. *Mass Media and Education.* 53rd Yearbook, Pt. II. Chicago: University of Chicago Press, 1954.

Osborn, Alex F. *Applied Imagination.* New York: Charles Scribner's Sons, 1953.

Peterson, Houston, ed. *Great Teachers.* New Brunswick: Rutgers University Press, 1946.

Rasey, Marie I. *This Is Teaching.* New York: Harper and Brothers, 1953.

———. *It Takes Time.* New York: Harper and Brothers, 1953.

Simpson, Ray H. *Improving Teaching-Learning Processes.* New York: Longmans, Green & Company, 1953.

———, and E. S. Brown. *College Learning and Teaching.* Urbana: University of Illinois Bulletin, 1952.

Snygg, Donald, and Arthur W. Combs. *Individual Behavior.* New York: Harper and Brothers, 1949.

Taylor, Harold, ed. *Essays in Teaching.* New York: Harper and Brothers, 1950.

THE TWO ENDS OF THE LOG

Tead, Ordway. *College Teaching and College Learning.* New Haven: Yale University Press, 1949.

Tyler, Ralph W. *Basic Principles of Curriculum and Instruction.* Chicago: University of Chicago Press, 1950.

Umstattd, J. G. *Instructional Procedures at the College Level.* Austin: University of Texas Press, 1947.

Wilson, Louis R., M. H. Hawlesworth, and Sarah R. Reed. *The Library in College Instruction.* New York: H. W. Wilson Company, 1951.

Faculty Personnel Policies

Abbott, Frank C. *Faculty-Administration Relationships.* Washington, D.C.: American Council on Education, 1958.

Barzun, Jacques. *Teacher in America.* New York: Little, Brown and Company, 1945.

Blegen, T. C., and R. M. Cooper, eds. *The Preparation of College Teachers.* Washington, D.C.: American Council on Education, 1950.

Diekhoff, John S. *Domain of the Faculty in Our Expanding Colleges.* New York: Harper and Brothers, 1956.

Marshall, Max S. *Two Sides to a Teacher's Desk.* New York: The Macmillan Company, 1951.

Research Division. *Teacher Supply and Demand in Colleges and Universities.* National Education Association, 1958.

Riesman, David. *Constraint and Variety in American Education.* Lincoln: University of Nebraska Press, 1956.

Wilson, Logan. *The Academic Man.* New York: Oxford University Press, 1942.

Evaluation of Outcomes

Dressel, Paul L., ed. *Evaluation in the Basic College.* New York: Harper and Brothers, 1958.

————, and Lewis B. Mayhew. *General Education: Explorations in Evaluation.* Washington, D.C.: American Council on Education, 1954.

Furst, Edward J. *Constructing Evaluation Instruments.* New York: Longmans, Green & Company, 1958.

Jacob, Philip E. *Changing Values in College.* New York: Harper and Brothers, 1957.

Lindquist, E. F., and others. *Educational Measurement.* Washington, D.C.: American Council on Education, 1950.

Remmers, H. H., and N. L. Gage. *Educational Measurement and Evaluation.* New York: Harper and Brothers, 1955.

Index

313

Index

Tape recordings: use in evaluation of teaching, 174, 184; use in classroom, 201

Taylor University, 263

Teachers: importance of, 80–81; preparation of, 137–38; in-service growth of, 139–48. *See also* Professors

Teaching: history of, 101–18; three kinds of, 119–21; evaluation of, 140–41, 170–77 *passim*, 182–83; good practices described, 149–63; as means of stimulation, 161–62; student appraisals of, 184–86; essentials for improving, 191–92; methods of, 191–208; need for realism in, 195–200; panels and reports in, 233–37; with student helpers, 262–72; use of community in, 282–92. *See also* Education; Learning; Professors

Television: limitations of, 136, 195, 198–99; use in teaching, 199–201, 209–21; partial list of educational stations, 201; cost, 221; definitions, 222–25; types, 224–25; closed-circuit, 225; discussion method used on, 259; at Stephens, 263; student involvement in, 271

Testing, 32, 52–63, 168. *See also* Examinations

Textbooks, 93, 202–3

Thomas, Allen C., 114

Training vs. education, 45, 193

Transfer of training, 31

Tyler, Ralph W., discussed by Morse, 178–81

Typology of students, 17–20

Under-achiever, defined, 18

United States National Student Association, 64

University Film Producers' Association, 203, 228

Utah, University of, 286–87

Values: in students, 11–14; stimulating students to use, 86–98; methods for teaching, 92–93; faculty as creators of, 151–52; of personnel workers, 278–79. *See also* Conformity of students; Jacob, Philip; Students

Vassar studies, 3–4, 8, 11–14, 16, 17–18, 88

Virginia, University of, 108, 286

Washington University (St. Louis), mathematics aids, 92, 230–31

Washington, University of, 290–91

Wayne State University, 197

Western Reserve University, 196

White, Andrew Dixon, 104, 106, 108

White, R. W., 7, 8

Whitehead, Alfred North, 226

Williams College, 107

Wilson, Woodrow, 111, 196

Winona State College, 298

Wisconsin, University of, 114, 155

Xenophanes, 192

Yale University, 104, 106, 108, 109, 297, 298

378,082
Cooper

Date Due